Visionary Architecture

ONE WEEK LOAN

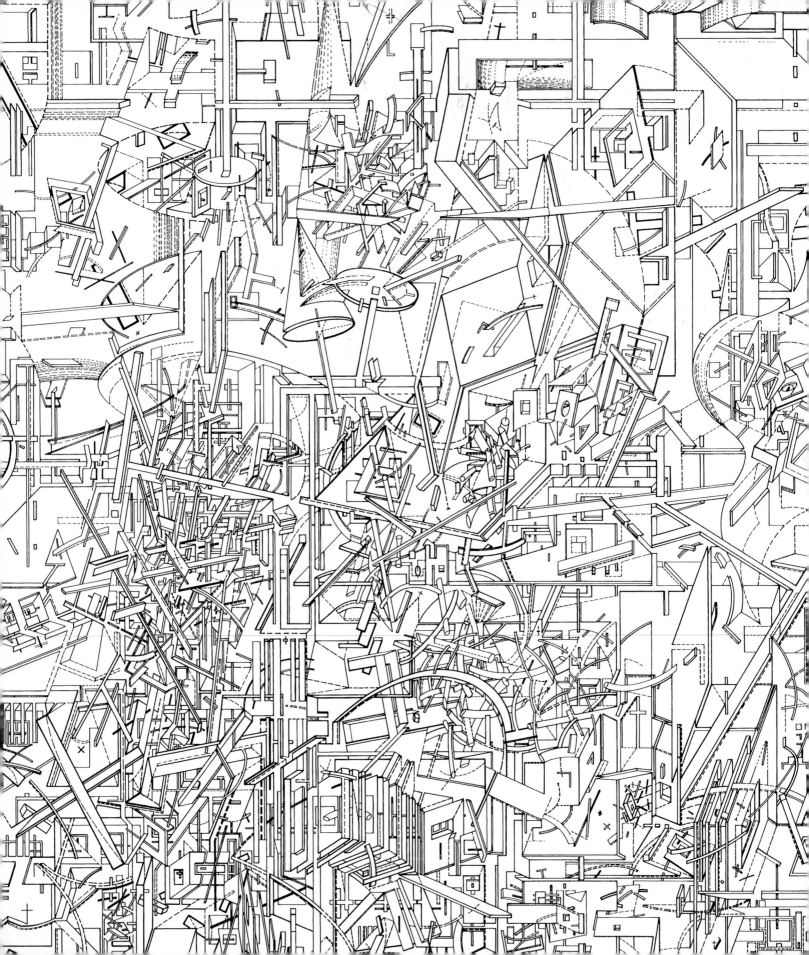

Visionary Architecture

Blueprints of the Modern Imagination

Neil Spiller

With over 450 illustrations

Thames & Hudson

Foreword

This book is intended to be the definitive history of twentieth-century visionary architecture. This history is linked to the metamorphosis of the 'machine' and the technologies that embody it. Whether 'machines' are the conceptual ones of Marcel Duchamp, the mechanized armatures of cranes on a building site, the virtual machines 'within' computers or the cabbalistic machines of Daniel Libeskind – to name but a few – they have all influenced the course of architectural vision. The vicissitudes of the machine have far outgrown the primitive machinations of the building industry, and many visionary architects have become disappointed with the limitations of traditional practice, its cheese-paring economic straitjacket and the political machinations of clients.

It is important to define the term *visionary* in the context of architecture. There is a long and noble tradition of visionary architecture; it is often unbuilt and sometimes might be unbuildable. It may take the form of polemical drawings, models (real or virtual) or texts about buildings or whole cities. Architects create such work for many reasons, some to 'inject noise into the system' (to quote Archigram), some for political ends, some to pursue their own idiosyncratic architectural languages and some with pedagogical aims. Such architects often form cliques and coteries, finding comfort in the company of like-minded designers. Some gain control of schools of architecture, making them centres of visionary discourse at certain times. Often groups of visionary architects develop projects that can be seen as contributing to a meta-conversation.

This book focuses on the second half of the twentieth century but contextualizes visionary work in two introductory chapters: One presents pre-twentieth-century visionaries such as Piranesi and Ledoux; the other is a critical essay on the visionary movements of the first half of the century. The book unfolds further with chapters on Situationist architecture from the 1950s, the emergence of Pop art and its architecture of the late '50s, hippie techno-play and the architecture of the 1960s. It then discusses – as a sort of case study – the evolution of the home and its assimilation of technology. The 1980s – an extraordinarily fecund decade for architectural visionaries – are represented by several chapters. Finally, the book brings us up to date with a chapter on the emergence of cyberspace and casts an eye to the future. My aim throughout is to illustrate the full potential of architecture and its discourses. Visionaries teach us to be optimistic and ambitious and not to accept the mundane shams that are often presented as acts of architecture in the world.

Contents

Arcadia, Alchemy, Antiquity and Machines

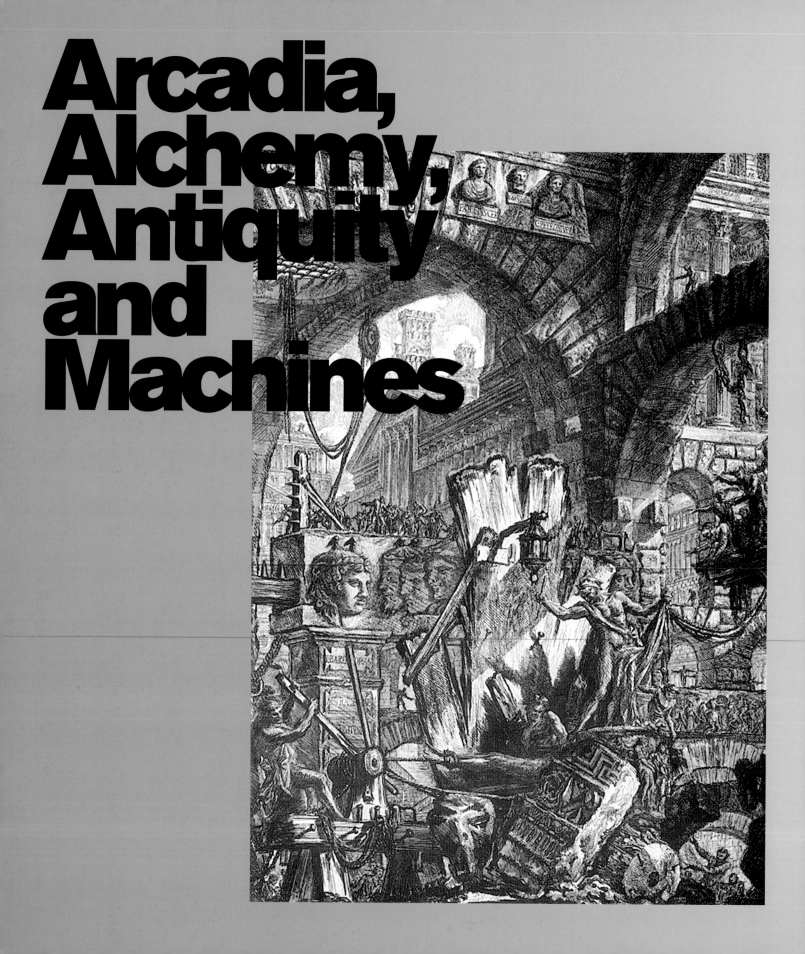

Visionary architecture could be said to have taken a hugely significant step at the end of the fifteenth century with the publication of the *Hypnerotomachia Poliphili*; many of the *Hypnerotomachia*'s Arcadian and symbolic aspirations and preoccupations are consistent with those of the 1900s. In the eighteenth century, Piranesi produced his pseudo-antiquarian renderings of an idealized Rome, as well as images of unbuildable prisons. In the 1800s, Ledoux created his astounding salt-works at Chaux, while his fellow Frenchmen Diderot and D'Alembert started fastidiously to document the use of tools, working practices and products in relation to architectural space. All of these events were harbingers of the visionary architecture of the twentieth century.

1
Exterior view from
Carceri
Giovanni Battista
Piranesi, 1761

'I gazed insatiably at one huge and beautiful work after another, saying to myself: "If the fragments of holy antiquity, the ruins and debris and even the shavings, fill us with stupefied admiration and give us such delight in viewing them, what would they do if they were whole?"'
Francesco Colonna

Imagine that a pious yet highly passionate young man, an admirer of a nubile young woman, awakes to find himself in a strange land. This land of dreams assaults his senses. Every nuance, every man-made and natural thing, is a sensual reminder of his love and unrequited, deep ache. This verdant land is full of highly ornamented sculptures, cavernous monuments, intricate rituals, beneficent banquets, inspiring inscriptions and gorgeous, tempting nymphs dressed in intoxicating finery (figs 2–3). It is an ideal world in which polytheistic prayers are answered, where good foils evil, and where the fecundity of nature is sacred and celebrated in a thousand different ways.

Poliphilo, as the ardent youth is called, stumbles along fuelled with a lusty interest in all that is animate or inanimate. He is the desiring observer full of hunger for aesthetic and sensual titillation. His journey is documented in a substantial book, *Hypnerotomachia Poliphili*, published in 1499 and written by Brother Francesco Colonna, a Dominican monk. Poliphilo's journey is told in the first person; the prose is immediate and evokes a tangible empathy in the reader. Even after more than five hundred years, the trials and tribulations, desire and despair of the book's hero are instantly recognizable. Poliphilo drifts through one aesthetic set piece after another. He hardly understands the full import of what he sees, yet he is entranced and blindly ecstatic.

Poliphilo yearns for a halcyon world, a noble, half-imagined Antiquity – and here it is, sparkling in its bejewelled and flowery abundance. It is a heightened rhetorical paraspace, a place of cathartic revelation. Poliphilo calls on a wide pantheon of gods and goddesses to bring him solace and sanctuary from his fears, troubles and lusts. His fervour is reflected in dense, often impenetrable, highly wrought yet detailed and sumptuous text. The following sentence is an example: 'In this horrid and cuspidinous littoral and most miserable site of the algent and the fetorific lake stood saevious Tisiphone, efferal and cruel with her viperine capillament, her meschine and miserable soul, implacably furibund.'[1] The book also seeks to deconstruct the traditional boundary between text and illustration. Some of its illustrations are of texts or inscriptions, and sometimes text forms shapes. A similar blurring of the ontology of text, image and building has been the almost constant predeliction of many twentieth-century architectural visionaries, as we shall see.

In fact the *Hypnerotomachia Poliphili* is a milestone in architectural vision; its content, its Baroque prose and its multi-sensual attributes make it truly exceptional – a synaesthetic extravagance. It negotiates fictional architectures as if they are real. To talk of the 'not there' as if it is there is a common trait in visionary-architectural discourse. The *Hypnerotomachia*'s knowledge of architectural proportion and detail was gleaned from Vitruvius and Alberti. Among the preoccupations and ways of seeing the world that are found in its pages and that characterized the visionary-architectural debate throughout the twentieth century are descriptions of the feelings of viewers about their conception of space, the Arcadian landscape and the architectural power of the fragment. The book is a Renaissance harbinger of some

of the most extraordinary architecture ever imagined.

The *Hypnerotomachia Poliphili* is an extraordinary achievement. It is almost viral; it sits in the subconscious awaiting moments of recognition as another of its analogies or symbols is unravelled and it again flashes into its readers' thoughts. Robert Harbison has written of it in terms of a highly effective machine, 'an artificially animated thing which goes on doing work'.[2] Some have theorized that this marvellous book has encrypted within it a massive alchemical message. Medieval and Renaissance adepts of alchemy often used systems of code – some visual, some poetic – to communicate with one another. This made sense in an era when the price for evoking the alchemical heresy was often death by burning at the stake. There are many great texts that sought to explain the magnum opus of alchemy in terms of allusion or analogy, a mixture of nature, artifice and symbolism. Some have also seen the *Hypnerotomachia Poliphili*, with its highly specific iconography and its definitive descriptions of places, as a 'memory theatre'. Memory theatres were mnemonic devices that, in their simplest form, consisted of images of icons and architectural settings constructed and recalled, in the virtual space of the mind, in order to provoke the remembering of songs, of the litany, of spells and of epistemologies. The alchemists often used memory systems as ways to encode and remember their complex work. Frances Yates in her seminal book *The Art of Memory* describes the *Hypnerotomachia Poliphili* as 'Perhaps an artificial memory gone out of control into wild imaginative indulgence … [it] makes one wonder whether the mysterious inscriptions so characteristic of this work may owe something to the influence of visual alphabets and memory images, whether, that is to say, the dream archaeology of the human mingles with dream memory systems to form a strange fantasia'.[3]

The symbolism of alchemy is one of kings and queens, incestuous royal beds, death and resurrection, rebirth and androgyny, and the reconciliation of

opposites such as the sun and moon, water and fire, male and female. ⬛⬛⬛odus operandi is one of cyclic distill⬛⬛⬛ solution and dissolution with ⬛⬛⬛e of heat and acid. Contrary to p⬛⬛⬛belief, the alchemist's search was not to turn lead into gold but to reach a point of philosophical understanding about the fundamental nature of the universe and its workings. The chemical quest was a mere microcosm of this overall objective. Claims that the *Hypnerotomachia Poliphili* is alchemical in nature are given credence by passages such as 'I saw a carving of a noble matron who had given birth to two eggs in the royal bedchamber of a marvellous palace. To the astonishment of the midwife and of many other matrons and nymphs present, there issued from one egg a little flame and from the other two bright stars.'[4]

The alchemical analogy also resonated throughout artistic and architectural practice during the twentieth century. For example, Marcel Duchamp's and Max Ernst's *oeuvres* can be seen to be heavily laden with alchemical symbolism. In the last decades of the century, architects such as Daniel Libeskind and Diller and Scofidio were influenced by this symbolism. As technology became more and more powerful, the art of architecture could progressively be likened to alchemical cycles. By the late 1990s, technology had started to assume the alchemist's mantle with its manipulation of atomic substance and its adoption of organic reproduction and growth paradigms.

Poliphilo's dreamland is above all Arcadian, but its sense of well-being is sometimes punctured by his trials in the Dark Forest or his face-to-face encounters with perilous creatures. In fact the *Hypnerotomachia Poliphili* firmly established the biological and mechanical dichotomy characteristic of twentieth-century visionary architecture and hints at some of the contemporary attempts to reconcile it. The book's epistemology is one that its learned author was constantly grappling with and rearticulating in his day job as a monk: reconciling Nature and the Sublime with worldly ideas and creations. All visionary architecture has

invented and positioned itself in relation to this continuum, which is fully biological at one extreme and fully mechanical at the other.

The *Hypnerotomachia Poliphili* deals with this dichotomy in its own original way. Poliphilo eventually arrives on the Isle of Cytherea, a place of continuous spring, a soothing place lacking all fears of tooth, claw and sting (fig. 6). Here he basks in the warmth of sunny glades: 'It was not invaded by hurtful wintry frosts nor in summer, by excessive sunshine or by torrid drought, nether did freezing plague it, but all was springlike … The place was planted with lawns, and with an impressive wealth of leafy trees that presented a wonderful display of verdure. Around everything there breathed a limpid air, redolent of flowers, the whole area was covered with grass and fresh rosemary and flowery meadows.'[5]

Mechanistic, Dreamy Outside Rooms

This description of architecture and landscape free from inclement weather, forever spring-like, can be compared with many of the utopian discourses of modern and contemporary architecture. Perhaps it was most influential during the hippie, free-love, portable-space, pod and inflatable era of the 1960s. For example, the *Hypnerotomachia*'s Arcadian vision was echoed by Peter Reyner Banham: 'The car … is already doing quite a lot of standard of living package's job – the smoochy couple dancing to the music of the radio in their parked convertible have created a ballroom in the wilderness (dance floor by courtesy of the Highway Department, of course) and all this is paradisal until it starts to rain. Even then you're not licked – it takes very little air pressure to inflate a transparent Mylar airdome, the conditioned air output of your mobile package might be able to do it, with or without a little boosting, and the dome itself, folded into a parachute pack, might be part of the package. From within your thirty-foot hemisphere of warm dry lebensraum you could have spectacular ringside views of the wind felling trees, snow swirling through the

2
'Awe-inspiring' pyramid from *Hypnerotomachia Poliphili*
Francesco Colonna, 1499

3
Three trophies from *Hypnerotomachia Poliphili*
Francesco Colonna, 1499

glade, the forest fire coming over the hill or Constance Chatterley running swiftly to you know whom through the Down pour.'[6] As a paradigmatic idea, this escape from weather and its restrictions on buildings is pervasive even today.

That the *Hypnerotomachia Poliphili* deals with the mechanistic is illustrated by the hand-anointing machine: 'The vase attached to the summit [of the machine] had been made so perfectly that when the chariot was in motion, the rod began to spin together with the vase, and the water sprayed out beyond the tree, stopping when the wheels did so. This is how I understood it: the power came from the motion of one of the wheels, which contained another, toothed wheel facing the turning spindle. This had

holes for teeth, and moved the stem of the vase … this marvellous device passed in front of us everyone wetting their hands and then their faces and making everything emit an unexpected fragrance, for when I rubbed my hands together, there was a perfume such as my senses had never known before.'[7] Here we have an enabling machine, an event-machine that is created and brought into play for a limited duration. This idea of expediency, anticipation and the architectures of events was, and continued to be, common parlance during the last century and greatly influenced the production of visionary architecture by such practitioners as Cedric Price, Archigram and Bernard Tschumi. The *Hypnerotomachia*'s depictions of

machines is also somewhat metaphysical and anticipates the deserted landscapes of De Chirico that so inspired the Surrealists. *Hypnerotomachia* machines are weird concoctions of ornament, mechanism and desire, and therefore they also anticipate the 'bachelor machines' of art and the 'Pataphysical texts of Alfred Jarry and Raymond Roussel that so influenced the anarchic nonsense of Dada. Both Dada and Surrealism had an influence on visionary architecture of the 1900s.

The twentieth century, like no century before it, was defined by technological development, particularly the exponential and accelerating power and dexterity of the machine. Twentieth-century visionary architecture was conditioned by mechanistic change and the search for new ways in which this change could help us respond to the new environments formed in turn by mechanistic evolution (figs 4–5, 7). Conversely, some visionary work of this period sought to purvey a more agrarian attitude, seeking non-industrialized materials, antique construction methods, figurative compositional protocols and naturally occurring phenomena that might create a meaningful architecture. We are in love with the machine yet simultaneously despise it. We love its promise of easy liberation from our daily grind, yet we fear its capacity to imprison and its portent of servitude.

Drawing Prisons

Twentieth-century visionary architecture had other important pre-modern precursors. Two such figures were Giovanni Battista Piranesi and Claude Nicholas Ledoux.

The Venetian Piranesi was a visionary who holds a special place in architectural history. Like the fictional Poliphilo, Piranesi's world attempted to construe meaning out of ruinous fragments of an antiquated architecture. He also attached himself to an antiquarian past – that of classical Rome. His father was a stone-mason and a master builder. Piranesi's architectural career started when he became articled to his uncle, an architect and hydraulic engineer who was responsible for some of the monolithic

4
Un-House: A transportable standard-of-living package, the Environmental Bubble
François Dallegret, 1965.

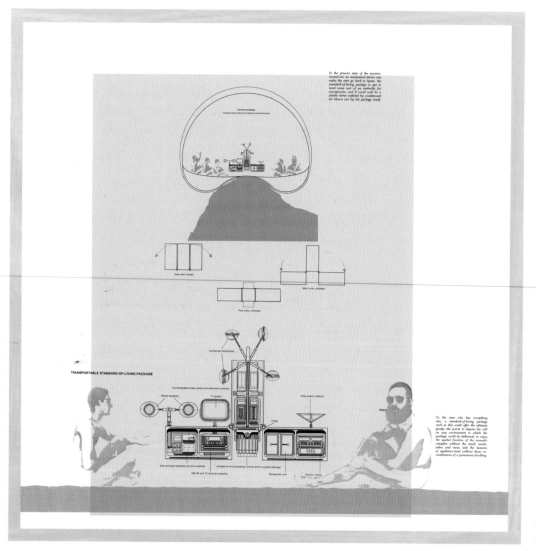

coastal walls around Venice's harbour. Contemporaneous with Piranesi's awakening architectural aspirations there raged a rigorous debate about the role of archaeology and the usefulness of following Vitruvuian ideas. In 1740 Piranesi travelled to Rome for the first time and was entranced by its beauty and history. The decaying fragments of the ancient city evoked a sense of wonder in Piranesi similar to that inspired by the strange land and its inscribed ruins in Poliphilo's dream. As a young man Piranesi also trained as a set designer and architectural illustrator, creating views of ancient Rome – a popular souvenir for the participants of Grand Tours. He was certainly the first 'paper architect' to purposely draw unbuildable propositions.

Piranesi's career seems to have divided into two halves. He spent the first half as a sort of constructor of retrospective histories. He would pictorially reconstruct the Antique fragments of Rome, not with the careful historical exactitude of the modern-day archaeologist but with

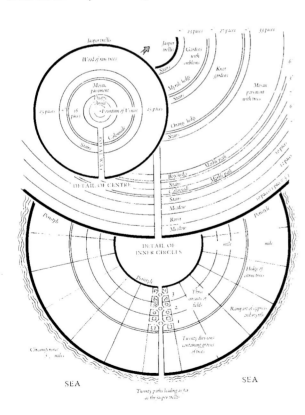

a kind of knowledgeable artfulness. He sought not only to glorify the Classical architectural lexicon but to rejuvenate it by 'finishing' these monuments to illustrate the continued vitality of the Classical idiom. This collaging of found objects and ideas combined with a preoccupation with polemic was also a major artistic and architectural tactic of the twentieth century.

Piranesi also anticipated the other great tradition of twentieth-century visionary architecture: exploring the gap between the architecture of architectural drawings and the architecture of real built buildings (fig. 8). In 1743 he published his *Prima parte di architetture* (figs 9–10). A portion of its dedication succinctly records his growing disaffection with philistine clients, his polemical inclinations, his yearning for an antiquarian vision and his determination to explore architectural progression through the drawn medium: 'The fact is that in our own time we have not seen buildings equalling the cost of a Forum of Minerva, of an Amphitheatre of Vespasian, or of a Palace of Nero, therefore, there seems to be no recourse than for me or some other modern architect to explain his ideas through his drawings, and so to take away from sculpture and painting the advantage that, as the great Juvarra has said, they now have here over architecture, and similarly to take it [architecture] away from the abuse of those with money, who make us believe that they themselves are able to control the execution of architecture.'[8] This sentiment is often at the hub of visionary ideas.

In 1749 Piranesi started to draw a series of massively overscaled imaginary prison interiors called the *Carceri* (Prisons for the Imagination). It is for this series of works that he is principally remembered. They are extraordinary. They seem to have come fast and furious from his hands, almost torn from a fevered soul. They are characterized by a frenzy of linework, deep, foreboding shadows, pulleys, cables, half-glimpsed torture machines and vertiginous Classical heights (figs 1, 11–14). For Piranesi to pick the prison as a motif was not unusual, as

8
Idealized representation of Rome from *Campo Marzio dell'Antica Roma*
Giovanni Battista Piranesi, 1762

9
Architectural fantasy from *Prima parte di architetture*
Giovanni Battista Piranesi, 1743

it was a popular theatre setting at the time. What is unusual is that a man who understood perspective implicitly finally let its dictums go and pushed his drawing style to the limit. His vanishing points are unaligned, and his projection planes multiply with unparalleled fecundity as he constructs the representation of an unrealizable group of objects and spaces. So, as with his historical representational endeavours, we see Piranesi as a schizoid artist/architect – one mode of thought dovetailing into, and contrasting with, the other. This testing of architectural limits and the differing modalities of the architectural drawing were the other large preoccupations of twentieth-century avant-garde discourse. The twentieth century's will to abstraction had a profound effect on its architecture.

The amazingly evocative images of the *Carceri* inspired Victorian Gothic Revivalists, John Soane, the Surrealists (particularly Dalí) and the Situationists, as well as more contemporary designers. These views of imagined, unbuildable, foreboding prison interiors are some of the most iconic images architects have ever produced. The *Carceri* are fraught with spatial conundrums, warped perspectives, incongruous and pendulous detail and shadowy machinery – war machines that can be set against the body. Indeed a later plate added to the collection features a poor soul on the rack. The cavernous, dark and dank spaces of Piranesi's imagination are analogous to Poliphilo's Dark Forest and likewise are full of fears and apprehensions: 'This made me suspect, not unreasonably, that I had arrived at the vast Hercynian forest, where there was nothing but the lairs of dangerous beasts and caverns full of noxious creatures and fierce monsters.'[9] As Robert Harbison has noted, the *Hypnerotomachia* is 'an architectural framework for a gothic novel without a heroine',[10] and so are the *Carceri*. Its influence can be seen time and time again in the pulleys, machinery and stretched cables of Lebbeus Woods's work (figs 286–8) and the hand-built timber machines and unbuildable scribings and perspectival conceits of Daniel Libeskind

(figs 263–5) and others. It can also be seen in park design and in the oversized fragment-figures in many modern and not so modern visionary-landscape propositions.

Prisons of Commerce

Ledoux was a contemporary French admirer of Piranesi. Although the two never met, the Italian was known to the Frenchman through his etchings. Ledoux's career was disrupted and rearticulated by the French Revolution; his Royalist sympathies had to be suppressed, and he had to cultivate an advocacy for the new government order. In 1804, two years after his death, his 'Architecture considerée sous le rapport de l'art, des moeurs et de la legislation' was published. This work not only speculates on the future of architecture but is a social blueprint for a noble and moral working community. It imagines a highly controlled society overlooked (both metaphorically and actually) by management, its surveillance methods aided and abetted by its architecture (fig. 15). Ledoux's career, post-Revolution, was as a public architect building churches, bridges, fountains, schools and even wells. In 1741 he was offered the job of Adjunct to the Inspecteur des Salines. He inspected, surveyed and posited designs for salt-works. It was in this capacity that he created his most extraordinary project, a design for the salt-works at Chaux in the Franche-Comté, up near the Swiss border. Its environs were deeply wooded, and the locals were prone to what Ledoux and his masters would describe as immoral behaviour; they were untrustworthy, inclined to drunkenness, pilfering and unreliability. Here again the forest was a place of danger, and architecture was its antidote.

Ledoux set about planning Chaux as an architectural expression of the rationality of the new order (figs 16–19). His first plan, the '*avant plan*' as it has been called, was essentially Classical; it drew on the geometry of the square as its ordering mechanism. It was symmetrical, and its columns were densely arranged.

10 (opposite bottom)
Ancient Capitol of Rome from *Prima parte di architetture*
Giovanni Battista Piranesi, 1743

11
Study for prison interior from *Carceri*
Giovanni Battista Piranesi, 1749

12
View of tunnel entrance
Giovanni Battista Piranesi, 1749

13
Study for prison interior from *Carceri*
Giovanni Battista Piranesi, 1749

14
Interior from *Carceri*
Giovanni Battista Piranesi, 1749

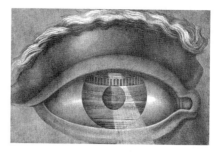

Its functionalism was criticised because the boiling pans for the salt were too close to the workers' dwellings, and it was criticised aesthetically for having too many grand columns.

Ledoux radically revised his plan, shifting the orthogonal geometry to a radial one. This facilitated the control-and-surveillance aspect of the scheme, and management's accommodation could be at the centre: the all-seeing 'eyes' at the centre of the 'eye', as it were. The 'Overseer's' and the 'Director's' houses were centrally placed. The project was clearly zoned and skewered itself forcibly into the Franche-Comté like a bullet hole or a dissection needle. Its radial lines sought to penetrate deep into the surrounding countryside, bending all to its will. This quantum shift from one spatial paradigm to another is clear if the first plan is seen as a manifestation of an industrial process, a sort of religious, contemplative space, and the second plan is seen as a village of noble artisans going about their business in a sober and ordered way. Ledoux's second plan had among many other aspirations the desire to remove the temptation of 'bacchic deliriums' through garden cultivation and honest toil. His architecture was pedagogic; it taught a way of life that achieved industrial economy by constantly occupying the workers' minds with rational ideas, hints about their station in life and the fear of being seen not to be conforming. This was a macrocosmic machine for the cheap and effective production of salt, the workers being merely the biological component in its biomechanical production processes. Like the mechanical parts, the biological ones needed to be strong, able, healthy and recursively accurate.

Ledoux's architectural lexicon consisted of a muscular, stripped-down Classicism that was sometimes prone to sparing, surreal ornamentation and always robustly conditioned by its primary geometry. Ledoux used a theatrical analogy for the organization of Chaux – it was a backdrop against which to act out French society's new-found productions. Chaux was a complex kit of parts fitted together seamlessly. Each part was analysed by Ledoux not just in architectural terms but also in societal, economic and political ones. During this time French society was debating and positing ideas that extended the gulf between itself and the old Order, which was seen as decadent, over-grandiose and metaphorically flatulent. The imperative was for a full, functional and new analysis of architectural form, to rid it of centuries of encrusted, costly but ultimately useless decoration and situate it firmly at the centre of a rational, new and supposedly equitable system of signs.[11] Ledoux's machine for the manufacture of salt was an epistemological model for French aspirations at this time. Chaux was treated by him as Denis Diderot treated the smaller machines of industry: 'In what physical or metaphorical system do we find more intelligence, discernment and consistency than in the machines for drawing gold or making stockings, and in the frames of the braid-makers, the gauze-makers, the drapers, or the silk workers? What mathematical demonstration is more complex than the mechanism of certain clocks or the different operations to which we submit the fibre of hemp or the chrysalis of the silkworm before obtaining a thread with which we weave?.'[12]

Avant-cybernetics

Diderot and Jean d'Alembert's *Encyclopédie* (the first volume, covering 'A', was published in 1751) was another attempt to define this rational mechanistic paradigm. Diderot and his associates drew and deconstructed machines and represented them in the *Encyclopédie* almost as one might create a tableau of a dissected human body (figs 21–22). Diderot was after a succinct, unambiguous system of classification for machines. He lamented the less than accurate naming of tools or parts that could be found across professions and crafts. He strove for a 'grammar of the arts'. He wrote about his 'dissections' of machines in these terms: '… the independence of the machine's various parts would seem to require one to talk about them, and illustrate them, all at the same time; and that is impossible – both in prose description, which has to be sequential (i.e. a matter of one thing after another), and in the plates, in which one working part will inevitably obscure the view of the other.'[13] This language recalls that of Norbert Wiener's cybernetics. During the late 1940s and '50s, Wiener began to see human beings and animals as complex systems which could be defined mathematically and mechanistically. One of his principle notions was that of the feedback loop. Cybernetic ideas in turn conditioned some of the most remarkable architectural work of the last century.

Diderot's approach continues to influence the way we see the world as sequential and machines as consisting of composite mechanical armatures, despite the efforts of Marcel Duchamp. Duchamp's mechanical elements in his famous *Large Glass* (1915–23) were bizarrely described and their functions highly contrived and ambiguous. It was Duchamp who – through his negation of static ideas and his preoccupation with shifting relational images and the emotional dynamics between viewer and object – anticipated notions of responsive architecture. His world continues to be highly influential on experimental architecture. It predates second-order cybernetics (first-order cybernetics recast to incorporate the observer), which itself was a major influence on the work of members of the Independent Group (1950s), on Cedric Price and Archigram (1960s onwards) and, allegedly, on the

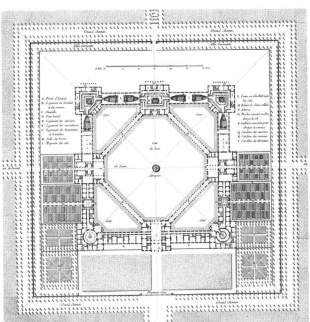

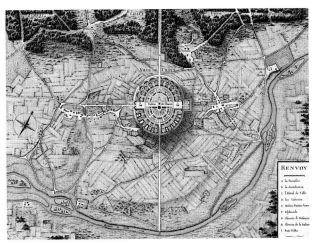

20
Cyclic epistemology drawing
Lebbeus Woods, 1984

21
Engraving of leather tanners gilding
Diderot and D'Alembert, 1751–

22
Engraving of the stages of casting a horse-and-rider statue
Diderot and D'Alembert, 1751–

Sculpture), Fonte des Statues Equestres.
Coupe de la Figure Equestre par le milieu de sa longueur, avec le Noyau qui remplit la capacité renfermée par la Cire, les Egouts des Cires, les Jets, les Events, et entourée de Brasquaillons. Et Figure Equestre couvert du Moule de Potée, recouvert du Bandage de fer.

FF

mid-twentieth-century Situationists.

Ledoux's fellow Frenchman the Situationist Guy Debord would have been able to ascertain the machinations of the capitalist 'Spectacle' in Ledoux's plan – even at this early stage in global consumerism. The Situationists despised the Spectacle – 'the collapse of reality into streams of images, products, and activities sanctioned by business and bureaucracy'[14] – and its inherent fragmentation of society, as we shall see (fig. 23). The Spectacle was present at Chaux, as plain as plain could be. It is interesting that Ledoux's epistemology is formed of concentric rings; other epistemologies and memory devices have also utilized this particular geometry and its implied dynamics. The Platonic geometry of the circle appears in the *Hypnerotomachia* as the otherworldly form of the Arcadian/utopian Isle of Cytherea: 'Its circuit measured three miles around, and it was a mile in diameter, which was divided in three parts. Each third contained 333 paces, one foot, two palms and a little more …'[15] The island consists

of geometrically planted herbs, patterned paths, topiary hedges, nymphs and numerous trophies. The trophies are yet more three-dimensional formal prompts for Poliphilo's take on things. They are images that make him remember the complex ideas and concepts of his world and their relation to each other – in short a memory machine.

Another example of the geometry of concentric circles informing an epistemology is the Renaissance work of the magus Giordano Bruno; like Colonna's it is also magico-mechanical. Bruno proposed a memory system consisting of concentric rings that rotated relative to one another. This rotation could be used to create juxtapositions of many mythological and alchemical concepts. Bruno believed that this system contained all the combinations and hierarchies in both the earthly and the spiritual realms: 'But Bruno's main interest was not the outer world but the inner world. And in his memory systems we see the effort to operate magico-mechanical laws not mechanisms. The translation of this magical conception

into mathematical terms has only been achieved in our own day. Bruno's assumption that the astral forces which govern the outer world also operate within, and can be reproduced or captured there to operate a magicomechanical memory, seems to bring one curiously close to the mind machine which is able to do so much of the work of the human brain by mechanical means.'[16]

So, from the simplistic representation of the circle as a form of surveillance, and its subdivision and symbolism, we have an evolutionary path to the computers of today – the virtual machines that had such an impact on the architectural work of the 1990s. In the eroticized drift of Poliphilo, the frenzy, impossibility and shadowy machines of the *Carceri*, the everyday, surveying social machine of Chaux, the architectural possibilities of memory theatres (those old precursors to computers) and the avant-cybernetics of Diderot are the genetics of the various architectural machines and technologies that conditioned experimental architecture of the twentieth century.

23
**Interior perspective
of New Babylon**
Constant, 1963

Improvising Body Space with Imagined Organs

Nat Chard

Nat Chard's work, like the other work discussed in this chapter, concerns observation, perception, distortion and the moving, visceral body navigating through architectural space. To the layperson, and even to many members of the architecture profession, visionary architecture can seem extreme, naïve or over-complicated. Architects who are interested in the expansion of architectural thought attempt to expand the realms of drawing, design and discourse. Fundamentally there is a simple reciprocal relationship at the bottom of any project in this book: if technology changes or augments the body, then – as the body is architecture's conduit – architecture must change and vice versa. Therefore developments in medicine are as important to the progression of architecture as advances in traditional building material, probably more so.

Nat Chard has been inspired by the chrono-photographs of Etienne-Jules Marey and Eadweard Muybridge to explore the architectural space between bodies, between parts of bodies and within bodies. Chard also sees the psychological perception of an individual's space as another important constituent of pure architectural space: 'Separated from a generic idea of programme, the architecture responds to the intuitive, the improvised and the accidental. The role of the architect is to propose the flavour – not its choreography. The spaces are driven by the desires and anxieties of the participants as well as practical programmatic requirements, such as supporting the body. As they learn from space, they can

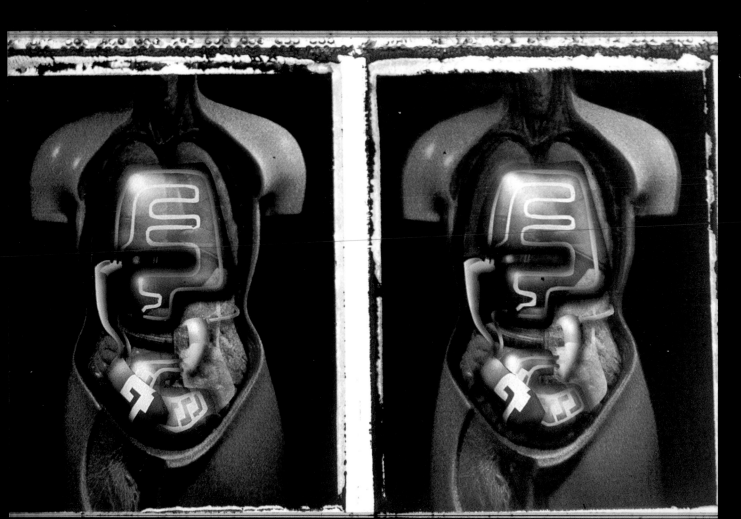

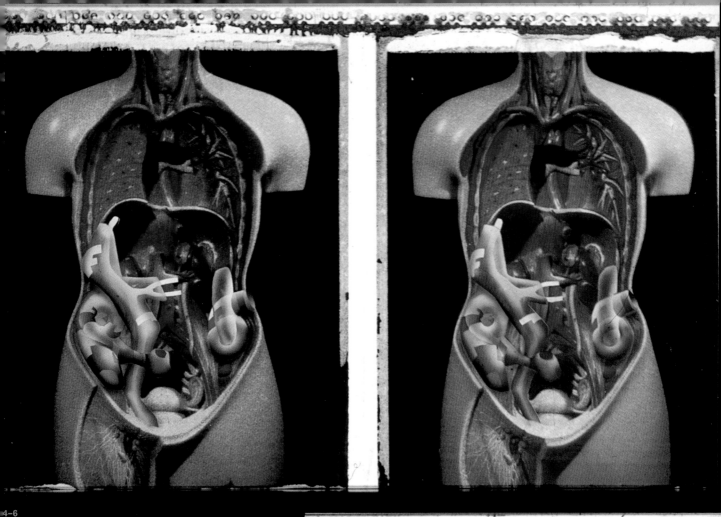

4-6
tereoscopic images
howing various
rosthetic devices
ugmenting bodily
uids
992

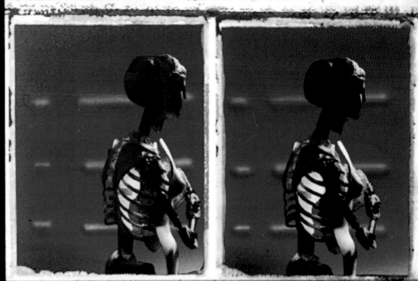

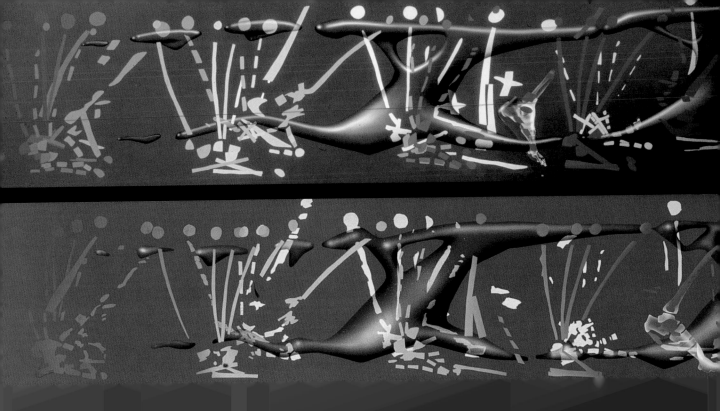

Casa Mila, a housing block; the Parc Guell; and his greatest work, the massive Sagrada Família cathedral.

The Parc Guell, named after Gaudí's patron, is on an elevated site to the north-west of Barcelona. Originally Gaudí planned it as a housing estate, but he only built a couple of houses on it. In the early 1920s it was bought by the municipality and named as a public park. It is choreographed by a series of meandering paths, and its focal points include a large public square and some happily deformed colonnades. The park's design features tilted columns which sometimes form drunken caricatures of Gothic vaulting. Gaudí used rough-hewn stone contrasted with crazy broken-tile mosaics. The overall effect is a cacophony of swirling forms and dazzling, fractured surfaces (fig. 46). His two housing blocks each have their own flavours, but one can see that they both come from the same seething imagination. Whilst both are characterized by skeletal fenestration and balcony composition, it at roof level that each has its own character. Casa Batllo's roof has the humped-back appearance of a sleeping dragon, all scales and spine, whilst Casa Mila creates a Surreal roofscape of twisted chimney stacks and undulating surfaces out of which a great gaping atrium is moulded (figs 44–5, 47).

The Sagrada Família was charged to Gaudí a year after it was begun, in 1883. It was to occupy his entire professional life and is an extraordinary architectural achievement. Its most remarkable façade was inspired by the Nativity. It has three portals, each with a theme: the Christian virtues of Faith, Hope and Charity. The cathedral was meant to have twelve spires of which eight have been built. Christian iconography melts into the foliage of the Tree of Life, and the whole façade has a rather cold, lava-like, droopy permanence. Dalí knew these landmarks of Barcelona from a young age and associated them with the vitality of the Catalan spirit and a Surreal future. As he put it in an essay, 'Concerning the Terrifying Beauty of Art Nouveau Architecture', in 1933, '... Everything that had been the most self-evidently practical and functional in the known architecture of the past, suddenly, in Art Nouveau, no longer serves any purpose at all; or, that which would be unable to win over pragmatic intellectualism to it, would only be of use for the "functioning of desires" – desires, moreover, that are the most shady, discredited and shameful.'[19]

The Imminent Morphogenetics of Gaudí

In 1917 D'Arcy Wentworth Thompson produced a book entitled *On Growth and Form*.[20] This book became an important precedent for architects interested in the metamorphosis of form. Thompson's book was dedicated to discovering the underlying geometric composition of natural shapes. It is illustrated by animals overlaid with a point grid. As the relationships between the points are repositioned, the animal changes into its geometric cousins. Some of these forms have been favoured by evolution and are therefore recognizable – others have not. Each family of forms shares a morphogenetic line. At the time the book was being read, Gaudí was designing the nave for the Sagrada Família.

Since 1979 Mark Burry has been Consultant Architect to the commission completing the Sagrada Família. Burry has developed speculative work that illustrates the extreme beauty and prophetic nature of Gaudí's masterwork (figs 32, 48–53). This work has not only enabled the geometric systems that Gaudí used to be rediscovered and the architectural work to continue. It has also opened the door to a way of conceiving of the future development of architecture in terms of a geometrical method with which to reconcile the demands of the real world with the amazing potential of the cyberplasmic virtual world.

Burry's work concerns the underlying 'second geometry' that Gaudí used to create his visionary work: 'The fundamental characteristic for second order geometry is that non-coplanar straight lines can variously describe warped surfaces with a pragmatism that is

masked by the apparent free-form composition. The principal practical advantage is the way each of these surfaces can be fragmented into individual components which, when combined, will form a seamless whole.'[21] In other words, Gaudí's work, whether detail, column, vault or decoration, is a representation of a frozen moment of a morphogenetic family. Gaudí settled on forms he found agreeable after tweaking (amazingly without a computer) the geometric points whose trajectories define a formal family. He had to decide which original form to throw into which geometric matrix. He stopped at certain points in these experiments as he was constrained by the dexterity of builders and the material characteristics of the stone or concrete he was using.

Burry has many fewer constraints. He is liberated by the computer, its visualization and its control of manufacture. Through his research the Sagrada Família can be viewed as a treasure trove of hyperforms waiting to be revealed. Burry can

virtually and structurally extend the family of Gaudian forms to create a cascade of related but extreme shapes by virtually changing the mathematical rules Gaudí set himself. This could produce the sort of 'edible' and 'soft' architecture craved by Dalí. Surrealist spatial protocols are shown to be of use in this possible hyper-Gaudian architecture, and the link between Dalí and Gaudí is affirmed: 'Read in this way, they are utterly indicative of humankind's striving for the ideal while one eye is kept on the monstrous, an ineffable benchmark and tally of extremes. The implied perfection is only skin deep. Closer reading provides the stimulation to extrapolate new ways to release the music and hear different architectural cadences to those with which we are more familiar.'[22]

Dalí admired the non-functional exuberance of Gaudí's work with, in Dalí's mind, its associations with scatological, erotic and digestive forms and processes. Dalí, around this time, started to create painted constructs which depicted hard objects as soft and malleable (his *Soft Watch* is an example). He wilfully conceived of Art Nouveau architecture as 'edible'. This 'edibility' was equated with its elements' non-angularity of form, their overt decorativeness, their animistic associations and, ultimately, their beauty. Dalí despised the white, clean lines of Le Corbusier and the formal purity of the ideas of the Machine Aesthetic. By the time he was writing his 'Terrifying Beauty' essay, Dalí had left the concerns of Purism behind him. At the end of the essay he becomes explicit about the importance of kitsch, lust and anti-intellectualism in his developing 'edible' aesthetic: 'Erotic desire is the downfall of intellectual aesthetics. "Venus in Furs" is heralded under the sign of the unique beauty of real ferment that is vital and materialist – Beauty is none other than the sum total of the consciousness of our perversions – Breton said: "Beauty will be convulsive or will cease to be." The new Surrealist Age of "cannibalism of objects" equally justifies the following conclusion: Beauty will be edible or will cease to be.'[23]

44
Casa Batllo (note the 'dragon-back' roof)
Antoni Gaudí, 1905–7

45
Casa Mila
Antoni Gaudí,
1905–10

46
Chapel interior in Parc Guell
Antoni Gaudí,
1900–14

47
Roofscape and chimney of Casa Mila
Antoni Gaudí,
1905–10

42 (opposite top)
Tower of Barbary, Dream Palace
Ferdinand Cheval,
1879–1912

43 (opposite bottom)
Exhibition composite drawing showing easels, lighting, plinths and layout
Spiller Farmer Architects, 1988–9

Dalí's and Gaudí's descriptions of objects and buildings as malleable, soft and metamorphic anticipated contemporary architectural notions of morphable materials and space made out of nanotechnology, cyberspace and biotechnology.

Children of the Revolution

Both the Russian art establishment of the early twentieth century and its young pretenders were effectively amputated from the rest of European artistic discourse and so started to evolve their own idiosyncratic way. Before the First World War, Paris had been a focus for Russian artists. Futurism, particularly the intellectually rebellious acts surrounding it, attracted Vladimir Tatlin, El Lissitzky, Naum Gabo and Anton Pevsner, who all lived in Paris. After the Russian Revolution, Kasimir Malevich, Tatlin and Alexandr Rodchenko, together with the writer Anatoli Lunacharsky, formed the nucleus around which Russian Constructivism would evolve. Lunacharsky, who had been made commissar for education, came up with the lexical hybrid 'agitprop', a combination of 'agitation' and 'propaganda'. Agitprop trains, boats and street floats were constructed to carry the Revolutionary message out to the wider Socialist Republic. Art schools were rearticulated to echo the new Revolutionary approach, including the hugely influential Vkhutemas school in Moscow. Malevich and Lissitzky were teachers there. Between 1914 and 1917, Malevich's work attempted to represent the underlying purity of mathematics, Cubism and nature. Preoccupied with the power of colour, he called this art 'Suprematism'. He was not interested in the notion of painting as a means of representing objects but as a way to conjure up an object's 'object-ness', as a way of provoking pure phenomenological feeling. Suprematist painting was beyond the object. His search reached a culmination with *White Square on a White Background* (1918).

The architectural visionary was Tatlin. In 1913 Tatlin had met Picasso in Paris and seen his Cubist sculptures. Tatlin developed his own series of sculptures/reliefs during 1914–15. *Corner Relief*, *Suspended Type* hailed a new direction in art and architecture that was to have an impact on the subsequent century. In 1919 Tatlin was commissioned to design a monument commemorating the Third Communist International. The design was first shown publicly in 1929.

It was a thousand-foot-high leaning tower consisting of three pieces, each piece rotating at a different speed. The tower was never built due to a shortage of materials. In 1920 Tatlin and some other colleagues posited the notion of Constructivism as an ongoing research programme in a paper entitled 'The Work Ahead of Us': 'In 1915 an exhibition of material models on the laboratory scale was held in Moscow (an exhibition of reliefs and counter-reliefs). An exhibition held in 1917 presented a number of examples of material combinations, which were the results of more complicated investigations into the use of material in itself, and what this leads to: movement, tension, and a mutual relationship between [them].'[24] Also in 1920, Gabo and Pevsner wrote the 'Realistic Manifesto': 'Neither Futurism nor Cubism has brought us what our time has expected of them. Besides those two artistic schools our recent past has had nothing of importance or deserving our attention … The realization of our perceptions of the world in the forms of space and time is the only aim of our pictorial and plastic art. In them we do not measure our works with the yardstick of beauty, we do not weigh them with pounds of tenderness and sentiments.'[25]

48 (right)
Elevation of Sagrada Família showing recent and older façades
Antoni Gaudí, 1884–

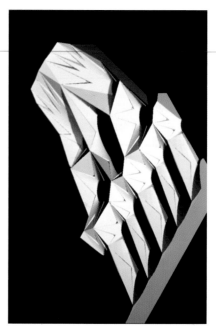

representation. New Babylon is represented through plans, perspectives, photomontages, models and dynamic concept sketches. At first Debord and the other Situationists welcomed Constant's attempt to define Situationism in urban terms and as an act of rebellion against the Modernism of Le Corbusier and his friends: 'We have a right to expect from truly impressive architecture – disorientation on a daily basis.'[4]

The first pieces of New Babylon were completed in 1958. In July 1959 the Situationists' journal *Potlatch* published 'The Great Game to Come', an essay setting out the major preoccupations of New Babylon. In this essay Constant emphasized the importance of swiftly constructing new cities and also commented that the 'total lack of alternatives involving play in the organization of social life prevents urbanism from attaining the level of creation and the gloomy and sterile appearance of most modern neighbourhoods is a shameful reminder of this.'[5] He demanded that the new city be ephemeral and diverse with playful animated ambiences always in flux. He believed that the *dérive* was an efficient way to study these phenomena. In his essay he also espoused the benefits of cinema projection, TV, radio, rapid transport and fast communications to contemporary urban existence: '[T]he investigation of technology and its exploitation for recreational ends on a higher plane is one of the most pressing tasks required to facilitate creation of a unitary urbanism on the scale demanded by the society of the future.'[6]

New Babylon is the only example of a city planned to reflect Situationist concepts and ideas. It is also a running commentary on the artistic and architectural predilections of the following fifteen years. Some of the first images Constant created of New Babylon are the most iconic. The *Constructie in Oranje* (Orange Construction) is vaguely reminiscent of Kiesler's Endless Theatre. Orange Construction again utilizes plexiglass and choreographs the plastic's surface by radiating model-wire lines that every now and then reveal a 'hub' (fig. 76).

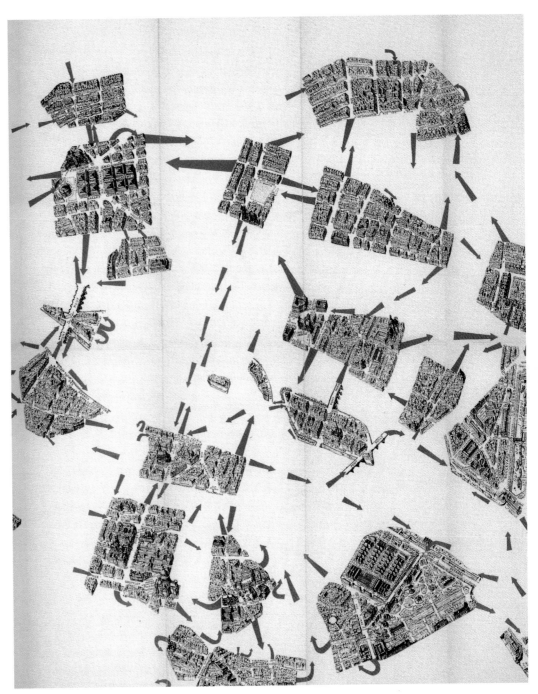

75
Guide psychogéo-
***graphique* de Paris**
Guy Debord, 1956

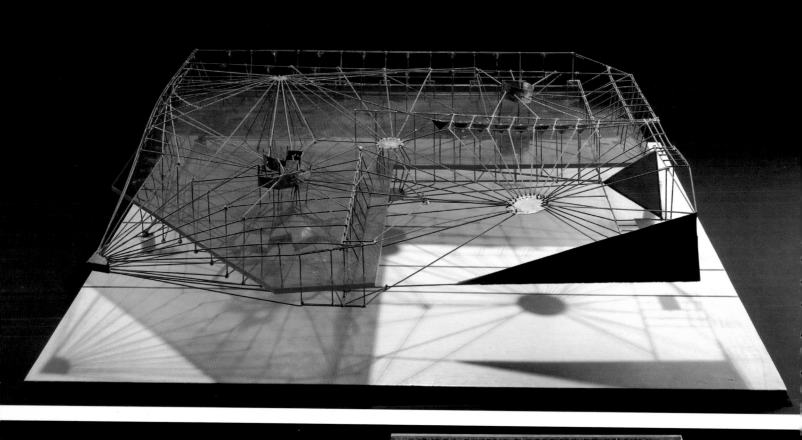

Again similar to Kiesler, Constant produced the architectural model as one might produce a sculpture. Throughout its long life, New Babylon consistently and cunningly declared very little about the spatial and societal ramifications of its architecture, nor did it specify the exact function of its key elements, whether they were hubs, cores or metallic armatures. Constant's work on the project hovered between abstraction and the mimicking of established modes of architectural representation. Models were photographed close in, to create the illusion that his plexiglass floor planes and spindly structure would translate into the massive objects they would be if built. They wouldn't be, of course; this project was not about building. Structure often consisted of complex webs of steel rods and tried too hard to escape the orthogonal preoccupations of real structural engineering (figs 76–81).

The first New Babylon models are rough-hewn, and their surfaces are speckled with small splashes of paint. *GeleSector* (Yellow Sector) (1958) added aluminium and copper to Constant's preferred model-making materials, and these started to form labyrinths. The labyrinth evolved to become one of the leitmotifs of the New Babylon project as a whole. Yellow Sector carried forward the aesthetic degradation of the surfaces of the model; a secondary language of pocking, corrosion and splats of paint and ink was artfully applied to it. During these early years the project progressed mainly in model form; a few plans supplemented this diet of plexiglass and wire. Some elements – for example the *Klein Labyr* (Small Labyrinth) (1959) – seemed to be essays in grungy Constructivism.

The surface patina of these works sometimes evokes movement patterns or denotes the messy memory of a recent unspecified event. In his second essay from 1959, Constant asserted that the traditional city was in disagreement with new forms of contemporary life. He believed that the human condition makes it necessary for us to seek thrills and adventure. He wanted to overcome nature, to control it fully. Again similarities with

Kiesler occur; Kiesler too wanted to eradicate the City/Countryside divide. Also in this essay, Constant demanded a new architecture of technology juxtaposed with the emotive and psychological play of the city's inhabitants.[7]

During this most productive of years, 1959, Constant started to show the relentless, unmitigated scale of New Babylon. It was revealed as an ubiquitous structure touching the ground with a Kieslerian intermittence. The proposed city was capable of covering the whole surface of the earth. It was like a biological growth, a vascular system of huge blocks linked together by skeins of arcing roadways that created the impression of mycelia. The year 1960 brought the first interior sketches of New Babylon. To begin with, they were carefully hatched and shadowed, but they quickly became inhabited by splotches, scribbles and deformed ladders made from trails of clotted ink.

In an essay written in 1960, Constant defined his brand of unitary urbanism as 'neither town planning, nor art, nor style; nor does it correspond to concepts like integration and the synthesis of cultural forms …'[8] In the same essay he evoked the cybernetic ideas of Norbert Wiener and stated that 'town planning should address this ongoing automation of life and the evolution of the robot.'[9] The time then spent on domestic and work chores could, he thought, be

usefully redirected towards creative play. By 1961 New Babylon had taken on the aesthetic of the fairground or carnival. Its representations were quickly and erratically sketched; concern in this suite of sketches was for movement, air currents and circular constructions. The following year Constant produced dioramas of wood and mirrors, exhibiting a strangely Cubist tendency. Comparative maps were drawn showing a sector juxtaposed on the city of Amsterdam. These drawings serve to illustrate yet again New Babylon's huge scale and extreme proportions. Whilst its internal labyrinth was the global stage set on which humanity's ludic tendency ran riot, it rode over other more historic urban labyrinths that it came upon.

By 1964 New Babylon was exhibiting artificial landscapes consisting of numerous crane-like pylons. In Constant's 1965 essay, 'New Babylon: Outline of a Culture', he returned to the theme of technology, reasserting that it was a critical tool for 'realizing an experimental collectivism'.[10] But details of this synthesis of technology and ludic living remained elusive. During 1965 and '66 a series of internal perspectives was drawn that oddly conformed to the tyranny of the grid so beloved by the rightist capitalists that Situationism was supposed to detest. Perhaps Constant's gridded interiors were attempts at *détourning* the grid. If so, they were poor ones. By this time he had resigned from the Situationist movement after much internal bickering about the role and form of architecture in a theoretical Situationist Utopia. One suspects that many of his colleagues failed to comprehend the extreme complexity and near impossibility of the full rejection of capitalist paradigms and legislation of space that a project such as New Babylon proposed to contend with. To design a scheme for a city that eluded the geometries, social organization and political implications of the capitalist 'Spectacle' was a great battle.

In 1966 Constant produced designs for the *Groot Labyr* (Great Labyrinth). This took the form of a collection of box-sectioned, angled and 'I' steel sections, arranged almost as a Constructivist installation (fig. 67). Around 1967 New Babylon began to feel what might be called the 'Francis Bacon influence'. The inhabitants of the city became blurred and strangely distorted. Stark planes of colour – blue here, terracotta there and yellow there – burst into the interiors, and the exterior became much more mesh-like. The year 1967's versions of New Babylon were 'straighter', more recognizable as architecture. Over the next few years New Babylon declined further into a chaos of scribble, haemorrhaging figures, smoke and general splatter. Enigmatic rooms appeared with bumps of organic, fleshy blobs heaped against walls, some even engaging in a bloated coitus. It is here that we leave New Babylon as it decays and disappears. The last model was an accumulation of small loudspeakers, lights and circuitry: 'The plexiglass control panel allowed the model to be played like a musical instrument.'[11]

The Cybernetics of Fun

In England, for almost a decade from 1960, another attempt to deal with performance, cybernetics, play, learning and leftist politics began to take shape. Superficially it had similarities with New Babylon, but these similarities were shallow. The Fun Palace was the result of a collaboration between its architect, Cedric Price, and Joan Littlewood. Littlewood was an advocate of street theatre and founder of the Theatre of Action in Manchester, which utilized methods of performance conceived to engage the working class and present the social ideas of the left wing. The Fun Palace site, just under 20 acres in area and situated in London's Lea Valley, was designed in opposition to New Babylon. The Fun Palace was anticipatory whilst New Babylon was intended to be destabilizing. The Fun Palace was a design for an entertainment centre rather than a proposition for a whole frenzied, delegislated, anarchist city that knew no boundaries. Again unlike New Babylon,

82
View of Fun Palace from helicopter
Cedric Price, 1962

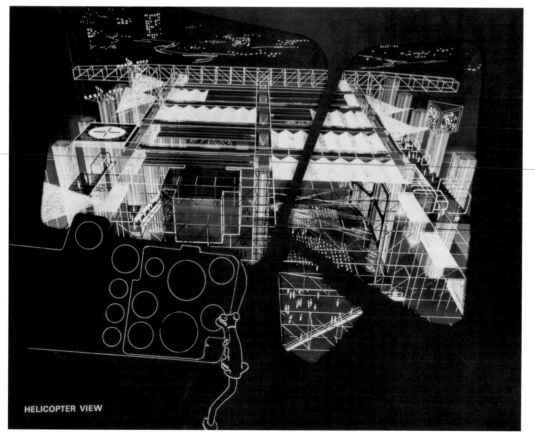

HELICOPTER VIEW

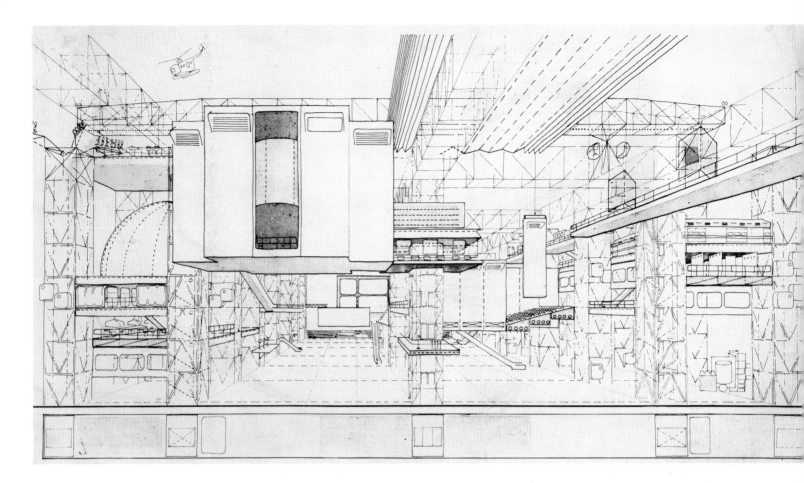

83
**Interior perspective
of Fun Palace**
Cedric Price, 1962

Price's preoccupation was with the provision of a highly defined kit of moveable parts which could be combined in numerous ways to enable and service a variety of uses and spatial configurations (figs 82–4). This kit included a selection of skin and servicing strategies. New Babylon's creator seldom had much interest in the make-up of the building envelope and the layered boundaries and conditions inherent in the transition from inside to outside. Constant was relatively vague on the technological hardware that would be necessary to create the project's dioramas, labyrinths and psychogeographical ambience. The Fun Palace was conceived as an articulate, dynamic spatial shipyard designed to encourage users to be responsible for their entertainment, their learning and their space.

Paradoxically, the drawings of the Fun Palace were lacking in the sort of artful representations that so beguiled architects. It was drawn as a complex machine, no more, no less. Price's drawings

were infinitely more accurate, descriptive and self-effacing than Constant's more pyrotechnic artistic approach. Functionally, the Fun Palace was founded and predicated on a massive services plinth that held sanitation, structure, vehicular access, loading bays and the like. Above this plinth, which stretched over the whole site, were latticed support towers supporting lattice beams and space frames which in turn supported escalators, pod-like enclosures, acoustic attenuators, louvres, a helipad, communication masts and moveable partitions and ceilings. Price could be very definite whilst specifying his constituent parts; he even navigated the project through the arduous London Fire Regulations with the aid of intumacious paint that would protect the steel members in case of fire.

The Fun Palace was to metamorphose in response to an ever-accelerating culture of change until eventually it was demolished. Price set a retirement age for the structural frame of ten years after

completion. Whilst Constant paid lip service to the notion of change over time, Price imbued every large and small element within the Fun Palace with a dimension of time, expendability and lifespan.

Price used others to complement his own expertise. Yona Friedman and Richard Buckminster Fuller were consultants on some aspects of the Fun Palace's elemental mobility. During 1963 the cybernetician Gordon Pask joined the team as a member of the 'Committee for the Fun Palace Cybernetic Theatre'. Pask and Price's vision of the Cybernetic Theatre had slight tinges of Kiesler's Endless Theatre (figs 68–9) as well as nuances of Constant's New Babylon. Pask's expertise was in the area of human learning as a cybernetic system; he was instrumental in developing second-order cybernetics. Pask called the observer's influence 'conversation'. So in the Cybernetic Theatre Paskian second-order cybernetics was integrated with Paskian

LEA RIVER SITE

**Photomontage
exterior perspective
of Fun Palace**
Cedric Price, 1962

Conversation Theory. Pask wanted the theatre to 'overcome restrictions in entertainment media such as the cinema and television'.[12] Following on from one of the primary notions in cybernetics, feedback – the ability of a system to self-regulate its actions – one of Pask's ideas for the Cybernetic Theatre was to wire the audience's seats into a feedback loop connected via computers to the performers.

Nowadays, the illustrations of the Fun Palace have a sedate charm, but between the lines a bustling building with a fast metabolic rate, adapting, responding and 'feedbacking', can be perceived. In contrast to frenetic New Babylon, the Fun Palace reveals deeper and more detailed thought and exhibits a pragmatism capable of delivering space that challenged the political and institutional status quo. New Babylon was a conceit conceived as a city, created by an artist masquerading as an architect for polemical reasons. It therefore often lacks full architectural understanding and

detail. The Fun Palace was a far more ambitious proposition than the rather staid version of some of its ideas built in Paris during the 1970s – designed by Renzo Piano and Richard Rogers and called the Centre Beaubourg.

Soft Babylon

The Fun Palace was designed nearly half a century ago. Has the growth of computer hardware and software facilitated a new cybernetics of Situationism incorporating new articulations of the *dérive*, *détournement*, psychogeography, unitary urbanism, expediency, delight and timely choice? One architect who believes this has happened is Marcos Novak. As we shall see, Novak first came to the fore as the author of the seminal 1991 essay 'Liquid Architecture in Cyberspace'. He equated the notions of cyberspace and virtuality as metaphorically liquid. The architectures of Price and Constant both attempted, albeit without the hardware and software drivers of Novak's virtual

world, to create fluid spaces that could quickly reconfigure and respond to their users' desires – a democratization of space.

In 1998 Novak created a notion of a cyberspatial Neo-Situationism which he christened Soft Babylon in Constant's honour: 'Over thirty years since its design, the multiple artificial landscapes first conceived in Constant's "New Babylon", for a space-frame structure over a city, are being realized through the medium of newspace, in manners both immersive and everted.'[13] Novak saw New Babylon as a utopia created to extend the concept of what is possible architecturally and socially. He argued that one must see Constant's propositions as an analogy for present-day technological and spatial environments: 'The megastructural framework that was to cover the entire planet has been replaced with the infrastructure of the global internet, the cellular telephony grid, and the constellations of low-earth orbit satellites that bring the whole earth within wireless

During the 1950s, the avant-garde spirit arrived in England, and younger architects and artists demanded a say in the running of the Institute of Contemporary Arts in London. The Independent Group, as they became known, began to propose exhibitions and instigate talks on mechanization, cybernetics, the automobile and the like. A fertile field of art practice developed, later known as Pop, and this inspired architects of the subsequent generation to be bold in their visions of the future. This small movement had its crescendo with the 'This is Tomorrow' exhibition of 1956. Peter Reyner Banham, Lawrence Alloway, Richard Hamilton, Eduardo Paolozzi and the Smithsons prepared the ground for London's pivotal role in the development of visionary architecture.

100
Instant City
Ron Herron,
Archigram, 1969

'[A]ccelerated changes in the human condition require an array of symbolic images of man which will match up to the requirements of constant change, fleeting impression and a high rate of obsolescence. A replaceable, expendable series of Ikons.'
John McHale

When the art collector Peggy Guggenheim left London during the early part of the Second World War, it was to escape the prospect of German occupation. It seemed at the time that she took with her the hope of creating a venue for British artists and architects that might have the same impact on art as the cafés of Paris or the bars of New York. The Guggenheim collection of Modern art would have been its centrepiece. The idea for such a venue had been mooted as far back as 1936 when the international Surrealist exhibition had galvanized all the strains of the Modern-art establishment. Artists, gallery owners, collectors and critics started to communicate with each other in unprecedented ways. Whilst nothing happened during the war years, the idea lay dormant in the mind of the English Surrealist Roland Penrose. When the war ended, Britain was in a dire state. Food and petrol rationing, for example, would continue for another four years. Many of Britain's major cities had been ravaged by the Blitz. Amongst the socialist-leaning population there were expectations for the future based on the dissolution of Britain's turgid and reactionary class system, the creation of a national health service and the formation of an equitable education system. This grey, bedraggled and expectant society saw little immediate benefit from being on the winning side in the war; taxes were high and scarcity ground every family down.

At the beginning of 1946, Penrose, with the art critic Herbert Read and a few friendly funding angels, determinedly created the Institute of Contemporary Arts. In February 1948 the ICA curated an exhibition entitled 'Forty Years of Modern Art' in the basement of the Academy Cinema in London's Oxford Street. The exhibition was swiftly followed by 'Forty Thousand Years of Modern Art' at the same venue. The ICA operated without permanent premises until June 1950. 17–18 Dover Street became its new headquarters, officially opened in December 1950. During that year the ICA hosted the exhibition 'James Joyce: His Life and Work'. A young artist called Richard Hamilton designed the catalogue. This exhibition was followed by another, 'Aspects of British Art', which featured the work of Eduardo Paolozzi and William Turnbull as well as Hamilton.

In May 1951 the Festival of Britain opened on London's South Bank. Many creative artists and architects felt that the Festival, like the Millennium Dome of 2000, was a lost opportunity. The Festival comprised a strangely watered-down traditional Modernism mixed with Art Deco motifs and was largely felt to offer nothing to the future. It was another example, if more were needed, of the artistic and intellectual bankruptcy of the British creative establishment. The ICA's contribution to the festivities was a show called 'Ten Decades: A Review of British Taste', a relatively traditional narrative journey through the major artistic events of the previous century which opened in August. But before this, the ICA shook the preconceptions of polite artistic society with another show: 'Growth and Form'.

The Evocative Sign

The initial ideas for 'Growth and Form' stemmed from Nigel Henderson. Henderson was a child of the old English establishment who had been sent down from Stowe school. His mother, Wyn, enjoyed life to the full; she had many lovers and was a good friend of the Bloomsbury Group, Dylan Thomas and James Joyce, to name but a few. In 1938 Wyn Henderson helped Peggy Guggenheim open the Guggenheim Jeune gallery in London. Nigel Henderson met Yves Tanguy, Max Ernst and even Marcel Duchamp. After the war, in which he served as an RAF pilot, he started studying art at London's Slade School.

Here he met Paolozzi. Hamilton joined the Slade from the Royal Academy and became another friend.

During the late 1940s Henderson was becoming interested in the underlying order of biological form and had the idea that the ICA might curate an exhibition themed around notions of seed dispersal. Paolozzi, at this time based in Paris, introduced his friend to D'Arcy Wentworth Thompson's *On Growth and Form*. Henderson lent the book to Hamilton, who then created the ICA proposal, which they presented to Penrose together. In the proposal document Hamilton wrote: '[T]he painter and the sculptor have much to gain from the enlargement of their world of experience by an appreciation of the forms in nature beyond their immediate visual environment. It is the enlarged environment opened by scientific studies that we would reveal for its visual qualities.'[1] The exhibition was also innovative because of its multimedia presentation. It included cine clips, photomicrographs, radiograms and much else. It illustrated the myriad ways people had developed to explore and record images of biological form. In effect it was a dictionary of scientific visual prostheses. Many establishment critics' feathers were ruffled, but the show did start to set the young ICA members apart from their more formal, older colleagues. At the close of 1951, these younger members began to suggest lectures and lecturers to the hierarchy at the ICA. In the spring of 1952 fifty or so individuals were invited to attend a 'Young Group', a decision presumably provoked by the need to quell discontent among younger members.

The first presentation to this group was of Paolozzi's collage material, which consisted of postcards, diagrams and advertisements. It was presented in no particular order and with no explicit narrative. At this time Peter Reyner Banham became the newly christened 'Independent Group' convenor. 'Independent' because the Group kept a healthy distance from the more formal activities of the ICA yet had a presence on its management committee. Also around this time the architects Alison and Peter Smithson, Henderson and Paolozzi submitted a proposal to the management committee for an exhibition to be called 'Parallel of Art and Life'. Concurrent with the evolving exhibition programme was a series of discussion and presentation forums about such subjects as the 'Victorian and Edwardian Decorative Arts' exhibition at the Victoria and Albert Museum, helicopter designs, the uses of cybernetics, 'Are Proteins Unique?' and the 'Machine Aesthetic'. Other members of the Group include the architect Theo Crosby, the critic and author Lawrence Alloway and the artists John McHale and Magda Cordell.

In September 1953 'Parallel of Art and Life' opened. This show exhibited 122 photographic images. The gallery was used not as a series of planes on which to mount panels but as the structure onto which the work was tied back. The exhibition was hung from the ceiling, projected from the walls and even leant up against the walls on the floor (fig. 101). It presented work at different scales, not just physically but also in terms of subject. It featured images of organic cells, aerial photographs, primitive stone heads, biplanes, patterns on eggshells, X-rays and women exercising. Again the art establishment accused the Group of being confused or just plain esoteric. Some reviewers did see the point of the show and the similarities it revealed in its search for a new optimistic language of form and graphics. One of the members of the '60s avant-garde architectural group Archigram, Ron Herron, saw the exhibition: 'It was most extraordinary because it was primarily photographic and with apparently no sequence; it jumped around like anything. But it had just amazing images; things that one had never thought of looking at in that sort of way, in exhibition terms. And the juxtapositions of all those images! I was just knocked out by it.'[2]

'Man, Machine and Motion'

During 1954, Independent Group activity focused on the human body and the effect

of the machine and the proliferation of mechanical reproductions of images and appliances. In July, John McHale was included in an exhibition held at London's Building Centre called 'Man versus Machine'. McHale was developing an interest in urban culture and information technologies and their impact on humanity. To McHale technology was good its imperative had to be understood in order to be able to predict its development and mitigate any of its downsides. In 1954 Reyner Banham stepped down as convenor of the Group due to his commitment to work on his PhD, later to become *Theory and Design in the First Machine Age*. Later the same year McHale and Lawrence Alloway assumed the role of joint convenors. The group discussed the work of Buckminster Fuller, the human image, mythology and psychology, and Le Corbusier's 'Modulor' system of proportion. In October the 'Collages and Objects' exhibition opened at the ICA. This exhibition, curated by Alloway and designed by McHale, showed work by McHale, Paolozzi, Henderson and Turnbull amongst work by Picasso, Ernst and René Magritte. Paolozzi aired his scrapbook *Psychological Atlas* for the first time; it featured selections of 'found' images similar to his 1952 presentation to the Group.

Also during 1954 the proposal for the exhibition 'Man, Machine and Motion' (then called 'Human Motion in Relation to Adaptive Appliances') was made by Richard Hamilton. Hamilton had developed the proposal for Newcastle's Hatton Gallery, but it needed an injection of funds to secure its development. It opened in July 1955 (fig. 102). Hamilton had been inspired by the motion photographs of Muybridge, and his work at the time was all about machines in motion. The exhibition consisted of two hundred or more photographs of the machines and suits developed to enable human beings to navigate through terrain that is alien to their physical make-up or to traverse landscapes at speed. The exhibition had four sub-themes: aquatic, aerial, interplanetary and terrestrial. In effect this was another exhibition about the prostheses

101
'Parallel of Art and Life'
Independent Group,
1953

102
'Man, Machine and Motion' exhibition, Newcastle
1955

IDEAL HOMES

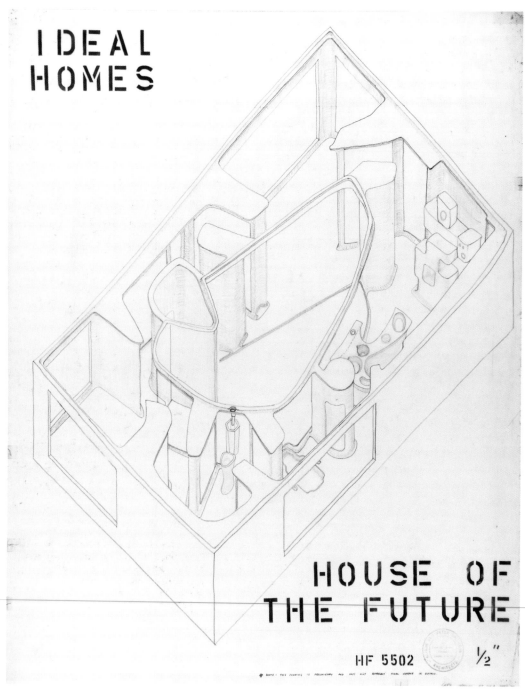

HOUSE OF
THE FUTURE

HF 5502   ½"

103
Axonometric of
House of the Future
Alison and Peter
Smithson, 1956

created by human beings to expand their conquest of time, space and distance, all shortly to be preoccupations for the new generation of visionary architects of the '60s. Also around this time Reyner Banham started to formulate his aesthetic criticism of cars, speed and streamlined styling – the 'Borax' aesthetic. These ideas are believed to have influenced Hamilton's work.

'This is Tomorrow'

During March 1956, the Smithsons premiered their House of the Future at the Ideal Home Exhibition in London (fig. 103). This was a curvaceous construction that sought to utilize as many modern appliances as possible: 'The structure: the house is moulded in plastic impregnated fibrous plaster, a kind of skin structure built up from separate parts with flexible joints to allow for the thermal movement and to provide structural discontinuity … The Outside Surface: The roof is doubly curved and dished to allow sunlight penetration, which dishing carries the rainwater to a single point from which it flows down a gargoyle into a container in the garden. To reflect the sun's rays the top surface is covered with aluminium foil.'³ The Smithsons were never to evoke this particular flowing aesthetic again, and it was left to the '60s pioneers Archigram to pick up the double-curved, prefabricated and lightweight mix a few years later.

The year 1956 was also the defining moment for the Independent Group: the 'This is Tomorrow' exhibition at the Whitechapel Gallery in London (figs 107–8). The show, which featured not only the Group but also some London Constructivists, was the brainchild of Theo Crosby. Consequently, it was a mix of Constructivist protocols, adverts and marketing, technology and the primitive search for a graphic and sculptural form with which to describe the technological upheavals of the '50s. The exhibition consisted of twelve groups of artists, architects and the occasional engineer. Each group also had to design its pages in the catalogue. There was no homogenous

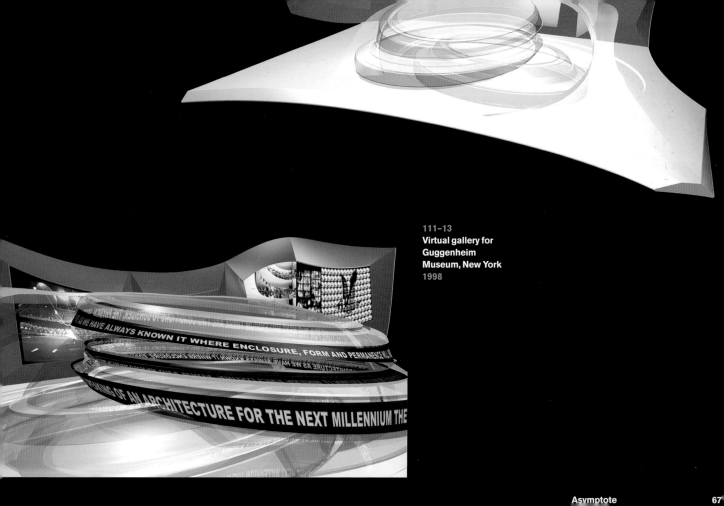

111–13
**Virtual gallery for
Guggenheim
Museum, New York**
1998

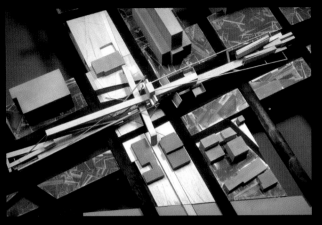

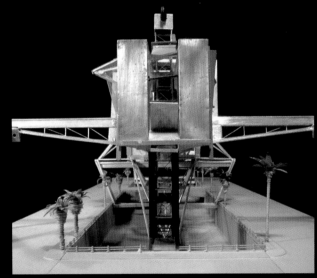

114–19
Views of competition model for Cloud City, Los Angeles Gateway
1989

The Second Poverty of Heroic Structures and Arcadian Networks

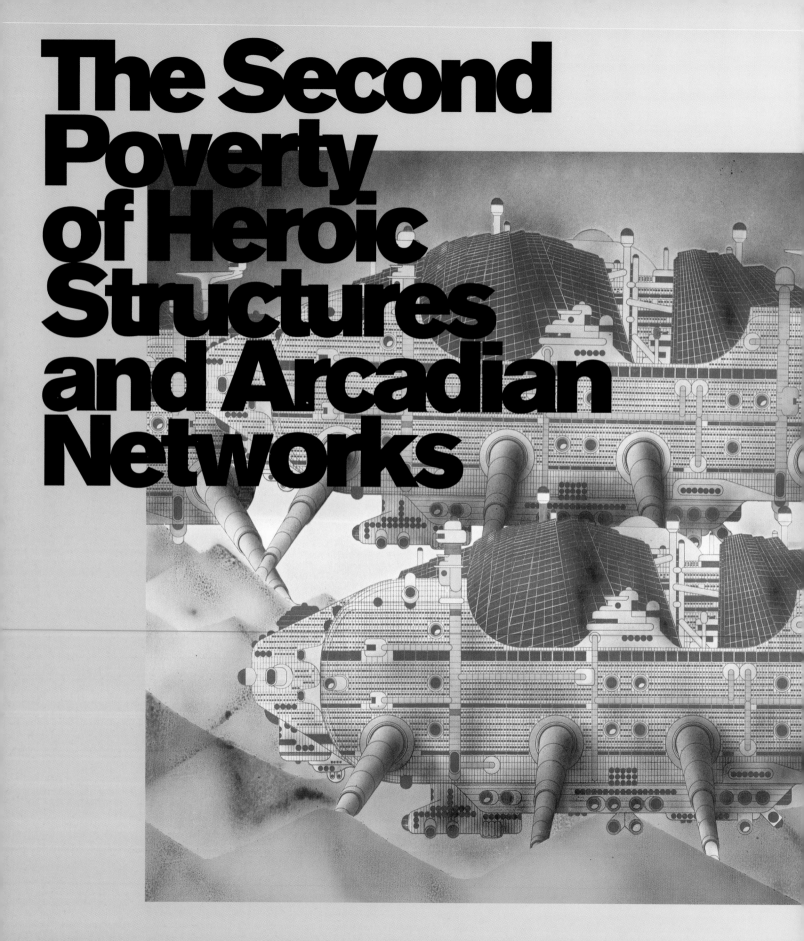

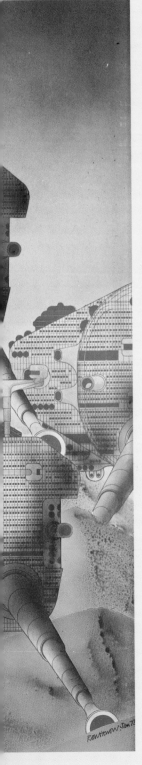

It might be argued that after the Second World War, technology liberated the West from war, famine, pestilence and political tyranny. During the 1960s, technologically optimistic architectural groups began to form, the foremost being Archigram in Britain. These groups created proposals that explored the world of advanced communications, consumerism, hippie social aspirations and transient 'happenings'. At the end of the decade, however, this optimism was already failing. Other groups, most significantly Superstudio in Italy, began to question the idea of technological utopias, contorting their imagery into disturbing representations of dystopian ubiquity and conformity.

120
Walking City
Ron Herron,
Archigram, 1964

'These products [of mass production] may be identical, or only marginally different. In varying degrees, they are expendable, replaceable and lack any unique "value" or intrinsic "truth" which might qualify them within artistic canons. Where previously creation and production were narrowly geared to relatively small tastemaking elites, they are now directed to the plurality of goals and preferences of a whole society. Where previous cultural messages travelled slowly along restricted routes to their equally restricted, local audiences, the new media broadcast to the world in a lavish diversity of simultaneous modes.'
John McHale

'An Archigram project ... provides a new agenda where nomadism is the dominant social force; where time, exchange and metamorphosis replace stasis; where consumption, lifestyle and transience become the programme; and where the public realm is an electronic surface enclosing the globe.'
David Greene

Some architects and artists, such as London's Independent Group of the 1950s, praised the machine-made, the liberation and protection that came about through co-existing with the machine, global advertising, cars and their sleek styling, and the conduits of mass communication. Other commentators felt they saw society becoming one-dimensional and feared that the single societal focus fostered by mass production and consumerization would in time create the same type of problems that other one-dimensional societies (Stalin's and Hitler's) had suffered from. Chief among these critics of the 'new' world was Herbert Marcuse. Marcuse, who had been a student of the Frankfurt School's Edmund Husserl, Martin Heidegger and Theodor Adorno, was concerned that conformity to the standardization of mass production would create a society in which individuality was outlawed. In his

1964 book entitled *One-Dimensional Man*, he opined that the only way to frustrate this universal imperative was by means of a 'great refusal'.

Architects in the late '50s were as usual caught between a rock and a hard place. They wanted the liberation of a healthy economy based on market-led mass production, and they wanted the ability to express their individuality. Likewise they wanted the users and owners of their buildings not to experience them as obstacles to a mobile and hedonistic lifestyle. There was an expanding realization that the promised dynamic, technologically advanced architecture of the Modern movement had failed to materialize. Most of the old firebrands were failing to progress and re-address their architecture in line with evolving societal and technological progress, though some had attempted to do this. For example, the various members of the Independent Group – James Stirling and the Smithsons in particular – were developing New Brutalism. Yet to the younger members of the profession, New Brutalism largely seemed pretty staid. The Smithsons' House of the Future (fig. 103), Buckminster Fuller's Dymaxion House (1927–9) and his prefabricated bathroom system of 1938–49, as well as Constant's New Babylon (figs 74, 76–81) were beacons to the young suggesting a light-weight, modular and daring future.

In 1956 Yona Friedman wrote his 'Manifesto: L'Architecture mobile', which succinctly set out the 'democratic' preoccupations of young designers of the time. Friedman's manifesto was predicated on the notion that all occupants of the new architecture should be the designers of their own spaces. But first, occupants had to be tutored about the implications of making design choices. This liberation of occupants to provide appropriate accommodation for themselves and change it at will was vitally important for Friedman, who felt that architects always build to their own stylistic and spatial preferences. In 1960 he added ten points to his manifesto. These included a demand for more leisure facilities (as production was

becoming automated and less in evidence in domestic agglomerations); a housing surplus of 10 per cent (to avoid market-led ghettoizing with areas stratified according to income); climate regulation; the recognition of the importance of the urban farmer; high-technology structures; three-dimensional urbanism; and architects left only to provide structural skeletons and buildings to facilitate bigness and the continued expansion of cities.

At this time some students and young architects began to conceive and talk about urban developments as organisms within a larger organism: the city. This future city was idealized as a writhing mass, powered and manipulated by playful, intelligent, honest, relatively well-off people. To these young thinkers, the city was a Futurist organism configured primarily for the car and consuming goods and services. The individual pieces of this meta-organism – the buildings – consisted of skins, spines, tubes and plates, and were designed to respond to fluctuations in use patterns, changes in the demand for accessibility to space, sudden events and the vicissitudes of the weather. Peter Cook called such ideas and propositions the 'lost movement of Bowellism'.

The late '50s marked a watershed, a catalytic moment for a new thrust from a new generation towards the goal of designing a contemporary urbanity. One of the truly original designers of this period was Mike Webb. In 1957 Webb was still studying architecture at London's Regent's Street Polytechnic. For his fourth-year project he produced the Furniture Manufacturers' Association Building for a site in High Wycombe. Its elevations have become one of the most instantly recognized icons of Webb's generation (fig. 121). This project has the aesthetic of a knot of pipes under the kitchen sink or the back of a '50s refrigerator. Conceptually the building has three independent parts; each part is linked to the others by stairs, lifts and ramps. The parts consist of vertical circulation, an auditorium, and offices/showrooms (some of which would have been available to rent). Forms are rounded and tubular,

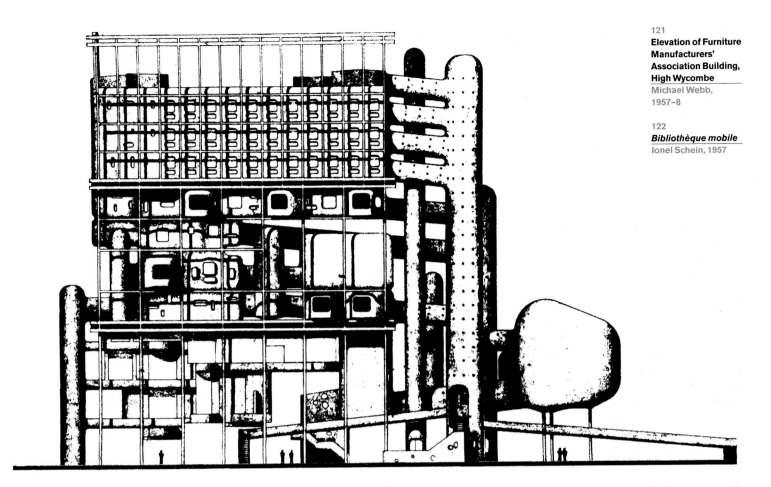

121
**Elevation of Furniture
Manufacturers'
Association Building,
High Wycombe**
Michael Webb,
1957–8

122
Bibliothèque mobile
Ionel Schein, 1957

and windows are punctures in the in-situ or precast ferro-cement. Similarities in construction and expression can be seen in Fredrick Kiesler's Endless House (figs 71–2). Webb was also inspired by Luigi Nervi's Turin Exhibition Hall (1948–9) and his Gatti Wool Factory (1953).

Webb's work anticipated four of the main architectural preoccupations of the '60s and '70s. One was Heroic Structure, where one could see the structure pulled away from the surfaces of enclosures and expressing itself, its circulatory pattern fed in, duct-like, to this rigid grid. The structure embraced a series of pod-like accretions which looked like they might be moved, re-articulated or added to. Function was expressed by the separation of difference, and this separation required an articulation of the connection and jointing of spaces. The building in effect meandered around inside and outside its formal structural array. This arrangement was similar to the juxtaposition of building and structural

support in Yona Friedman's vision of new cities. The building became a celebration of circulatory events. Webb was starting to equate the vehicular, the pedestrian and the movement of goods – one might even call it 'hardware' – as a knot of time-based activity that needed to be controlled yet remain flexible. Much was made in this era of the movement, speed and storage of goods and cars, and their integration into the city's rich mesh.

While the forms of the Furniture Manufacturers' Association Building are naturalistic, like a concoction of the entrails of animals, it is also bubble-like, similar to the ergonomic curves of our bodies. As the '60s progressed, these curvy yet functional bubbles, in Webb's projects and those of other architects, became more and more dissolved, light-weight and mobile, finally detaching from their structures and disappearing altogether.

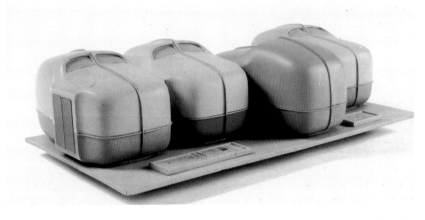

123
Structural model for Sin Centre
Michael Webb, 1959–62

124
Structural perspective for Sin Centre
Michael Webb, 1959–62

125
Sectional perspective of Fun Palace
Cedric Price, 1964

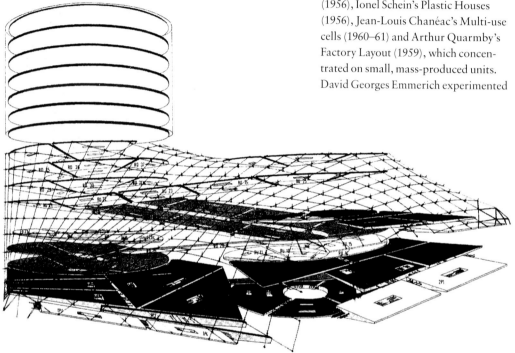

As the bubbles started to drift across our landscape, connection ports back to our communications meta-skin became necessary; we needed electronics to escape the plastic grey carapaces of our desk-bound gizmos. The gizmo had to camouflage itself or run above or below us in such density that we could jack in wherever and whenever we wanted to, but only rarely did its bundles of conduits become visible.

Other significant projects of the late '50s included Pascal Hausermann's *Maisons Spatiales Novery* (plastic houses) (1956), Ionel Schein's Plastic Houses (1956), Jean-Louis Chanéac's Multi-use cells (1960–61) and Arthur Quarmby's Factory Layout (1959), which concentrated on small, mass-produced units. David Georges Emmerich experimented with prefabrication and tensegrity structures starting in 1958. Other architects explored large-scale urban design; Paolo Soleri's Mesa City (1959) and Ekkehard Schulze-Fielitz's Space City (1960) were interested in high-density, non-prescriptive living in conjunction with massive support structures. Mesa City was important because of its rich matrix of layered life that cleared the ground of urban sprawl: 'The natural landscape [said Soleri] is not the most apt frame for the complex life of society. Man must make the metropolitan landscape in his own image: a physically compact, dense, three-dimensional energetic bundle, not a tenuous film of organic matter. The man-made landscape has to be a multi-level landscape, a solid of three congruous dimensions. The only realistic direction toward a physically free community of man is toward the construction of truly three dimensional cities. Physical freedom – that is to say, true reaching power – is wrapped around vertical vectors.'[1] Two projects by Japanese Metabolists – Arato Isozaki's Space City (1960) and Kisho Kurokawa's Helecoid – also contributed to an evolving aesthetic of huge straddling structures. What they were developing was the city as creeping parasite.

Webb followed the Furniture Manufacturers' Association Building with an even more audacious project.

The Sin Centre, as it came to be called, started life as the Entertainment's Centre for Leicester Square (figs 123–4). In this final-year project at the Polytechnic, Webb anticipated the other preoccupation of the '60s: hedonistic fun. The project's development was slightly ahead of, but never in the sort of detail as, Cedric Price's real commission for the Fun Palace (fig. 125). However, Webb imbued this student project with a wealth of detail and programmed both its construction and its methods of spatial re-articulation. It had a much more light-weight construction and was therefore more aesthetic than the Furniture Manufacturers' building. Ductwork broke free of its cosseting risers and infiltrated the building, whose primary organization was around two cores which formed the structural, vertical circulation and servicing focal points of the plan and section. Ramped floor plates then zigzagged from one core to another. Bowling alleys, department stores, dance floors and bars were strung along these route ways. The car was not separated from the hedonistic users who accompanied it to the integral drive-in cinema, remaining close by like a second skin as they shopped and partied. Webb has always been interested in the car, and many of his projects have sought to explore the closer and closer symbiosis of car and user, particularly in the domestic context. The Sin Centre was essentially half drive-in and half ravey nightclub with the opportunity for retail therapy along the way. Advertisements populated its glass roof-skin, reminiscent of the Vesnin brothers' Pravda building, yet here we were truly in a neon night. One was sure that half-hidden interstitial places in the structure could be used for more interesting sins.

In 1960 the Museum of Modern Art in New York presented an exhibition entitled 'Visionary Architecture'. Webb's work was featured alongside projects by Soleri, Buckminster Fuller, Louis Kahn and Kiesler. Meanwhile in London the arcane machinations of English academia continued to fail his Sin Centre and deny him his diploma.

The Poetry of Countdown

In late 1960 a small group of young architects began to meet to discuss ideas, show each other projects, and talk about their preoccupations and what the future might hold for their discipline. This group included Webb, Peter Cook and David Greene. Cook was a graduate of London's Architectural Association, and Greene was a graduate of the School of Architecture at Nottingham. Webb had been tutored by Stirling, Cook by the Smithsons and Arthur Korn, and Greene by Buckminster Fuller, so the baton had in some sense already been passed. All the participants in this group were dissatisfied with the staid nature of architectural practice, the refusal of the profession to grab hold of real technological innovation, and the upper middle-class smugness of the English architectural scene.

In May 1961 the first 'Archigram' pamphlet was published (fig. 126). It was hoped that it would fill a lacuna among publications willing to feature student work. 'Archi-gram' was a lexical hybrid of 'architecture' and 'aerogramme'. The pamphlet consisted of collaged images of student projects and competition entries and some poetry by Greene: 'A new generation of architecture must arise – with forms and spaces which seem to reject the precepts of "modern" – REJECT curtains – design – history – graphpaper.'[2] The featured projects in some way tried to evade the straitjacket of prescriptive Modernism, so many of them sought to evade its orthogonal compositional protocols. Webb's Furniture Manufacturers' building was joined by Greene's Bud scheme (1960) for a mosque in Baghdad, in which 'Light pushes through the skin which comes to meet it.'[3] The overall feel of Bud was that of a relative of the starfish. John Outram's concert hall at Westminster (1959) had an aphid aesthetic, while Cook and Gordon Sainsbury's complex of hotels and offices at Piccadilly in London (1961) bucked the Bowellist trend by means of a fragmented circus with projecting cores, the circus containing a series of overlaid roads and service arteries. Greene's poetry

126
Archigram 1
Peter Cook and David Greene, May 1961

invariably added a hippie-techno narrative to Archigram productions:

'The love is gone.
The poetry in bricks is lost
We want to drag into building some
of the poetry of
Countdown, orbital helmets,
Discord of mechanical body
transportation methods
And leg walking
Love gone.'[4]

By late 1962 Cook had produced his first design essay in prefabricated metal accommodation with his Metal Cabin Housing, and Greene had pushed his own Bowellist aspirations much further and conceived of his unruly and strangely shaggy Cliff-side Entertainments Stalk (1961) and Spray Plastic House (1962). At this time the fledgling trio of Archigram was conscious of another trio of young architects whose names were appearing in the press and on placed competition entries. This group consisted of Ron Herron, Dennis Crompton and Warren Chalk; all were working for the London County Council. Cook had won the 1961 Gas House competition, and with some of the

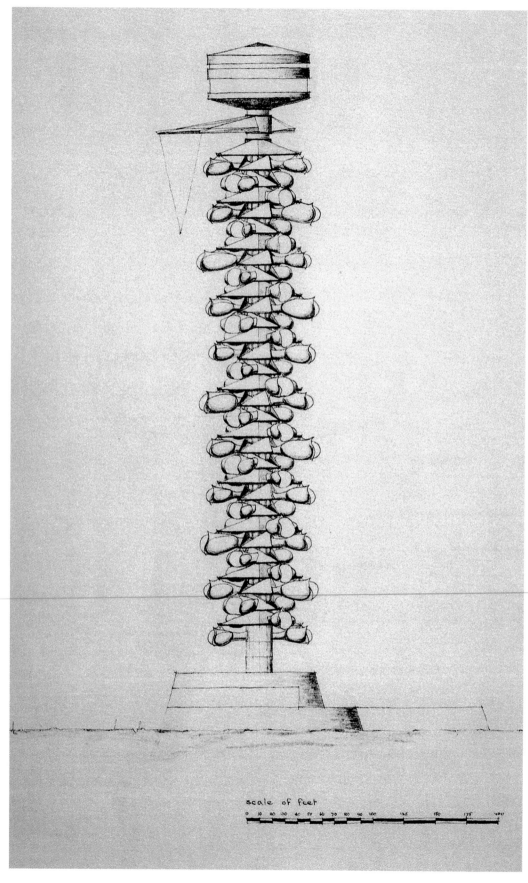

scale of feet

proceeds a larger Archigram publication was conceived. The LCC group was asked to contribute, as was Cedric Price. *Archigram 2* appeared in April 1962, and the LCC group joined Archigram.

Living City of Towering Entertainments

By June 1963 the expanded fledgling group was being given its first break. Ex-Independent Group activist and architect Theo Crosby managed to secure £500 for an Archigram exhibition installation at London's ICA, scene of many of the exhibitions and discussions that had inspired them. Almost simultaneously the group moved wholesale into Crosby's architectural group in the building contractor Taylor Woodrow's design section in London. The exhibition, conceived by Archigram, was called 'Living City'. It is inevitable that it should be compared with the triumph of the Independent Group's 'This is Tomorrow' exhibition.

'Living City' was organized in seven 'Gloops', each gloop defining 'an area of basic constant and reasonably predictable fact. Man. Survival, Crowd, Movement, Communication, Pace and Situation: all contributing and interacting one on another and sum totalling to Living City'.[5] The structure was enclosed and had a kaleidoscopic effect. Time or bombs were represented by 'tick-tick'; cigarette packets, ketchup bottles, Robbie the Robot (a reference to 'This is Tomorrow'), Superman, a Coca-Cola sign, geodesic domes, the cyborg from the film *Metropolis* and all manner of juxtaposed consumer semiotics were brought together to give a flavour of Archigram's world. It was a world of burgeoning technological advancement, of optimism, of liberation from Victorian moral codes and class, of bright colours, of in-your-face corporate identity and lifestyle marketing. Like all good exhibitions of the twentieth century, it featured a mannequin. Archigram's mannequin was not adorned with the impossible corsets of Raymond Roussel, or the sexualized feathery and fishy whoredom of the Surrealists, or the blank other-world robotics of the Independent Group's Robbie, but was totally naked, mounted on a Heinz baked-beans can as a parody of the Classical plinth. Like all the other mannequins, and like John McHale's Ikons, it was a microcosm of aspirations, preoccupations and blind spots. Here in its unadorned splendour was Archigram debunking Classical proportion, geometry and propriety and declaring its allegiance to the fast world of brand, expendability and expediency, and the city of mass-produced tastes, desires, situations and lusts. Whereas the street signs of the Surrealists suggested real and literary locations within a memory machine of preoccupations, Archigram's street signs were the ubiquitous signs for products, signs of the times and embracing the Spectacle. 'Living City' was not a blueprint for a city, however: 'Architecture is not in evidence here, our aim is to capture a mood, a climate of opinion, to examine the phenomena of city life, to create an awareness within the spectator of himself, his attitudes, and the significance of the throwaway environment about him.'[6]

Archigram 3, published in August 1963, concerned itself with expendability and the consumer. It elucidated many of the 'Living City' preoccupations in more architectural terms. Buckminster Fuller's geodesic domes and prefabricated bathrooms, the Dymaxion car, garden sheds and consumer goods proliferated. 'It's all the same,' one page shouted. Thus the connection between the expendable packet of soap powder and buildings or bits of buildings was explicitly made. As Cook's editorial put it, 'Our collective mental blockage occurs between the land of the small-scale consumer-products and the objects which make up our environment. Perhaps it will not be until such things as housing, amenity-place and work place become recognized as consumer products that can be bought "off the peg" – with all that this implies in terms of expendability (foremost), industrialization, up-to-date-ness, consumer choice, and basic product-design – that we can begin to make an environment that is really part of a developing human culture.'[7]

127 (opposite)
Corn on the Cob
Arthur Quarmby, 1962

128 (left)
Tower elevation for Montreal Expo, 1967
Peter Cook for Taylor Woodrow Design Group, 1963–4

The year 1963 was a busy one for Archigram. Two other significant projects manifested themselves. Herron and Chalk collaborated on the Interchange project, a study for a multi-transport exchange. This portion of an imaginary city contained tubular route ways and stacked towers of car parking and other accommodation. The city became a network of functional silos and penetrating skyways with a subterranean service root-system.

Within the Crosby group at Taylor Woodrow, a competition was set up to design propositions for the Montreal Entertainments Tower, which was to be part of the 1967 Montreal Expo. Cook won the competition with one of the great iconic towers of the twentieth century. The first thing worth remarking on is its phallic associations (fig. 128). Indeed, this could account for its seminal place in male critics' minds. Its formal concept is simple: a central shaft with platforms supporting geodesic accommodation at top, middle and ground levels – all linked by means of vertical and tilted lifts and escalators. The final model was made by Dennis Crompton, who had already emerged as the group 'Mister Fix-it'.

In May 1964 Amazing Archigram 4 – Zoom was published. Archigram 4 was designed in a playful comic idiom. As well as illustrating some of the Montreal tower entries, it evoked the technologies of the spaceship and the hovercraft, and wondered whether, in the future, we would all be travelling around cities of outdated Modern-movement ideas in such vehicles. It argued against the stasis and immobility of much of what was then seen as contemporary architecture.

From 1962 to 1964 Cook was also working on what was to become another classic Archigram project. This scheme for a plug-in city was initially a continuation of some of the ideas contained within the earlier Metal Cabin Housing project. In Plug-in City all elements were expendable and could be dismantled and reassembled (figs 130, 132). Small living capsules were plugged into megastructural frames. Plug-in City

even had weather balloons ready to inflate to block out the unruly and unpredictable climate of the UK. Cook described it as being '"heroic", apparently an alternative to the known city form, containing "futurist" but recognizable hierarchies and elements. Craggy but directional. Mechanistic but scaleable'.[8] Plug-in City hinted at a place where consumer choice and mobility were everything. Architects' taste was a thing of the past; what one did as a contemporary architect was to facilitate well-serviced choices of location and architectural apparel. Predicting the metabolic rate of a city's various parts was seen by Archigram, Price and others as the critical factor in continued urban rejuvenation. Whilst its individual segments would become obsolete, the city itself would remain vital if new, updated segments could be incorporated to replace them. Plug-in City was zoned; Cook explored university nodes, office areas and a 'Maximum Pressure Area'.

Concurrent with the Plug-in City proposal, Crompton produced Computer City, which embodied many of the effects Archigram felt the fast evolution of the computer and the digital transmutation of data would have on urban areas. This city, much like Norbert Wiener's conception of the biological organism, comprised electronic switching and components which in turn could be described as a series of electronic states, feedback loops and fluctuating sensitivities. Computer City was conceived as a series of motile field dynamics; the paraphernalia of the traditional city was dispensed with (fig. 145). Its visual configurations and materiality had nothing to do with the city's effectiveness; what was important was how wired it was and how fast one could connect to its information flows. This project anticipated the ongoing dematerialization of Archigram's works. The overriding imperative of the Archigram phenomenon was one of disappearance. Technology was evolving into smaller and softer pieces – software was overtaking hardware as the most important product to own. The city had to become informationally denser and capable of swift response.

Loose-fit Human Learning Machines

The importance of life-long education, the democratic accessibility of information, its swift digital transmission and the ability of the university to educate beyond its echoing hallowed halls were catalysts for two greatly different yet (aspirationally) strangely similar projects. Cook's Plug-in University Node and Price's Potteries Thinkbelt were exactly contemporary schemes. Cook constructed a nodal network through which pedestrian walkways and information were piped (fig. 129). The main enclosures were tensioned skins on 'trays' which were the fundamental building blocks of the nodes. Each node was then inhabited, infiltrated or plugged into by

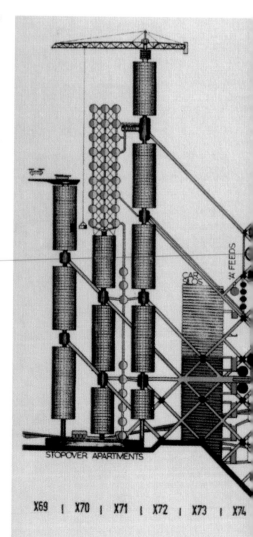

STOPOVER APARTMENTS

X69 | X70 | X71 | X72 | X73 | X74

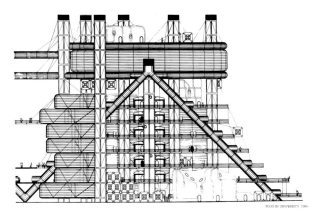

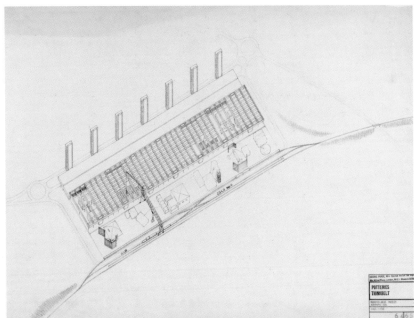

129
Elevation of Plug-in University Node
Peter Cook/
Archigram, 1965

130
Axonometric of Potteries Thinkbelt, Madeley Transfer Area
Cedric Price, 1964–6

131
Plug-in City, Maximum Pressure Area Section
Peter Cook/
Archigram, 1964

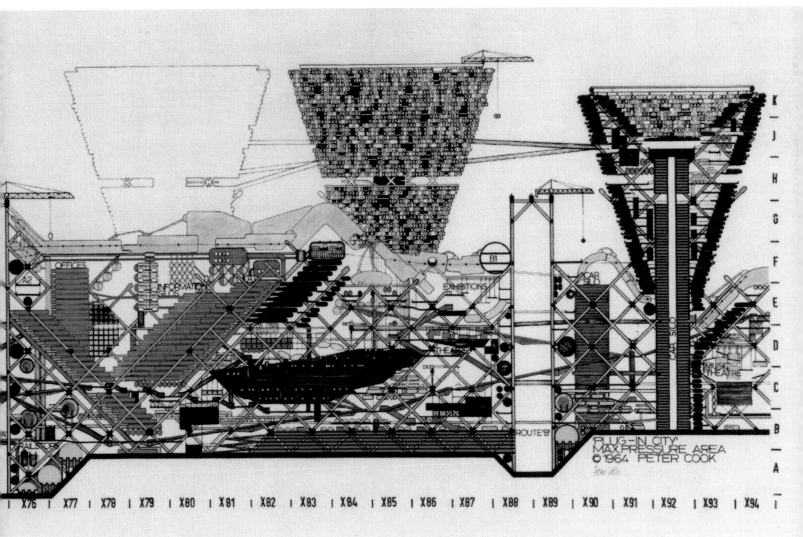

132
Axonometric of Plug-in City
Peter Cook/
Archigram, 1962–4

function-specific accommodation such as lecture halls, gyms or games rooms. Other less specific or less environmentally controlled areas flowed around these parasitic pieces. Each student was based in a metal box located according to his or her wishes.

Price's Potteries Thinkbelt was a lesson in his conception of 'expediency' (fig. 131). It was socially targeted, existing within the problems of a specific area and conceived as a tool for alleviating those problems. Its site in North Staffordshire was, and still is, an area in decline. In previous years it had been a centre of pottery, steel and rubber production. With the advent of '60s disposable and plastic culture, these industries and the communities they supported began to fall into disrepair. Price knew that an area such as

this required a new social impetus, which he decided should be 'Education'. He could foresee the further fragmentation and dissociation between craft-based employment and training and the more academic training of the professions. Theory, practice, prototype and profession must somehow be integrated. Price believed that historically students had resided in the cheap peripheral areas of cities in slum housing and deprived neighbourhoods or in the huge ghettos of university campuses. His Thinkbelt encouraged students to live in real communities and help to regenerate them. He carefully considered the impact of large numbers of people suddenly converging on such areas. For example, schemes for packaged water-purification plants were envisaged to avoid the further

disintegration of existing Victorian drains and works.

Price proposed a university on and around trains and their sidings and stations. Its network – bounded by Madeley, Pitts Hill and Meir – was vaguely triangular in master-plan (if you can call it that) form (fig. 135). Price saw Thinkbelt travel as continuous, as having no rush hour and no congestion. The network consisted of packaged facilities, faculty sidings, 'Transfer Areas' (where modes of transport from cars, trains, bicycles and aeroplanes could be switched), and four types of housing based on site ground condition, number of inhabitants and length of stay. Housing was constructed from 'appropriate' materials; no aesthetic axe was ground. Price was not seduced by the fashionable plastic and metal aesthetic of the '60s. Above all, his belief was that inflexibility of building encouraged inflexibility of thought and therefore inflexibility of education. His theoretical projects always dealt with highly specific statistics, sites and phenomena.

The Pod Leaves the Frame

In 1964 Warren Chalk was the first member of Archigram to connect the word *capsule* with homes. In November of that year *Archigram 5*, entitled *The Metropolis*, followed hard on the heels of *Archigram 4*. It was full of pods, clusters, capsules and ziggurats; schemes by Cook, Greene, Moshe Safdie and Arata Isozaki were featured among others. Back at Archigram HQ (at the behest of Taylor Woodrow), the group developed a research project for 'Capsule Homes'. These were stuck around a central structural and servicing tower: 'The capsule was a set of components: whilst snugly and efficiently fitting together they were capable of total interchangeability … Perhaps a dream machine as well as a mere "house"?'⁹

Gasket Housing was a development on the Capsule idea; its authors were Herron and Chalk. The basic premise of this elegant project was to maintain the plugged-in structural and servicing infrastructure (figs 153–4). The space of the capsule was to be sculpted of thin, highly articulated plates or gaskets, similar to those found in car engines but pod-plan-sized. Small differences from one gasket to another would produce the fundamental nooks and crannies for contemporary living and its necessary privacies.

For the first time Archigram featured Greene's Living Pod Stack. In a sense this took off from his earlier Cliffside Entertainments Stalk. Like Greene's mosque Bud, it was influenced by the craggy skins of Kiesler's Endless House (figs 71–2) of pods on a structural stick; the pods had the architecture of whelks or naked mussels. Living Pod was Archigram's most developed pod

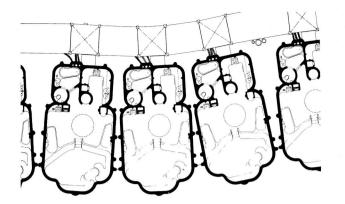

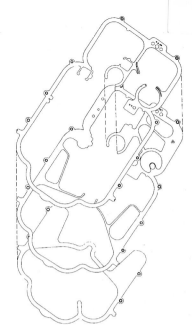

133–4
Gasket Housing
Ron Herron and
Warren Chalk/
Archigram, 1965

135
Master plan showing infrastructure network, Potteries Thinkbelt
Cedric Price, 1964–6

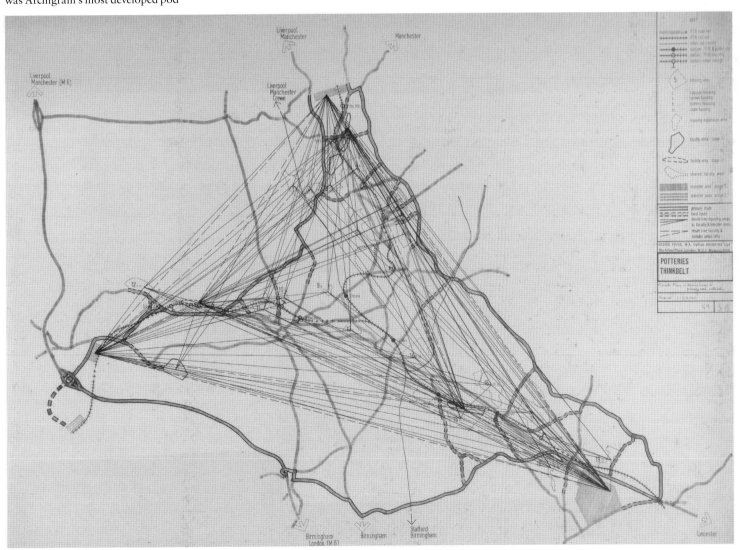

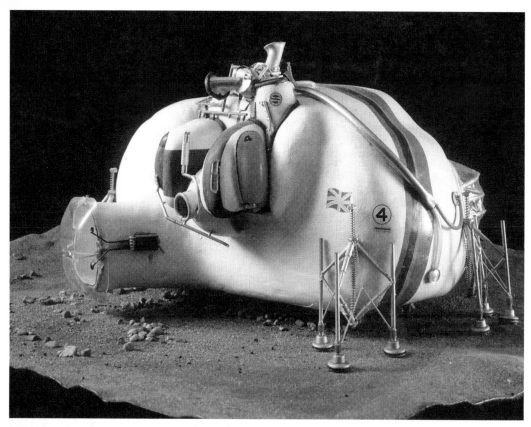

proposition (fig. 136). Greene also made propositions about stacking pods; in this respect they were reminiscent of Arthur Quarmby's Corn on the Cob (fig. 127). Living Pod was highly articulated, anticipating the Apollo 11 space module with its padded feet (cunningly represented in the model, in true English style, by beer-bottle caps). This was a seminal moment for Archigram. The pod was separating from the frame; things would never be the same again. As Greene put it, 'With apologies to the master, the house is an appliance for carrying with you, the city is a machine for plugging into.'[10]

Ron Herron's contribution to the 'mobile house'-or-'pod on heroic structure' dichotomy was to postulate the hybridization of both concepts. Thus Walking City (fig. 120) was born. Walking City in a sense returned to the aphid-like aesthetic of a few of the Bowellist schemes; it did not have the craggy but directional laissez-faire of Cook's Plug-in City. Walking City was at once Pod City

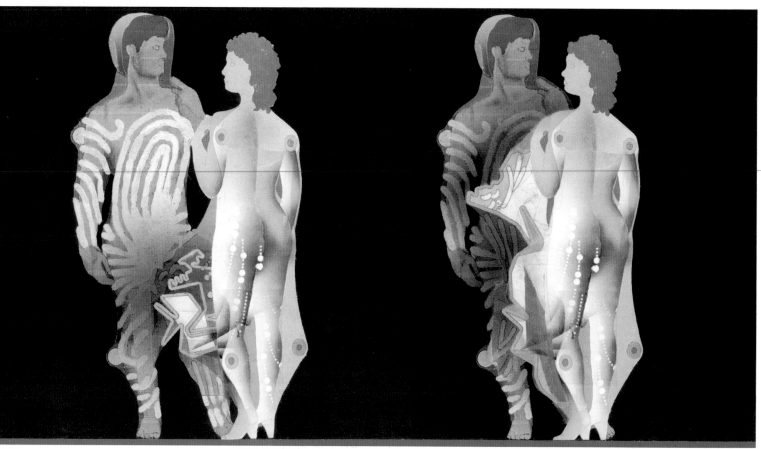

city, and that could be used in any way the user wished. Taken to their illogical extreme, they became the 'Continuous Monument' series (1969–71). These collages were not representations of a positive utopia but illustrate the ubiquity of ascalar architectural ideas, the unfailing allure of the grid and cube and their invisible capitalist rationale of machine production (figs 149–50, 52–4). In Toraldo di Francia's words, 'Eliminating mirages and will-o-the-wisps such as spontaneous architecture, sensitive architecture, architecture without architects, biological architecture and fantastic architecture, we move[d] towards the continuous monument, a form of architecture all equally emerging from a single continuous environment the world rendered uniform by technology, culture and all the other inevitable forms of imperialism.'[16]

Primarily the vehicle of Andrea Branzi, Archizoom's works were also a sideways swipe at the Modernist architectural utopias of groups that were more

interested in abstract notions about the future of architecture than in dealing with evolving social structures of the contemporary city. Residential Park, part of the lengthy Non-Stop City proposal (1969), was an attempt to show a user-'negotiated' positioning of parks and housing. Archizoom's political stance centred around this notion of 'negotiation': 'Freed from the armour of its own character, architecture must become an open structure, accessible to intellectual mass production as the only force symbolizing the collective landscape … The clash no longer takes place in the fields of ideology but in quantitive terms: quantitively, it becomes possible for different phenomena which apparently have no link with one another to interrelate positively … Freedom, as an end, becomes an instrument of struggle.'[17]

The year 1968 saw the publication of *Archigram 8*. This issue had an editorial entitled 'Open Ends'; 'Metamorphosis' and 'Nomad' were the watchwords. Ron Herron conceived Tuned Suburb (1968)

149
Continuous Monument
Superstudio, 1969

150–1
Continuous Monument
Superstudio, 1971

and Oasis (1968). The former was about how one might tune up a suburban home by adding conduits, receiving masts and inflatable extra spaces. Presumably informed by Price's Fun Palace (figs 82–4), Oasis was a cosseting trussed structure that allowed choice, response, emancipation and metamorphosis. The underlying idea was that '[i]f architecture laid claims to human sustenance, it should surely have responded as human experience expanded. For architects the question is: do buildings help towards the emancipation of the people within? Or do they hinder because they solidify the way of life preferred by the architect? It is now reasonable to treat buildings as consumer products, and the real justification of consumer products is that they are the direct expression of a freedom to choose.'[18]

While Archigram had already signalled its disillusion with the Megastructure concept of the future, others were still in its thrall. One of the most memorable such propositions of the '60s – the definitive Megastructural model of its generation – was Gunter Domenig and Eilfried Huth's Graz-Ragnitz project (fig. 156). This project was given much of its presence by its spectacular and highly wrought model. Structurally the project consisted of 'alternating layers of deep trusses and open faced cubes, separated by layers of paired diagonal struts which accommodated the cubes of the trusses above and below'.[19] This was how Reyner Banham, in his seminal genealogy of these leviathans, 'Megastructure: Urban Futures of the Recent Past' (1976), described its complex layered anatomy. Through this intricate ordering system, an equally complex series of woven circulation, roads, goods and service runs was positioned. Capsules could be plugged into the system at many optional points.

Networking in the Garden of Digital Delights

A package of seeds was inserted into each issue of *Archigram 9* in 1970. *Archigram 9* marked the final phase of the Archigram odyssey. But first another break. Cook,

Herron and Crompton won a research award from the Graham Foundation for Advanced Studies in the Arts, and Instant City (figs 146, 155) was born. The project had two linked but different incarnations. Herron had relocated to Los Angeles for a short period, and therefore his scheme happened to alight there. Cook remained mostly in the UK, and his version dealt with the quirkiness of rural and small-town England. Instant City consisted of a mobile kit of parts such as light-weight structures, televisual monitors and inflatable, packaged environmental services – indeed the whole gamut of Archigram mobile playthings developed over the previous decade (fig. 100). Instant City was about special events when the normal infrastructure of an area could not cope with an 'instant' yet rare occurrence – a music festival, for example. Instant City was the equipment, '60s style, with which to control a flash flood of hedonistic humanity: 'The programme was seen as augmentary and anticipatory. [It gathered] information about an itinerary of communities and the available utilities that exist (clubs, local radio, universities etc.) so that the city package [was] always complementary rather than alien.'[20]

Today Instant City has the familiar resonance of the large pop or rock festival and seems a perfectly natural series of ideas and devices that can be used to cope with the sudden influx of thousands of hungry, slightly stoned and worshipping fans. Obviously it wasn't just conceived for big gigs, yet its baroque technological dangling-gizmo architectural language is at its most appropriate in this arena. The Instant City approach can be seen to have been refined and reused time and time again in the work of Mark Fisher, a one-time student of Peter Cook who has become the most renowned stage and event designer in the world. Fisher can boast of having created the sets of Pink Floyd's 'The Wall' (with its inflatable characters), the huge urban happenings of Jean Michel Jarre, and the demonic 'Ozzfest' as part of a lengthy list of achievements. All, even in small part, influenced by Archigram.

The other trend that characterized the end-phase of Archigram's development was their interest in the wired Arcadian network. Here their ideal environment became, give or take a little electronic wizardry, very similar to that of our Renaissance hero Poliphilo. Poliphilo sees ghosts and phantoms, his information network is secreted in glades or woods and accessed by symbolic software protocols, and his world is occasionally populated by quirky machines that seem to have minds of their own. The prime mover in the Archigram Arcadian repertoire was David Greene, who foresaw that technology would become so small that the styling of its outer box might be more important for issues of camouflage or expediency, and therefore what it might look like could be almost surreal. The functional requirements and efficiency of an object could become totally divorced from its form. In 1968 Greene's first forays into the fecundity of the Arcadian idyll were Rokplug and Logplug (fig. 157). His writing of the time hit a sort of evangelical techno-hippie post-apocalyptic optimism. He described Rokplug and Logplug as being indistinguishable from natural rocks and logs. The artificial species, camouflaged among natural examples, were wired with electronic and water services. Rokplugs and Logplugs were found by wireless 'Plugfind' tracking devices. Greene produced a series of collages in which the Rockplugs and Logplugs were totally indistinguishable from their natural peers. This snippet of poetry accompanied his proposition:

'I like to think
(right now please!)
of a cybernetic forest
filled with pines and electronica
where deer stroll peacefully
past computers
as if they were flowers
with spinning blossoms'[21]

Here we see Greene yearning for a synthesis between the natural and biological, the artificial and the electronic.

The Plug project was followed by An Experimental Bottery – L.A.W.U.N. Project No. 1 (1969), billed by Greene as 'the world's last hardware event'.

L.A.W.U.N. is short for 'Locally Available World Unseen Networks'; a 'bottery' was a fully serviced natural landscape. Conditioned and tended by robots, Greene's landscape was predicated on the fact that, no matter how light hardware is, it is still a drag to lug it around. Why not have a set of robotic attendants with interchangeable additions that can cater for all your needs and, more importantly, attend to your chores? Greene understood the full architectural ramifications of this notion: '[Y]ou might say that the development of portable hardware produces an architecture of absence.'[22] Bots could be called up with a small, portable, hand-held device, which was all that had to be carried. Greene dedicated an actual site to the development of a prototype bottery. Oddly, this site was in the picturesque county of Dorset between Poole Harbour and the small B3351 road. Greene presumably picked it to cement the proposition's agrarian, Arcadian feel. This was not the styled plaything of trendy urban bohemians

152–4 (previous, above and right)
Continuous Monument
Superstudio, 1969

155 (opposite)
Part of Instant City in a Field
Peter Cook/ Archigram, 1969

The Second Poverty of Heroic Structures and Arcadian Networks

the organization is handled, the procedural magic of the heroic floors, the wit of the escape stairway that clutches on the exterior cliff … all the time we are being tempted by the cries, the reminders, the whispers of various pieces of shaft, ramp, stair or hanging box that we will encounter as we move up the building …'[27] The building is a simple design with a changing translucent façade. The play of aperture and opened-up vignette choreographs its perception and streetscape. This is digitized, hyperized townscape, sometimes here, sometimes there, always somewhere.

More recently Lim has become more interested in narrative, ecology, boundary conditions and architecture for animals. All of which have spawned publications and numerous unsolicited and solicited designs. Lim is a doer rather than a talker, a creator of fine spaces, and a painter and draughtsman of cool representations of these spaces.

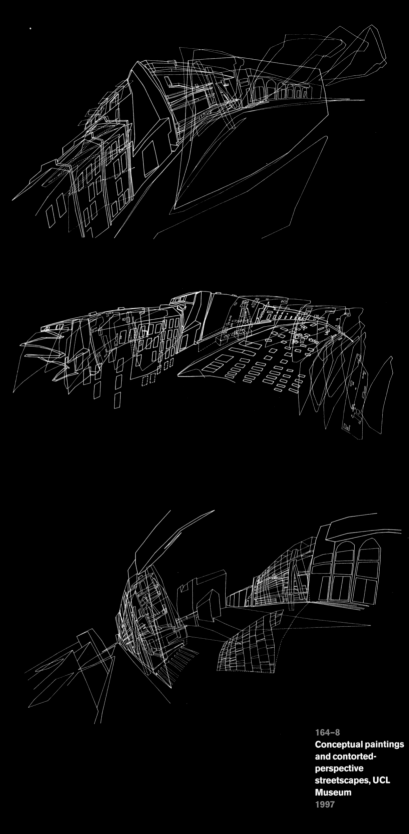

164–8
Conceptual paintings and contorted-perspective streetscapes, UCL Museum
1997

A Gizmology of Visionary Housing

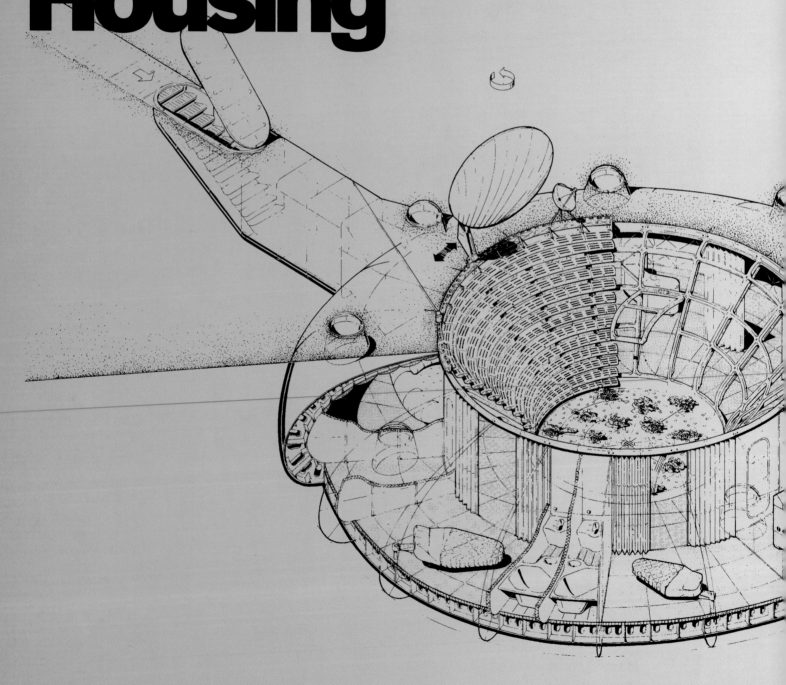

It is instructive to examine the building type of the house as a microcosm of visionary architecture. Designs for houses, unlike many other building typologies, have to grapple with the necessity to accommodate technology and social change. This chapter charts the evolution of the house from the beginning of the twentieth century to the contemporary cyberized moment. The house has had to come to terms with a variety of mechanical gizmos, including the car, the washing machine and the computer; sometimes the house itself has been subsumed into a massive gizmo, thus giving new meaning to Le Corbusier's 'A House is a Machine to live in' trope.

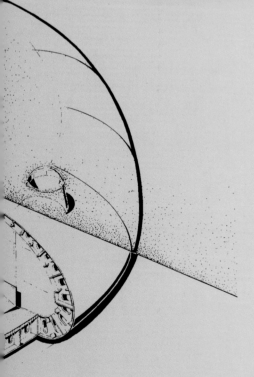

169
Doughnut House
Future Systems, 1986

'The "modern" style has its merits and it has come to stay, I think. But we will probably witness a considerable change in it. Some elements of grace and suavity will surely redeem its starkness. Its begetters were actuated with the desire to create something essentially of our own day. The clean lines of the aeroplane, the functionalism of the motor-car, the machine inspired them. In the realm of architecture they essayed a similar development. Tradition was discarded, the stock-in-trade of design cast overboard.'
Randal Phillips

'The machinery of society, profoundly out of gear, oscillates between an amelioration, of historical importance, and a catastrophe. The primordial instinct of every human being is to assure himself of a shelter. The various classes of workers in society today no longer have dwelling adapted to their needs; neither the artisan nor the intellectual. It is a question of building which is at the root of the social unrest of today; architecture or revolution.'
Le Corbusier

It might be instructive at this point to examine the house as a microcosm of visionary architecture and its metamorphosis from the beginning to the end of the twentieth century. From the early 1900s, the evolution of experimental design in architecture found its model in housing design, particularly in one-off houses. A house is the condensation of the ideas, aspirations and preoccupations of its designer and owner. A house can be read in this respect like a text, and such a text can reveal much about the time of its construction and its attitude to domesticity, privacy, technology, formality and gender.

The history of the house can also be calibrated by its denial or acceptance of mechanical and electronic products and processes. We will call these elements gizmos. A gizmo is a mechanical appliance in the home – the computer, the telephone, the washing machine, the sink,

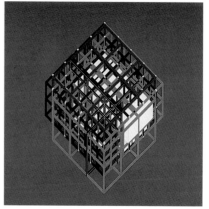

Dad's electric razor, the hi-fi, the DVD and the battery-operated child's toy are all gizmos.

During the first half of the century, the technological and social imperatives that conditioned Archigram's propositions were in place but not yet as strong as they would become. What later manifested itself as nomadology and ubiquitous servicing on the wired meta-skin of the world started, relatively slowly by our standards, to deconstruct the staid, sacrosanct spatial relationships of the nineteenth century. Homes had to change as the horse lost its place to the combustion engine, central heating started to invade some of the more prestigious houses, and structural systems displaced old load-bearing walls. Light and space were starting to be seen as social resources.

Frank Lloyd Wright's work is often discussed as the architectural fulcrum between the Victorians and the Machine Age of the twentieth century. One of the high points of Wright's early career was the Darwin Martin House (1904) in Buffalo, New York. This house also illustrates the beginning of the impact of technology on dwelling in the new century. It is a synthesis of four main elements: the main house itself, the pergola and conservatory, the stable/garage block and a smaller house for one of Martin's relatives. This constellation of structures is integrated into the landscape. Wright's work from this time is remarkable because of the sureness and subtlety of this integration. The whole equally balances the natural and the artificial. Space is formed from either column and beam or hedge and tree. As the viewer perambulates around the building, a series of spaces, internal and external, open up for aesthetic inspection.

Winter in Buffalo can be harsh. The Darwin Martin House articulates itself around two fireplaces. One double-sided fireplace defines the entrance hall and the living room; the other forms a welcoming focal point in the reception room. Main features of the plan are the quadripartite columns that inhabit the interstices of the tartan grid; it is these tight areas that make up both the main vertical structure

and the service risers. Heating equipment is contained in the space created by the hollow columns, delivering warm air out of small windows in the face of each column. Wright believed in using technology to facilitate the occupants' comfort or to create masterful designs, but the idea that this technology should be naked and proud was anathema to him. Such a notion would pollute the visual purity of his work. The factory-made could not be relied upon to fit into his contrived interiors.

The Darwin Martin House seeks to control and legislate space mostly without the aid of doors. Wright used many devices such as ceiling heights and lowered beam soffits to define useable space and make a distinction between it and circulation space. Therefore this building is little different in broad terms from Ron Herron and Warren Chalk's Gasket Housing (fig. 133) because it too layers a series of thin planes, each slightly different, to create an overall three-dimensional space. With Wright this tactic also facilitates subtle transitions from inside to outside. So here, at the beginning of the century, the gizmo was penetrating the house. Yet Wright faced its risers and runs in brick and stone. The car, the ultimate mobile gizmo, was hidden at the back of the plot along with the horses.

In contrast to Wright's banishment of the car, Le Corbusier welcomed it. The ground floor of the Villa Savoie (1929–31) was configured to facilitate vehicular turning circles, and the car was 'docked' into its ground floor. Drivers were decanted within the building, accessing higher floors by means of a ramp. The ground floor was essentially a whole floor given over to the gizmo. Washing machines and other utility machines had their home at the base of the house. The gizmo had gained a floor, and its aesthetic was starting to inform the machined shapes of handrails and other mechanistic details of the domestic environment. Naturalistic reliefs and decoration had become a thing of the past.

Whilst Le Corbusier the architect was excited by his Modernist architecture, Richard Buckminster Fuller, the engineer, went far beyond him, both technically and gizmologically. In 1927 Buckminster Fuller produced designs for the Dymaxion House. Its forms were not conditioned by the arcane aesthetic preoccupations of the art-architect; they were formed by simple engineering concerns of light-weight structure, prefabrication, speed of erection and the lifetime of elements. Buckminster Fuller's first biographer, the Independent Group's John McHale, expanded on the house's rationale: 'The basic structure of the Dymaxion house was organized around a central duraluminium mast on which were suspended two hexagonal decks, the lower totally enclosed the double-pane vacuum glazing. Suspension and structural rigidity, on the wire-wheel principle, were effected by triangulated tension cables. The mast contained mechanical core elements which provided lighting, plumbing, air conditioning etc. The internal labour saving mechanics designed into this house were extremely sophisticated for this period, and many of them … tagged as

"impractical"… Space division was effected by use of floor to ceiling units. These contained some of the mechanical utilities and provided space for food, clothes, books etc. … Auto storage was tied into this system, as was the mechanized dishwashing and drying. Photoelectric cell-operated doors were foldable and, like the floors, pneumatic and soundless … Cleaning and dusting [were done] by compressed air and vacuum units.'[1]

Here the domestic potential of the gizmo was realized for the first time. Architecture was never the same again. Fuller was to further elaborate on this conception of industrialized, prefabricated, gizmocentric housing in 1945. His Wichita House was produced in the Wichita Aircraft plant and was the big brother of the Dymaxion House. Its outline was circular; Buckminster Fuller maintained the central-mast structural organization and its tensioned aluminium primary material, which has a low-maintenance non-oxidizing surface. As McHale put it, 'In aircraft terms the house was "no trouble at all to produce" having only 200 parts as opposed to 2500 parts in current aircraft. At full-volume run of 500,000 dwellings a year, the cost of a house was put at 50 [cents a pound] – $3700 complete. In limited production this would have worked out at $6500. Houses were designed to come off the production line completely crated as shippable to any part of the U.S. for $100. A mast boomed truck would deliver, erect and connect up to utilities in 16 man days. In the end, although 3,700 purchase applications were registered, the war's end brought a redirection of capital investment in the aircraft industry and tooling up funds could not be raised.'[2]

After the Wichita House, Buckminster Fuller continued to explore advanced structures and started to develop many projects that exploited the lightweight structural integrity of the geodesic dome. Geodesic domes could be built from prefabricated uniform elements that could be flat-packed. In 1949 he developed his Autonomous Living Package, an 8-by-8-by-25-foot pack that

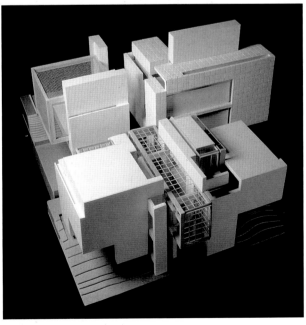

170
House VI, Connecticut
Peter Eisenman, 1972–5

171
Axonometric diagram of House VI, Connecticut
Peter Eisenman, 1972–5

172
House VI, Connecticut
Peter Eisenman, 1972–5

173
Model of House X, Michigan
Peter Eisenman, 1975

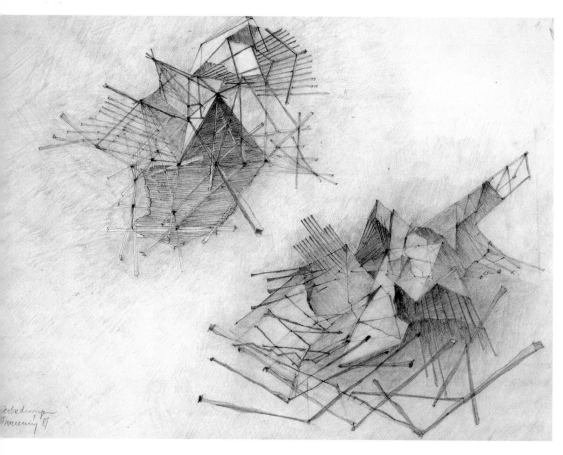

than impressed with her perfect, privacy-defying house.) The Farnsworth House is also Victorian about its gizmos. They are not to be seen but are confined in the tight internal 'core' that creates the various open-plan spaces and includes the toilet and kitchen. So this is a step back for the gizmo. There is no garage. Electrical appliances are held in a compacted space within the core and are never meant to stray.

Whilst the Villa Savoie lifts itself off the ground to accept the penetration of the car, the Farnsworth House lifts itself off the ground because its control-freakery cannot bear its underbelly to be caressed by the ground's filthy dirt. The white steel frame is inviolate. Nothing can be allowed to knock or abrade its beautiful industrial sheen. This is a very demanding architecture. It must be microscopically maintained; its users must be monastically disciplined and not prone to the lazy, decadent behaviour of which Mies would not have approved.

Enabling Gizmos

In 1956 the Smithsons, as we have seen, displayed their House of the Future (fig. 103). Over the next twenty years, many other experiments in the prefabrication of housing occurred. Of all the architects who began to practise at the beginning of the '60s, Cedric Price's work was perhaps the most influenced by Buckminster Fuller's method of designing and asking difficult questions about architecture.

Price recognized that the time of day radically affected how a house was used as well as the resources of space and energy it consumed. He also recognized that traditional housing stock consisted of objects that were obstacles to the evolution of the family and also that the house was a commodity. He saw occupants attempting to rebel against, recondition and rejuvenate their houses with superficial changes in wallpaper, garden gates or carpets and knocking down a wall once in a lifetime if they were lucky. Part of the problem, Price believed, was the particularity of planned space. What was needed was adaptable space within which a

could be assembled to create a 50-foot dome, mounted on five hydraulic jacks and then elevated to account for weather conditions. Within the dome, circular tracks mounted at various heights could reposition living containers and levels, the domestic environment moving in line with weather and whim. Le Corbusier's maxim 'A House is a Machine to live in' became 'Roam home to a Dome.'

Buckminster Fuller developed larger and larger geodesic domes, eventually positing one to cover a large proportion of Manhattan. His influence on the cutting edge of architecture in the second half of the twentieth century was extraordinary. Archigram and Cedric Price were clearly influenced by him.

Meanwhile architects were still far behind the other great architectural master of the twentieth century. Ludwig Mies van der Rohe was grappling with the imprisonment of the unruly gizmo. His view on the domestic gizmo was paradoxical. On the one hand he wanted to celebrate the unwavering exactitude of

industrial construction technology, and on the other hand he was searching for a purity of internal space that sought to reduce the gizmo to nothing or to confine it in a cupboard.

The culmination in Mies's housing work was the Farnsworth House (1945–51) in Plano, Illinois. This house is the final, extreme version of Le Corbusier's 'Free' façade. It is a total glass box; roof and floor are formed from steel beams and their infill panels; finishes are of the highest quality of material and detailing. Mies liked the idea that the Farnsworth House was light and essentially consisted of nothing. The house's second paradox is to do with its relationship to nature. It is perfect, white, clean and very neat. It can't tolerate the free-ranging spider, the organic detritus of the autumn or the step of a muddy boot. Yet it is a simple prototype of Reyner Banham's air-filled, transparent, highly serviced mobile balloon. Its spaces in one sense reach to the nearest ring of trees. (Interestingly, Mrs Farnsworth was less

178 (opposite top left)
**Peanut House
photomontage**
Future Systems, 1984

179 (opposite top
right)
**Mandarin House
photomontage**
Future Systems, 1981

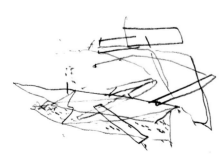

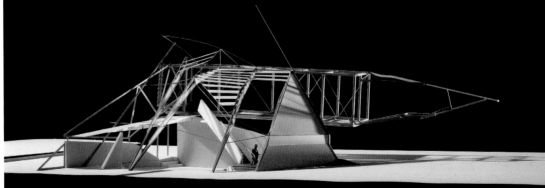

180 (opposite
bottom)
**Blob proposal for
Grand Buildings
competition
(unentered) showing
Trafalgar Sq., London**
Future Systems, 1985

181 (top)
**Photomontage
interior of Open
House**
Coop Himmelb(l)au,
California, 1983–92

182 (above)
**Structural model of
Open House**
Coop Himmelb(l)au,
California, 1983–92

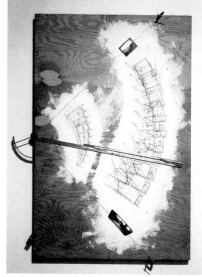

The Open House further destabilizes the orthogonal, logical geometries of the 'house'. The architects' creative sensibilities and reason are subjugated to a sort of 'automatic' composition akin to Surrealist and Dada practice. Here the house becomes an architecture of 'pick-up sticks', any configuration of which will do. The architects' role is to find a sort of codification of this stick-pile by imbuing the wayward, illogical sketch with hierarchies of structure, skin and floors. Fighting the illogicality of the first sketch in a search for architectural novelty – the next fleeting fashion for the invisible gizmo: this is the second reaction against historicism.

The third such notion was influenced by Daniel Libeskind's teaching at the Cranbrook Academy of Art in Michigan, and was a direct result of searching for a Modernist architecture that did not reject the classical canon. This idea conjoined with an interest in the ritual phenomenology of the house and its accoutrements. The Grunewald House (1980) was designed by Ben Nicholson whilst he was still a Cranbrook student. It was another attempt to create an architecture in response to theoreticians arguing for the medium's demise and rebirth: 'By seriously addressing thinkers such as Freud, Heidegger, Baudelaire, Poe and Magritte, Munch and Bachelard, it is possible to form a house that no longer responds to long-worn and debatable notions, but rather evokes dormant desire and is a response to an urban world teetering on the brink.'[7] Nicholson's house utilized ideas of decay, found objects and despised sheets of colourful veneer as a concept for modern life: 'The proposed dwelling is anthropomorphic, while simultaneously using devices of the machine age. It is to be tuned and structured so that the parts fit upon themselves as a series of wedges; no longer being stone standing on stone, but part wedged on part, stretching or compressing laterally …'[8] This was both a real and a virtual place in which to dwell. Normal domestic acts were intensified across their normal scales. The house was both a hermetic laboratory and a series of normative rooms with normative functions. Nicholson here rejoiced in the extraordinary events, products and tools of everyday life and their surrealism when tweaked, spliced and disentangled. Again the gizmo was everywhere and nowhere. Its vectors, its double-curved surfaces and its sinuous wirings and pipings were

everywhere yet hidden deep within the more architecturally normative.

Mechanizing Poliphilo's Dream

As the 1980s drew to a close, the by-now-ubiquitous gizmo, sometimes fully exposed and sometimes hiding, suddenly received a boost of power that imbued it with a new vicious, fecund imperative – that of cheap, transmittable memory. Computers had been around for half a century or more, and their impact had been astonishingly speedy. This was reflected, yet again, in the contortion of the house, now prone to a spate of remembering gizmos. Simultaneously we were reminded of the awesome power of the military gizmo by the East European civil wars and the even more awesome power of natural disasters. Houses were developed for these situations as well.

The Slow House in North Haven, New York was developed from 1988 to 1991 by Diller + Scofidio (figs 183–4).

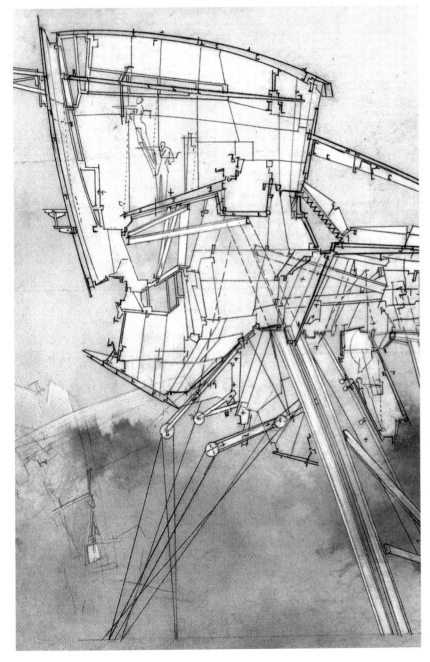

183 (opposite)
Model of Slow House
Diller and Scofidio,
1991

184 (opposite top)
Conceptual plan of Slow House
Diller and Scofidio,
1991

185 (left)
High Houses
Lebbeus Woods,
1994

186 (above)
Fault House San Francisco
Lebbeus Woods,
1995–6

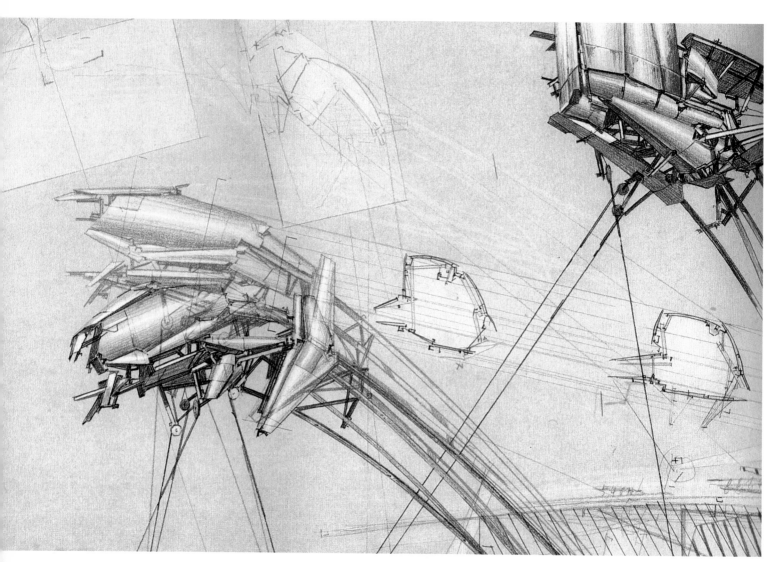

187
High House
Lebbeus Woods,
1994

It is situated on a beach; it is a vacation home. The house revels in confounding the owners' ability to consume its views in the hungry way of a city dweller – it 'slows' the user down. It also plays on subverting the traditional relationships of taking in the view. The power-window of the television set is relocatable because the view from the window is shown on the TV. The games of virtual and actual surveillance and of replaying and recording are a typical Diller + Scofidio tactic. The house is turned inside out and inverted as the owner is forever traversing the boundaries between reality, actuality and virtuality – all laid out and synthe-sized in the horn-shaped structure. The gizmos play with their own sense of reality and its speeds and inertias.

During the early to mid-'90s,

Lebbeus Woods created a number of houses. The High Houses (figs 185, 187) were an attempt to occupy the site of an old, destroyed factory in Sarajevo but also an attempt to exploit the air rights above it. The trauma of ethnic battles is echoed in the long, fine arcs of the houses' supports, which are reminiscent of bullet and shrapnel trajectories. These poignantly balanced structures are described by Woods as follows: 'These houses respond to people's powerful need to achieve freedom of movement in space through a fuller plasticity of experience, and to exist in the full dimensionality of space – to fly and yet, paradoxically, to be rooted, to belong to a particular place and time.'[9]

Woods then became interested in the climatic and geomorphic conditions

that affect the city of San Francisco. He proposed a set of houses with which to negotiate natural disaster. These were the Wave Houses, Slip Houses, Fault Houses (fig. 186) and Shard Houses. The Wave Houses had 'ball-jointed frames that flex and re-flex in [a] quake, supple metal stems and leaves [that] move in the seismic winds'.[10] These were buildings for shifting terrains and arduous circumstances in which nature conspired against the normal relative inertness of a house.

In the High Houses, the gizmo's destructive side was mimicked to provide liberation; spaces within the house that were not circumscribed by function were 'free'. The new computerized gizmos could extend space freely. The spaces and craggy metallic outcrops were to be used as the occupier felt appropriate. The strict

In twentieth-century art there was often a reuse of found objects and ideas. This chapter looks at this artistic practice when it is assimilated into architecture. The first architectural structure using this notion, the Dadaist Kurt Schwitters's *Merzbau* (1920), sets the scene. More contemporary work includes Tschumi's *Manhattan Transcripts* (late 1970s), which compare architectural design to film story-boarding. Ben Nicholson's polemical Appliance House (1990) takes a dark look at American consumerism and its sleek exterior, while Nigel Coates's NATO group (1980s) explored an architecture of reused, flowing urban detritus. Kevin Rhowbotham and Nic Clear's Non-Specific Urbanism is also featured.

'Every acquisition, whether crucial or trivial, makes an unrepeatable conjuncture of subject, found object, place and movement. In sequential evolution, the collection encodes an intimate narrative …'
Roger Cardinal

'Detournement, the reuse of pre-existing artistic elements in a new ensemble, has been a constantly present tendency of the contemporary avant-garde both before and since the Situationist International. The two fundamental laws of detournement are the loss of importance of each detourned autonomous element – which may go so far as to lose its original sense completely – and at the same time the organization of another meaningful ensemble that confers on each element its new scope and effect.'
Guy Debord

If we return to the 1920s, we can determine another trace in the history of visionary architecture: that of the reused fragment. In or around 1929, Kurt Schwitters, a Dada artist and poet based in Hanover, started to build a 'column' of 'found' materials in his house. He found these materials in the street: tram tickets, shoelaces, sweet wrappers, cigarette butts, old newspapers, advertising flyers, a myriad of things discarded by a busy society. The column grew and grew. The floors and ceilings of the house had to be removed as Schwitters nourished his creation with more flotsam and jetsam. As well as the column he made other objects and pictures. He called the column a '*Merzbau*', his reliefs '*Merzbild*' and his two-dimensional collages '*Merzzeichnung*'. His was the lonely interior world of the obsessive collector and collagist. This combined with his geographical distance from his Berlin-based Dada colleagues led them to accuse him of provincialism and bourgeois aspirations. Schwitters's art was conditioned by stringent financial constraints, but he succeeded in reinventing street detritus by constructing

highly evocative artworks that spoke of the urban dynamics of his time: 'Out of frugality, I drew on what came to hand, for we were a poverty stricken country. One can still cry out by way of bits of rubbish and that is what I did, by gluing or nailing them together. This I call Merz … Nothing was left intact anyway, and the thing was, to build something new out of broken pieces.'[1]

The word *Merz* comes from '*Kommerz- und-Privatbank*', a 'found' term whose allusions to the French word *merde* ('shit') and the German word *ausmerzen* ('to eradicate') Schwitters liked. His response to his indigenous cultural environment was to utilize its rubbish for political effect. The detritus therefore became imbued with meaning and reason. The act of collage removed the notion of capitalist expediency from each object he honoured.

Over the years Schwitters's column grew up into the attic and down into the cellar. As it grew, he formed spaces within spaces. Over time these were sealed and other spaces momentarily formed. Some of them were of such a scale and content that Schwitters named them. The Cathedral of Erotic Misery, the Grotto of Love and the Cave of Deprecated Heroes were but three such spaces he made as the column engulfed his house. These spaces and many others within the *Merzbau* can be seen as chambers of transformation – alchemical alembics. Schwitters can be perceived as the alchemical adept involved in a series of distillations to achieve the transmutation of objects and spaces. His modus operandi was to make his work subject to the ecstatic dislocation of his creative self by creating it from what he found; in this sense *Merz* was out of control. It depended on the chance meeting of the scavenger and the debris discarded by human bodies in physical and psychological motion. One is reminded of the old saying that refers to the nature of the *prima materia*, the alchemist's most base substance that he must make into philosopher's gold: 'It is familiar to all men, both young and old, is found in the country, in the village, in the town, in all things created by God; yet it is

despised by all. Rich and poor handle it every day … no one prizes it, though, next to the human soul, it is the most precious thing upon the Earth and has the power to pull down kings and princes. Nevertheless it is esteemed the vilest and meanest of earthly things.'[2]

Perhaps Schwitters would have recognized these words as describing his own *prima materia*: 'rubbish'. Ironically, his growing, degenerate, parasitic *Merzbau* was turned back into rubbish in one last, quick act of mechanistic fragmentation. In 1943 an Allied bomb destroyed it: a fitting end for the organic, reticent monument in an explosion of vectors.

Another German Dada (and Surrealist) artist, Max Ernst, understood the alchemical power of the collaged fragment, and his early work, particularly *Une semaine de bonté* (his collage novel of 1933), illustrates how far this technique could be used in the service of Surrealism: '[Collage is] an alchemical compound of two or more incongruous elements, resulting from their unlooked-for juxtaposition, this being due to a will to systematic confusion and thorough going derangement of our senses, or else to mere chance or a purposeful exploitation of the vagaries of chance.'[3]

Appliance House

What might happen when objects are liberated from the tyranny of function, appropriateness and the subservient confinement of hidden utility spaces? To become the altars, decorative reliefs and fetishized surfaces of a collaged church dedicated to the 'Appliance'? The Appliance House by Ben Nicholson is such a 'purposeful derangement'. Its ambitions are high; it and its designer seek to create a new ontology for architecture. Nicholson created this artful enigma using as a main compositional tactic the divining of the reciprocal energy of collaged pieces. His intention was to create a work of architecture that somehow honoured, but also consisted of, the mechanical objects and appliances

205
**Appliance House,
Telamon Cupboard
genesis**
Ben Nicholson,
1986–90

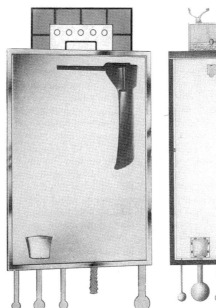
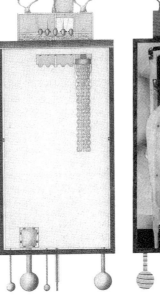

that make a house a home. These Banhamesque gizmos were not just washing machines and vacuum cleaners but included, for example, scissors, axes, rope, grommets and metal extrusions. This concoction of disparate elements was rescaled as they were collaged and *détourned* into a wild container for themselves. The Appliance House as Nicholson describes it is an 'orphanage for consumerist detritus'.[4] His first act of creation, as he calls it, is raping books. The two books on which he focused his loving violence in the case of the Appliance House were the Sears catalogue – the bible of mail-order consumerist desire – and the Sweets catalogue – the pantheon of door furniture as well as a Diderotian taxonomy of screws, nails and fixings. (Both publications in fact form the bedrock of design and architectural production throughout the US.)

Nicholson uses his scalpel like a surgeon. His incisions are predetermined, artfully arranged and rearranged. He has written of the alchemical act of 'blowing life into inert substance'.[5] Like Ernst and Schwitters, he is fully aware of the awesome impact of the collage and the fear the establishment has of its implied negation of disciplinary boundaries and of its fecund radical suggestiveness: '[C]ollage encounters monopoly and it

terrorizes guilds of knowledge. Every profession, academy, institution or organization is vulnerable to collage, as orders of logic are broken apart by the collagist.'[6] Whilst making the collages for the Appliance House, Nicholson spent hours studying Schwitters's work, attempting to understand the order in which each collage had been constructed. The precision and delicate forethought of the collaging process greatly entranced him, seems almost to have become a meditative device.

Once one of Nicholson's collages reaches a state nearing completion, it is named. The act of naming is conditioned by a series of 'hunches' about what the collages might become. This naming tactic is also an instrument of *détournement*. It carries with it the potential for another order of distortion and subversion. The idea that one doesn't need to know what one is designing whilst designing it is anathema to Modernist architectural dogma. Notions such as these foresake the functionalist liturgy of design that is embedded in architectural discourse and therefore constitute heresy. Nicholson's practice glorifies in such fundamental affronts to a staid profession.

The collages of the Appliance House are a type of hyper-*détournement*; *détourned* elements are further *détourned*

and *détourned* again (figs 206–7). First the fragmented image of a consumerist desire is exhumed from its 'Spectacular' tomb (as Debord would have us believe). This image is further fragmented, its functionality is torn from it, and what is left is the seductive, sleek husk, which in turn becomes more material to be chopped, slit and cut, both metaphorically and actually. The end results are grafted together as if by a mechanoid reverse butcher. The house is a deliberate museum conceived to save objects from the throw-away infatuation of the Debordian Spectacle. It is intended to be a corruption of the Spectacle devised by hyperizing it into its own negation. Prior to gluing, each piece of paper is held in place by hand-made tabs of drafting tape measuring $\frac{1}{16}$th to $\frac{1}{32}$nd of an inch. The Appliance House simultaneously has the wide-eyed innocence of the child and the extreme particularity of a control freak.

Nicholson rejoices in the divinity that can be discovered in the mundane. For example, he has a deep sympathy for the plastic tags used to secure packages of bread: 'It is objects such as these, that are produced in millions and discarded in exactly the same number, that will be kept safe in the Appliance House.'[7] The house has a simple spatial arrangement: 'Three pairs of small rooms facing onto a hall

whose doors to the street and garden are pierced at either end. Each room encloses an accentuated state of normal, everyday, suburban living, but the rooms have all changed their ceramic nameplates. Where there used to be the cosy nook with an open fireplace, there is a fireplace to suit the pyromaniac within us all. Where there was once a study, in which stood a Toby jug collection and family sports trophies were displayed, there now exists the Kleptoman Cell, a room given over to the face-to-face confrontation of what it means to have in one's possession any object gained by any means, fair or foul.'[8]

The house is skewered by the 'Pin', which is tapered like a knight's lance and counter-balanced by an exterior pendulum. The Pin dances above the head of the house's owner. It can be set in motion by the odd breeze, nudge or push, and is punctuated by numerous small, close-able compartments meant to contain things of autobiographical importance (much like Schwitters's *Merzbau*).

Within the house's Kleptoman Cell are the Telamon Cupboard (fig. 205) and the Flank Walls. What becomes clear very quickly is that Nicholson is the house's owner, the unnamed personality who inhabits this subverted world. The Kleptoman Cell is the sort of space in which the owner/Nicholson collects things that might be of use later. It is analogous to the cellar, the attic and the garage (figs 208–9). It is a private museum of stolen objects, taken or borrowed but never returned. The Telamon Cupboard is 'a great wooden cabinet of immense roundness, stability and gravitational force. Constructed as if it were a liberated kitchen appliance, it has finally come to terms with the mechanism enclosed by the skin-tight panels that surround and imprison it. The cupboard permits the appliance's pristine skin to be handled, yet it protects its mechanical workings'.[9] The Telamon Cupboard consists of forty sliding panels; it takes on the airs of a confessional yet evokes the voyeur's satisfaction with the quick, furtive touch of a

double-curved, sleek, shining, voluptuous body. In fact the whole of the Appliance House is a memory theatre. The Flank Walls stretch and compress the contents of the Kleptoman Cell and the Telamon Cupboard. So the house is contained by walls made out of itself projected anamorphically.

This level of detail and subversion continues at every scale, from walls to door handles. The Appliance House choreographs a series of interior narratives about the subversive power of the collage and the seductive desire evoked by consumer objects. These narratives construct an architectural piece that makes its own rules of composition and construction. Nicholson's *détournement* is rich and constantly reworked; each generation of reuse reinvents the appliance, continually slapping the Spectacle in the face. The irony of the Spectacle, of course, is that it is somehow disarmed by fleeting events and narratives yet always recovers to fully assimilate its adversary.

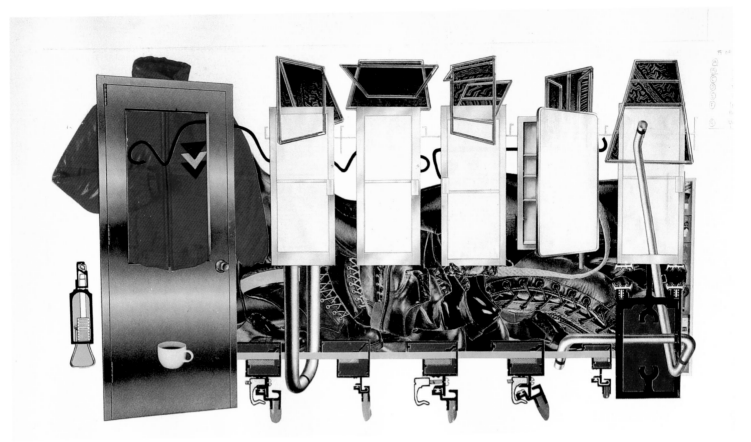

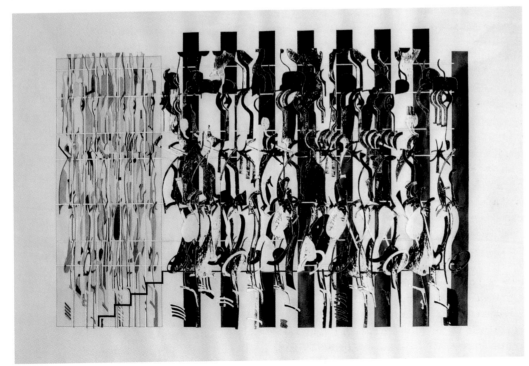

207 (above)
Appliance House, Saggital Name Collage
Ben Nicholson, 1986–90

208 (left)
Appliance House, exterior elevation of Cell wall
Ben Nicholson, 1986–90

209 (below)
Appliance House, Kleptoman Cell plan
Ben Nicholson, 1986–90

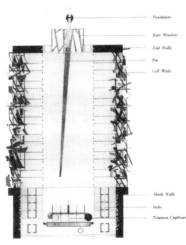

THE KLEPTOMAN CELL

There is No Space without Event

Nearly two decades before the Appliance House was created, Bernard Tschumi had also grappled with the production of architectural space, its Spectacular reality and its dependence on capitalist imperatives, and had come to the conclusion that architecture must rework itself. This necessary reworking coincided with the social upheavals of 1968 and a general questioning of what constituted architecture and of how much of its established language and semiotic carapace could be discarded without losing its essence.

Even the notion that architectural output was just the production of buildings was questioned. As Tschumi put it, 'At a time when architectural memory rediscovers its role, architectural history, with its treatises and manifestos, has been concurrently confirming to architects that spatial concepts were made by writing and drawings of space as much as their built translations. The question is [whether] there [is] any reason why one cannot proceed from design that can be constructed to design that concerns itself with only ideology and the concept of architecture … and if architectural work consists of questioning the nature of architecture, what prevents us from making this question a work of architecture in itself.'[10] One is reminded of Piranesi and his *Carceri* project, which sought to question the role of the drawing and posit it as an architectural object in itself (figs 1, 11–14).

In Tschumi's influential series of essays entitled *Questions of Space* (1990), written to supplement his earlier theoretical work of text and collage drawings *The Manhattan Transcripts*, he reminds us of the important contribution the Futurists, Dadaists, Surrealists and Situationists had made to new modes of spatial exploration as a reaction to the speeding machine and the dream worlds of psychosexual theory. One can immediately see the nuances of psycho-geography in Tschumi's conception of the city: 'My body carries in itself, spatial properties and spatial determination: up, down, right, left, symmetry, dissymmetry.

It hears as much as it sees unfolding against the projections of reason, against the absolute truth, against the pyramid, here is a sensory space, the labyrinth, the hole. Dislocated and dissociated by language or culture or economy into the specialized ghettos of sex and mind, Soho and Bloomsbury, 42nd and West 40th Street, here is where my body tries to rediscover its lost unity, its energies and its impulses, its rhythms and its flux.'[11]

Tschumi's polemic was grounded in his assertion that 'there is no space without event,'[12] and it was his collaging of events, his mixing of programmatic considerations and his development of a personal architectural space-time notation that formed his contribution to the progress of twentieth-century architectural vision.

In *Questions of Space* Tschumi noted that the Russian Revolutionary architects made the mistake of thinking of architecture as an instrument of social change that would create an equitable Soviet society. According to Tschumi, they misinterpreted the notion that space can influence immediate behaviour. He understood that space and architecture cannot be torn back from the grasp of the demon Spectacle. He foresaw the survival of architecture, but the cost was the negation of the formalism that society expected from it. This was what would give the new architecture, whatever that might be, its power: 'I would therefore suggest that there has never been any reason to doubt the necessity of architecture, for the necessity of architecture is its non-necessity. It is useless but radically so.'[13] The commodification of space had somehow to be made subject to *détournement*. Tschumi believed that it was not through the materiality of construction nor through the semiotic decoration and elaboration of structure that this might be achieved, but through the subversion of space and event.

In *Questions of Space* Tschumi set out sixty-four questions about the meaning and understanding of the concept of space and architecture. Question 4.7 seems most apposite: 'Does the truth of Revolution lie in the

permanent expression of subjectivity?'[14] Subjectivity seems key to the *détournement* of space and architecture. The Spectacle legislates space and architectural production by manipulating the definition of what is considered objective and therefore functional. The capitalist imperative that demands that architects are clinically objective in terms of function and cost is its weapon against the incorporation of a whole lexicon of marginalized concepts, spaces and actions. These changing 'objective' criteria manifest themselves as architectural styles, dogmatic doctrines and the weight of patronage. When one chooses a style in architecture, one subscribes to numerous intellectual and formal protocols of bondage: 'The Classical vocabulary of architecture is Piranesi's chosen form of bondage. Treating Classical elements as fragmented and decaying symbols, Piranesi's architecture battled against itself, in that the obsessive rationality of building types was "sadistically" carried to the extremes of irrationality.'[15] Tschumi noted that during the 1970s the history of space was surreptitiously appropriated by reactionary historians as the history of style.

Tschumi's seminal theoretical work was *The Manhattan Transcripts* (fig. 210). Though first published in the UK in 1981, the initial airing of some of the ideas and work within took place in New York in 1978. *The Manhattan Transcripts* was a device for notating and choreographing space and events. Tschumi saw this work as a necessary way to understand the twentieth-century city. The *Transcripts* are in four parts: The Park, The Street, The Tower and The Block. Their plot concerns a 'murder'. The Park utilizes Tschumi's 'three square' principle: 'Photographs direct the action, plans reveal the architectural manufacture and diagrams indicate the movements of the main protagonists.'[16] The Street is about 'the borders of spaces, the events they contain and the movements that transgress it'.[17] The Tower illustrates the flight and fall from a Manhattan tower, while The Block notates the confrontation between different movements and

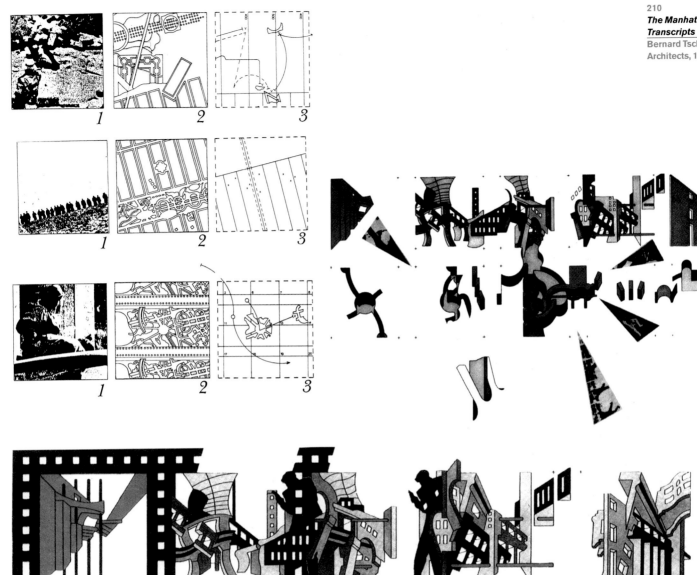

programmes and posits extraordinary hybrid events. Tschumi required the reader to participate in an act of revolutionary subjectivity if they wished to 'enter' the work. The *Transcripts* did not apply themselves to the polite asides of architectural endeavour. Murder, prison and perverse sexual activity were all grist for Tschumi's event-driven mill. The established codes of the representation of architecture – plans, sections, elevations and the cyclopian perspective – are also notations of spatial repression. Film scripts, story boards and choreography provide other ways to describe architectural events. Tschumi asked: 'Is there such a thing as architectural narrative? A narrative presupposes not only a sequence but a language. As we all know, the language of architecture, the architecture that "speaks" is a controversial matter. Another question: If such architectural narrative corresponds to the narrative of literature, would space intersect with signs to give us a discourse?'[18] He was instrumental in awakening architects to the notion that architecture was a rich space-time weave. He showed that this weave could be enlivened by narrative, emotion, story-boarding, events, situations, and (as Cedric Price had realized before him) duration and time.

Baroque Neo-Situationism

Tschumi was attracted to London in the late 1960s because of its artistic and cultural vitality. The Architectural Association proved to be a welcoming home for his particular brand of architecture. His unit of students set about rearticulating and subverting the everyday objects and spaces of contemporary life. Tschumi believed this was the only way to change architectural discourse. One member of the unit was Nigel Coates. Coates later returned to the AA to teach in Tschumi's Unit 10 in 1977, inheriting it in 1979.

For Coates, an architectural epiphany occurred sometime in 1981. His work became more artful; it concerned itself with vectors of people, movement

recognizable three-dimensional items such as nutcrackers, breasts and the products of glass-blowing and created highly worked pieces that conjoined and hybridized objects. These new functionless objects were exquisitely made. (Rhowbotham cynically recognized that the craft of an architectural object and the flawlessness of its surface always affect its perceived value.) These forms were then ascribed functions, thus becoming a total inversion of the form/function dialectic. This tactic was used polemically to illustrate the notion that form comes before programme, thus disenfranchising function as a generator of architectural form and turning Modernist spatial protocols on their heads.

During the late '90s Rhowbotham returned to the vicissitudes of the city. (He had been a student of Matthias Ungers and Colin Rowe at Cornell University in the US.) Rhowbotham was not concerned with the continuing project of many architectural historians, which was to document the evolution of a city of the past. He was more interested in the evolution of virtual space and the 'dirty speed' of the computer and its impact on the city: 'Dramatically improving communication speeds are fostering greater market sensitivity and, by degrees, a progressive fragmentation of market production, catering for ever finer differences in consumer taste. What seemed to be a recipe for the creation of new markets – the clean analogy – is in reality an implied fragmentation of existing structures. Rather than provoke a promised expansion of labour opportunities, the strictures of the dirty-speed economy have forced fragmentation upon existing industries with marginal increases in labour demand, exacerbating relative workload in the name of increased efficiency.'[35]

Rhowbotham sees the city as subject to another level of control, another level of the Spectacle that is independent of the old geographical shackles of position and subject to the conditions of time. His work thus started to exhibit an interest in fields, events and the multiprogramming of spaces, all within time-based systems. This particular topology was characterized by flux, the exchange and the changing figure and ground of the city's fluid virtual forces. He started to describe these notions as 'Field Event/ Field Spaces' (figs 225–6). In order to illustrate the potential extension of his insinuated fields, Rhowbotham asked viewers to consider the 1915 Suprematist painting *Eight Red Rectangles* by Malevich: 'By making a reading in which the canvas denotes an extensive void of space receding from the picture plane, it is possible to interpret the displacement of the object fragment as extended and scattered within a projected rectangle … Consequently a number of potential readings, that is to say the number of latent reconfigurations of the constituent elements within an extended space, is provoked by the work. This is the experience of FIELD SPACE.'[36]

Détournement and collage are intimately interlinked. They can be seen as a long and virulent tradition characteristic of the twentieth-century's artistic and architectural avant-garde. The old alchemical idea of transmutation was unprecedentedly powerful. The computer became the vessel of transmutation, a virtual machine of *détournement*. Computers can morph, collage and suck images from any source just by the light of a scanner. Paradoxically they are also the Übermachine of the Spectacle. The story

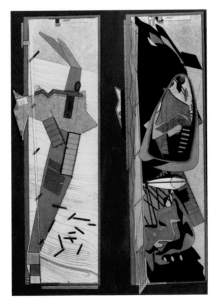

of *détournement* has a bright future that will stretch deep into the twenty-first century. The paradox of the computer, as ally and foe of the Spectacle, is ever deepening and more difficult to untangle. Rhowbotham's contribution is the way he repeatedly makes the architectural profession aware of such simple but potentially devastating facts.

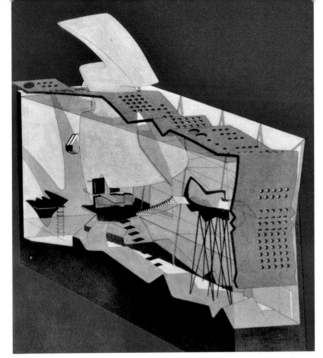

225 (opposite top)
Field Event/Space
Kevin Rhowbotham,
1995

226 (opposite bottom)
Field Event/ Field Space, Repetitive Landscape
Kevin Rhowbotham,
1995

227–9 (left and above)
Georgian Frontage, house plans, cutaway axonometric and interior model with Bloids
Kevin Rhowbotham,
1991–3

Détourning the Platonic House

Milenko Ivanovic

Milenko Ivanovic's architectural project is a studied *détournement* of Mies van der Rohe's Farnsworth House. Mies's iconic, transparent, jewel-box house is set in a wooded landscape, and represents everything he strove for in his architecture. It is fetishistically designed, every detail considered and every junction a lesson in forethought. It is clean and pure, and everything within and without must never stray out of place. Here an antiseptic architecture carves a rectangle of neutrality for itself. It is a palace of machine-making in the heart of the natural, and this severe sanctity is also applied to the domestic mess. The Farnsworth House lifts itself up above the ground on steel stanchions. The naturally uneven ground surface of

hillock, grass, and worm-cast is considered an inadequate datum for such a masterpiece.

Ivanovic's intervention is both an act of subversion and a necessary inscription of time-based contextual activities. First, he creates a hybridized device, at once machined but also organic. This device rests its belly in the dark, muddy no-man's-land under the Farnsworth House. This is the dead, barren, shadowy scar burnt by the Farnsworth House's presence into the landscape under itself.

Ivanovic's piece craves everything Mies's never did. It enjoys the stain of fruit, the organic energy of fruit juice, the fermentation of plum decomposition, the splat of home-made paint, the muddy

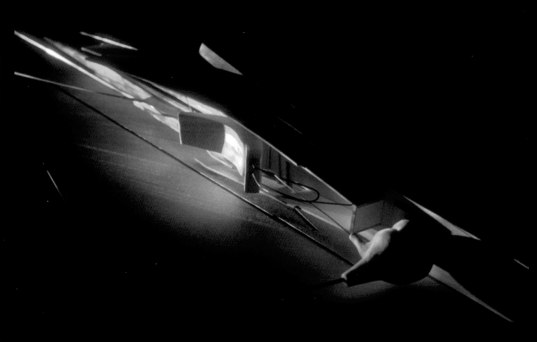

230–33
**Various views of
Farnsworth Machine**
2002

belly, the sweet scratch of needles and even its own decomposition. The device sucks juice and pigment from the soil, the fallen fruits of the surrounding trees and the nearby river. This material is mixed in its little vats and scratched into the blank canvas of the Farnsworth House's underside. This tattooing of wet material becomes the conceptual antidote to the house's space-time disablement. Ivanovic reintroduces the house to its context and introduces it to a new series of time-based, contextual relationships. He fills its hollow vessel with nature, chance, time, death and stain. The Czech philosopher Vilem Flusser wrote of the hollow vessel and our learning to use it: 'By using the word *hollow*, one gets to the root of things. From "hollow" there come "Hale" and "Hell", as one can see from the English "whole" and "hole". By using the word *hollow* you are talking of the Whole. For quite a long time, science, by thinking formally, has been disclosing what is behind phenomena, and it sees the hollowness (the curved space of mutually intersecting fields of possibility) behind them. But only recently have we begun to compute alternative contents out of this hollow-ness. Only recently have we begun to learn what pottery is all about: about producing empty forms in order to inform what is amorphous.'[137]

Ivanovic has done exactly this.

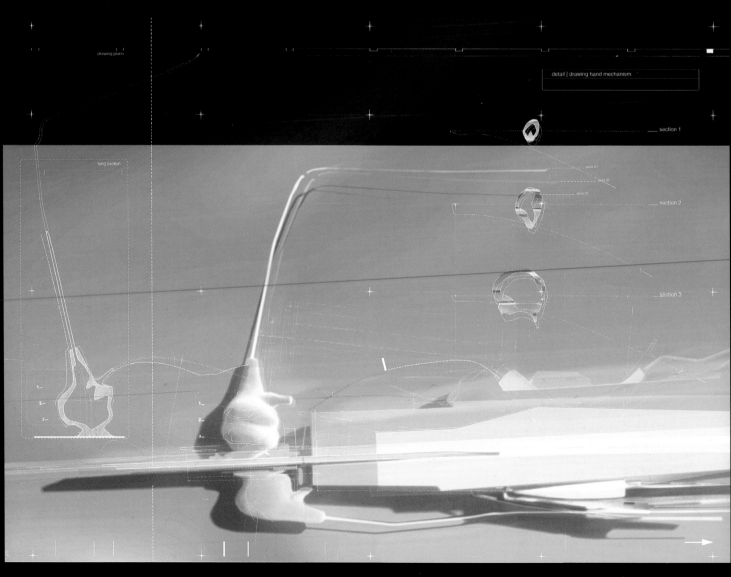

detail | drawing hand mechanism

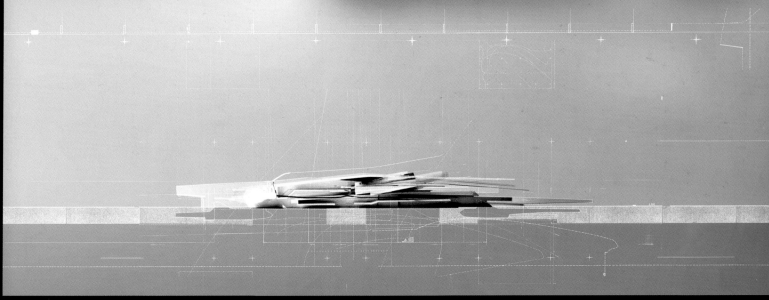

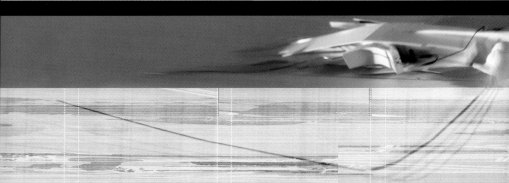

234-7
Various views of
Farnsworth Machine
2002

Walking in a Parkland of Ecstasy, Delirium and Disjuncture

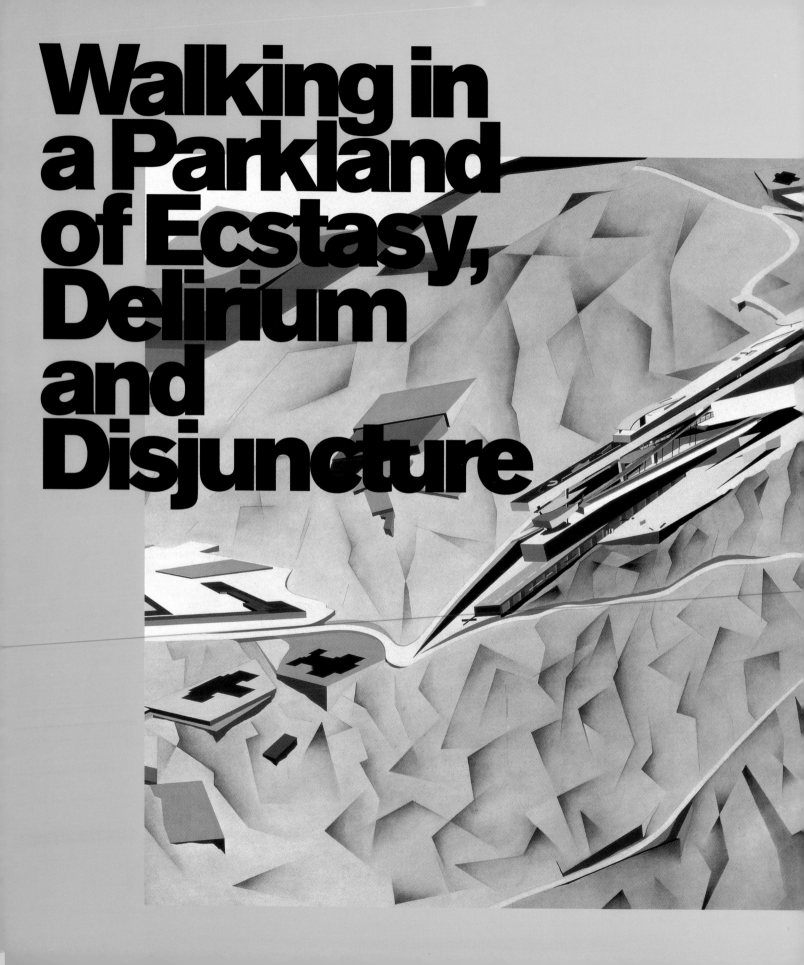

During the late 1960s, architects started to question the dogmas and doctrines of the Modernist masters. The old, established relationships between form and function and between ornament and crime seemed to have little relevance in a world of difference, of burgeoning information technology, of cold war and of the equivalence of value in all things. Architects began to develop an architecture of disjunction, of splitting, of shards and of follies. This era of deconstruction was defined by three major events: the Hong Kong Peak competition (won by Zaha Hadid in 1983), the Parc de La Villette competition (won by Bernard Tschumi in the same year) and the MOMA, New York exhibition entitled 'Deconstructivist Architecture' (1988). This chapter explores the evolution of the Deconstructivist style, discusses the cultural context of the time and illustrates the ideas that inspired these architects.

238
Peak Overview
Building

Zaha Hadid
Architects, Hong
Kong, 1983

'It is not necessarily that they consciously work from Constructivist sources. Rather, in dismantling the ongoing tradition, in which modernism participated, they find themselves inevitably employing the strategies rehearsed by the avant-garde. They are not capriciously imitating the vocabulary of the Russians, the point is that the Russians discovered the geometric configurations which can be used to destabilize structure, and that these configurations can be found repressed in high modernism.'
Mark Wigley

'In planning any given building, the architect must first assemble and compose only space, not concerning himself with material and construction. Construction enters into architecture only in so far as it determines the available material to obtain maximum results. This has nothing in common with art and can only serve the requirements of architecture accidentally.'
Nikolai Ladovsky

239
Blazing Wing
Coop Himmelb(l)au, 1980

240–41
Models of La Villette
Folie
Bernard Tschumi Architects, 1983

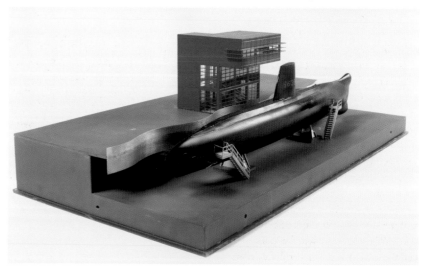

In the *Hypnerotomachia*, Poliphilo's dream world is Arcadian, and his journey through it, with heaving, lustful heart, brings him to different critical points in the landscape. These points are architectural pieces; they are intersections of meaning and form. These follies, ruins and statues are the vessels whose surfaces and internal spaces carry knowledge and epistemologies.

In 1980 Coop Himmelb(l)au built an icon for the final twenty years of the twentieth century. It was called Blazing Wing (fig. 239). A couple of years before this, their architecture had started to fracture; it and they began to foresee an architecture of the 'split' and the 'rupture'. This realization was expressed in the Reiss Bar, Vienna (1978), a project meant to observe (or corroborate) that *Reiss* was embedded in *reissen*, the German verb 'to split': 'The project postulates a 48 centimetre crack, zigging and zagging up opposite walls. The conceit of the crack is a small stretching of the room, a pulling apart, the split sustained by parallel vent tubes got up to look like giant bolts – their washered ends (as if) punching through the street façade – and by two benign spikes over the bar.'[1]

Blazing Wing was an architecture of event, a never-to-be-repeated architecture, an architecture of flame. Why flame? Flame embodied the zeitgeist, a fragile but dangerous beauty, hot yet cool, the heat of alchemical transmutation. Blazing Wing did not engage with its site or the ground on which it stood. It was beyond location and the specificity of geography. Its structure did not belong to an idealized Classical age, but it had some sort of structural integrity that was beyond simple description. It hung in the sky, unstable, a deadly, fiery guillotine, likely to plunge into the earth below it, branding it with an archaeology of cinders.

The Reiss Bar and Blazing Wing announced the onset of an architecture of beautiful, sublime confusion. This architecture of the 1980s has been called 'deconstructive'. It is a brimming cauldron of paradox. Here is an architecture that is abstracted yet literal, that is without scale yet precisely scaled, that is not contextual but that is very influenced by its context, that is revolutionary yet is not at all, that rejects Modernism but does not. It denounces architecture but is hugely architectural, and it celebrates the demise of the architect yet depends on the architect's formal talents. This is a dynamic architecture, but it is mostly static. It references the Constructivists, yet it does not.

'Deconstruction' was born out of nihilist confusion. The cracks of the Reiss Bar and the flames of Blazing Wing, together with Peter Eisenman's decomposition and drawn textural abstractions, the *détourned* cinematics of Tschumi, and Daniel Libeskind's Neo-Constructivist third way of palimpsestual symbolic vectors, offered a clue to an architecture that just might be appropriate for a world teetering on the edge of an abyss whose bottomless nothingness was draining architecture like some sort of black hole.

With all movements, cliques, call them what you will, catalytic events

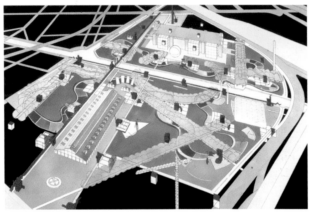

242 (above)
***Folie* No. 1**
Bernard Tschumi
Architects, 1983–

243 (left)
Aerial perspective
Bernard Tschumi
Architects, 1983

244 (below)
Exploded axonometric drawings showing organizational layers
Bernard Tschumi
Architects, 1983

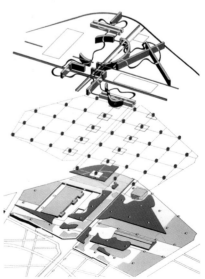

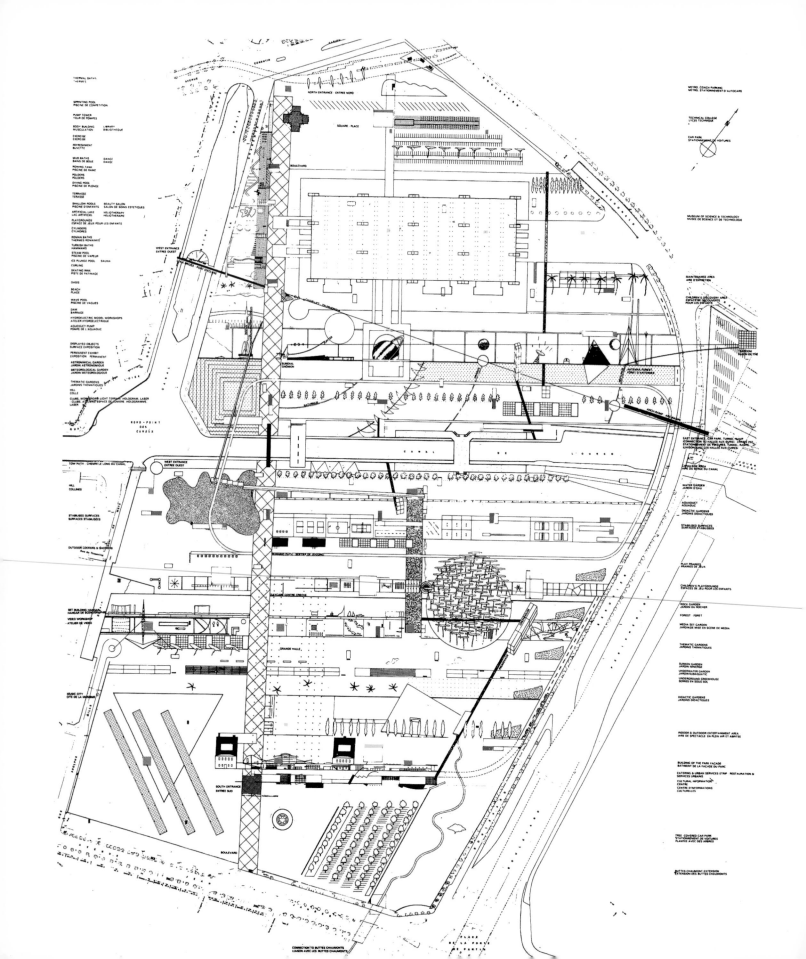

THERMAL BATHS
THERMES

SPRINTING POOL
PISCINE DE COMPETITION

PUMP TOWER
TOUR DE POMPES

BODY BUILDING   LIBRARY
MUSCULATION   BIBLIOTHEQUE

EXERCISE
EXERCISE

REFRESHMENT
BUVETTE

MUD BATHS   DANCE
BAINS DE BOUE   DANSE

ROWING TANK
PISCINE DE RAME

POLDERS
POLDERS

DIVING POOL
PISCINE DE PLONGE

TERRASSE
TERASSE

SHALLOW POOLS   BEAUTY SALON
PISCINE D'ENFANTS   SALON DE SOINS ESTETIQUES

ARTIFICIAL LAKE   HELIOTHERAPY
LAC ARTIFICIEL   HELIOTHERAPIE

PLAYGROUNDS
ESPACE DE JEUX POUR LES ENFANTS

CYLINDERS
CYLINDRES

ROMAN BATHS
THERMES ROMAINS

TURKISH BATHS
HAMMAMS

STEAM POOL
PISCINE DE VAPEUR

ICE PLUNGE POOL   SAUNA
ICE PLUNGE POOL

CURLING

SKATING RINK
PISTE DE PATINAGE

OASIS

BEACH
PLAGE

WAVE POOL
PISCINE DE VAGUES

DAM
BARRAGE

HYDROELECTRIC MODEL WORKSHOPS
ATELIER HYDROELECTRIQUE

AQUEDUCT PUMP
POMPE DE L'AQUADUC

DISPLAYED OBJECTS
SURFACE EXPOSITION

PERMANENT EXHIBIT
EXPOSITION PERMANENT

ASTRONOMICAL GARDEN
JARDIN ASTRONOMIQUE

METEOROLOGICAL GARDEN
JARDIN METEOROLOGIQUE

THEMATIC GARDENS
JARDINS THEMATIQUES

HILL
COLLE

CLUBS, WORKSHOPS LIGHT TERRAIN, HOLOGRAM, LASER
CLUBS, ATELIERS ESPACE DE LUMIERE, HOLOGRAMME,
LASER

STABILISED SURFACES
SURFACES STABILISEES

OUTDOOR LOCKERS & SHOWERS

MST BUILDING HAMEAU
HAMEAU DE SCIENCE

VIDEO WORKSHOP
ATELIER DE VIDEO

MUSIC CITY
CITE DE LA MUSIQUE

NORTH ENTRANCE ENTREE NORD

SQUARE PLACE

BOULEVARD

WEST ENTRANCE
ENTREE OUEST

WEST ENTRANCE
ENTREE OUEST

TOW PATH - CHEMIN LE LONG DU CANAL

HILL
COLLINES

RUNNING PATH / SENTIER DE JOGGING

GRANDE HALLE

SOUTH ENTRANCE
ENTREE SUD

BOULEVARD

CONNECTION TO BUTTES CHAUMONTS
LIAISON AVEC LES BUTTES CHAUMONTS

METRO, COACH PARKING
METRO, STATIONNEMENT D'AUTOCARS

TECHNICAL COLLEGE
LYCEE TECHNIQUE

CAR PARK
STATIONNEMENT DE VOITURES

MUSEUM OF SCIENCE & TECHNOLOGY
MUSEE DE SCIENCE ET DE TECHNOLOGIE

MAINTENANCE AREA
AIRE D'ENTRETIEN

CHILDREN'S DISCOVERY AREA
ESPACE DE DECOUVERTE
POUR LES ENFANTS

EAST ENTRANCE, CAR PARK, TUNNEL, RAMP
(CONNECTION TO HALLES AUX OURS)
ENTREE EST, STATIONNEMENT DE VOITURES, TUNNEL, RAMPE,
LIAISON AVEC LES HALLES AUX OURS

CANAL SIDE AREA
AIRE DU BERGE DU CANAL

WATER GARDEN
JARDIN D'EAU

AQUADUCT
AQUADUC

DIDACTIC GARDENS
JARDINS DIDACTIQUES

STABILISED SURFACES
SURFACES STABILISEES

PLAY PRAIRIE
PRAIRIES DE JEUX

CHILDREN'S PLAYGROUNDS
ESPACES DE JEU POUR LES ENFANTS

ROCK GARDEN
JARDIN DU ROCHER

FOREST GARDEN FORET

MEDIA SET GARDEN
JARDIN DE MISE EN SCENE DE MEDIA

THEMATIC GARDENS
JARDINS THEMATIQUES

SUNKEN GARDEN
JARDIN VINATIER

UNDERWATER GARDEN
JARDIN SUBAQUATIC

UNDERGROUND GREENHOUSE
SERRES EN SOUS SOL

DIDACTIC GARDENS
JARDINS DIDACTIQUES

INDOOR & OUTDOOR ENTERTAINMENT AREA
AIRE DE SPECTACLE EN PLEIN AIR ET ABRITEE

BUILDING OF THE PARK FACADE
BATIMENT DE LA FACADE DU PARC

CATERING & URBAN SERVICES STRIP   RESTAURATION &
SERVICES URBAINS

CULTURAL INFORMATION
CENTRE
CENTRE D'INFORMATIONS
CULTURELLES

TREE COVERED CAR PARK
STATIONNEMENT DE VOITURES
PLANTEE AVEC DES ARBRES

BUTTES CHAUMONT EXTENSION
EXTENSION DES BUTTES CHAUMONTS

conspire to solidify them, to give them added purpose. Deconstruction can boast three such events: the Parc de La Villette, Paris competition, the Hong Kong Peak competition (both 1983) and the 'Deconstructivist Architecture' exhibition at New York's Museum of Modern Art (1988).

When the Parc de La Villette competition was announced, it was entered by visionary architects of more than one generation. The Smithsons, Cedric Price, the Office of Metropolitan Architecture (OMA), Zaha Hadid and Tschumi all applied for its brief. Meanwhile the wacky Coop Himmelb(l)au lads were at it again, working on a design for a Rooftop Remodelling (1983). Here was a collection of shards, splinters and bent plates that on one level looked like the skeleton of a bird after cats had been at it, and on another level evoked the collapsed masts and rigging of a catamaran disabled by a storm. Only Himmelb(l)au and Tschumi were to see their works built.

The grand motif of Tschumi's winning design, *La Case Vide*, was the point-grid of red cubes in various states of corruption (figs 243–4). This grid was the datum against which every one of Tschumi's moves was calibrated. (One is reminded of Kandinsky's 'Red to excite activity'.) Red was often the emblematic colour of choice for the Deconstructivists. (And if red was Deconstructivism's colour, its patron saint of philosophy was Jacques Derrida.)

Tschumi's project was a juxtaposition of layers of points, lines and surfaces. Like the red cubes, these were initially Platonic, yet through the distortion of interference they became truncated, deformed or punctured. The point-grid cubes were microcosms of the design. The processes that conditioned the overall configuration of Tschumi's plan also conditioned the individual deformation, aggregations and erosions of the cubes. The cubes were follies, sometimes imbued with function, sometimes not (figs 240–2, 271–2). Tschumi discussed this design in terms of a search for something away from the traditional coherence of architectural

247–8 (left and below)
La Villette competition model
OMA, 1983

245 (opposite)
La Villette competition entry plan
OMA, 1983

246 (right)
La Villette competition drawing showing layers of landscape
OMA, 1983

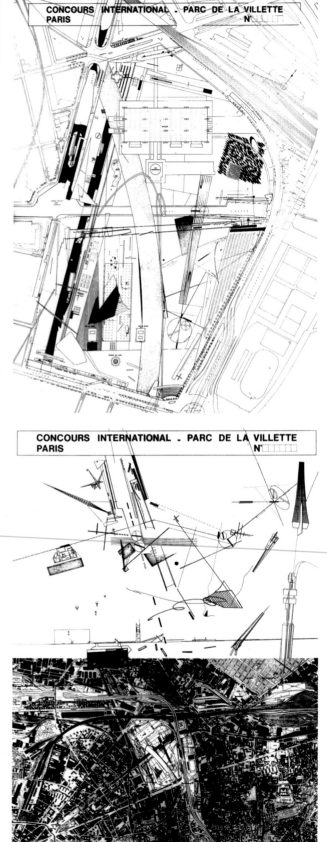

249
**Conceptual painting
for La Villette
competition**
Zaha Hadid
Architects, 1983

250
**La Villette
competition plan**
Zaha Hadid
Architects, 1983

251
**Location plan and
conceptual organiza-
tional diagram**
Zaha Hadid
Architects, 1983

structure, which he believed to be inappropriate at this time. This coherence of architectural thought had been at the centre of the Modern movement and of Russian Constructivism, and its success had stopped architects considering whether it was possible to create an architecture of incoherent thought. The latter, Tschumi believed, better reflected his own era. He felt that the fragmenting concepts of space and time, and the scientific and philosophical reliance on the relative, forced architects to consider architectures of hybridization, fragmentation, juxtaposition and shifting relationships. He described his Parc de La Villette plan as one that could only lead to a radical questioning of the concept of structure – to its decentring – since the superimposition of three autonomous (and coherent) structures (points, lines, surfaces) does not necessarily lead to a new, more complex and verifiable structure. Instead they open a field of contradictory and conflictual events which deny the idea of a pre-established coherence. Permutations and substitutions of elements within the three systems add to the disruption.[2]

The French landscape garden has a long and distinguished history. Tschumi's Parc de La Villette fit into this tradition. Notions of scalar inversion, reflection, function and non-function, absence and presence, and twisted symbols were nothing new within French landscape. *La Case Vide* was 'an empty slot or box in a chart or matrix, an unoccupied square on a chessboard, a blank compartment: the point of the unexpected, before data entered on the vertical axis can meet with data on the horizontal one. The matrix normally suggests endless combinations, permutations and substitutions'.[3] Here were the combinatory gymnastics of Giordano Bruno but without the iconic, epistemological memory. Tschumi's combinations revealed no further knowledge; they were essentially empty, the Joycean Machine chundering on with no memory, no past, future or present. The cubes were wrapped in Constructivist cloaks. This veneer did much to contribute to the notion that Deconstruction and Constructivism were similar movements.

Nothing could be further from the truth. As Tschumi himself explained, 'My concern with the early days of film montage and cut-ups, with Eisenstein and Vertov, or with the literary theories of the time that led to current post-Structuralist thought, found great relish in playing against the residues of avant-garde images. There was no stylistic concern. In no way was I interested in the sort of historical parallels with Revolutionary 1920s the way others have been in relation to the eighteenth century.'[4]

The architecture of Revolutionary Russia was conceived for bodies that were searching for a new art, a new way of life and a holistic, equitable future. These bodies were starting to speed up, starting to gleam within their metal and glass; their metabolic rate was slower than ours; the information to which they were subjected was thousands of times less than that to which we are. These bodies were conscious in real time, chained to geography and living life along time's arrow.

The Deconstructivist body of the 1980s was a whole other thing. It was fast; it was prostheticized with a zillion additives; its influence could be global. It was multi-focal; history and event were intertwined into hypertextual scratch-mix splendour. All that remained in common was fear. The Russian Revolutionaries and other turn-of-the-century avant-garde groups feared the lack of God and befriended the machine. God wasn't even in the architectural detail, as the Modern movement maintained. The Deconstructivists were gazing into the void caused by the death of God, perceiving Debord's Spectacle in a million twisted, alienated fragments and befriending no one and nothing, and their architecture reflected this. Anthony Vidler summed this up in a discussion of Tschumi's *Case Vide*: 'Where the upwardly spiralling ramps of the Tatlin tower stood, at one level, for the endless and regenerative calisthenics of the new society, the follies of La Villette presuppose no therapeutic ends. Analogically, the folly stands for a body already conditioned to the terms of dissemination, fragmentation and interior collapse.'[5]

252
Hong Kong Peak location plan
Zaha Hadid Architects, 1983

253
Hong Kong Peak level plans
Zaha Hadid Architects, 1983

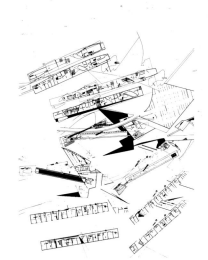

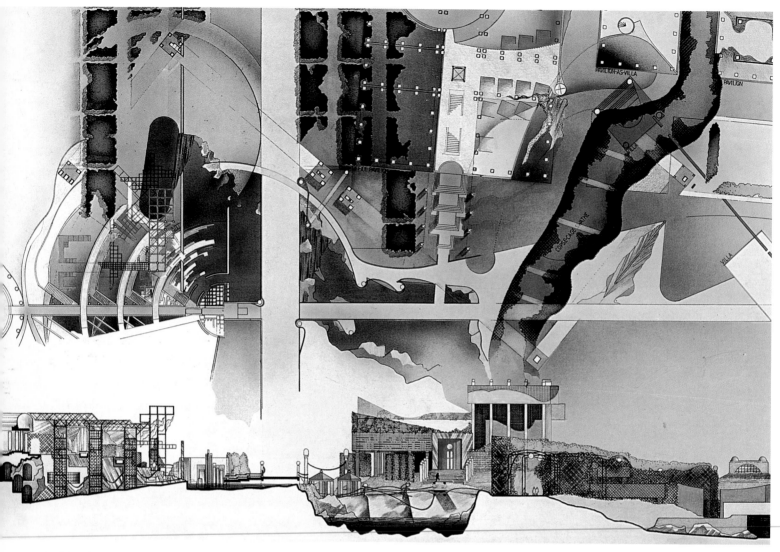

254 (above)
Layer City, south from the Shadow House
Peter Cook/Christine Hawley, 1981–2

255 (right)
Layer City
Peter Cook, 1981–2

256 (far right)
Way Out West
Peter Cook, 1988

257 (left)
**Drawing of hilltop
Academy, Arcadia,
Second Version**
Peter Cook, 1979

258 (above)
**Drawing of Outriders
of Layer City**
Peter Cook, 1981–2

259 (below)
**Drawing of Lump
(Mound), Side 3**
Peter Cook, 1973–4

Growing a Delirious Landscape of Expediency

Another well-known project for La Villette was that of Rem Koolhaas and Elias Zengelis's OMA. This project was for a series of banded zones; the point of departure was the hybridizing of some influential town-planning and architectural concepts (figs 245–8). OMA sampled Constantinos Doxiades, Team X, Cedric Price and Archigram. They proposed five meta-layers: Strips, Confetti, Access and Circulation, Composition of Major Elements, and Connections and Elaborations. The Strips comprised the functional pieces of the brief and included gardens, play areas and other programmatic segments. These were laid out east to west. The Confetti layer consisted of all the interstitial accommodation, information kiosks, picnic areas and such like. Access and Circulation was characterized by the north-to-south boulevard that intersected the Strips and provided a route between all major spaces in the park. The Composition of Major Elements was the layer of eclectic structures and features that were pre-existent or to be developed by other architects. Finally, the Connections and Elaborations were the points of connection and transition from surrounding urban areas: plazas, gateways and railway lines.

OMA augmented this spatial strategy with a planting scheme organized around three categories of nature: Surfaces, Screen of Trees and Vegetal elements. Surfaces consisted of play prairies, thematic gardens etc. The Screen of Trees was an 'east–west marking of the zones in the form of arboreal trees of differing height, species, transparency, density and homogeneity, produc[ing] curtains as in the theatre, which together act as "sliding landscapes"'.[6] The view from north to south would consist of six thousand trees with carefully carved vistas. On the east–west axis, the trees would capture views of various activities. The large Vegetal elements were to be the Linear Forest and the Circular Forest: 'The Linear Forest south of the canal and the Circular Forest at the centre of the Park have a didactic correspondence: from the natural to the artificial, from solid to hollow, from evergreen to deciduous.'[7] In a sense, OMA's scheme was a horticultural banded algorithm awaiting programmatic input to configure its green architectonics.

Cedric Price also entered the La Villette competition. His entry was all service conditioning, and he made no effort to aestheticize his project's graphics for the predilection of the press and judges. Price's work was an exercise in minimal intervention, minimal infrastructure, just enough to rearticulate the peculiarities of the existing park and augment them with a few other educational and delightful experiences and functions. It was an architecture of benevolent gantries and shadowy hillocks. Price's main concept was to see the park as a 'lung', a '24-hour workshop' for experimentation in the delight of learning. The park's construction and day-to-day workings and ordering were to be open to the educational observance and scrutiny of local residents. The scheme was a synthesis of urban farming, school, fishery and conservatoire: 'The growing, harvesting and consumption of vegetables, fruit and fish on the site logically interweave with the production and dissemination of music and science. People, services and activities are layered to enable a filigree of voluntary movement and self-choice activity. Not all areas are used, and not all the enclosures are designated. The individual is in control and the park is the intelligent, friendly toy that invites investigation. The size of the site must be celebrated and its uniqueness exploited.

The public thresholds contrast the familiar with the new.'[8]

OMA's old assistant Zaha Hadid also opted for a layered approach in her competition entry (figs 249–51). This time the gardens were often mobile and suspended in the sky: 'The terrain is seen as a flat landscape with all nature, that is, nature which is more refined in terms of texture, physically elevated. The green plateaux in a field in the sky constitute a new type of garden, not hanging but at certain instances, they are suspended … Their calligraphy in the land is imposed by a mechanical system, sometimes regular when controlled, at other times random if driven by man.'[9]

Hadid's architectural language for this project consisted of implied orbits, of galaxies of shards, of a Planetary Strip, and the ground plane was graduated so it made a transition from mud strip to composed floral garden and all the stages in between. She created a Discovery Garden that plunged through this miasma to provide necessary intersections with the park's major programmatic facilities.

Deconstruction, as we have seen with Himmelb(l)au's Blazing Wing, does not trust the inertia of the ground plane (fig. 239). The ground becomes the almost blank parchment for a new spatial calligraphy, a laboratory for inscription, collision and functional braiding. Much of Hadid's work has an almost scriptorial preoccupation. The programmatic criteria of a project somehow conjoin with more artistic preoccupations to create the emblematic incisions for an architecture. Hadid's inscriptions are not always informed by the dynamic desire-lines of context; often they are a revelation of the palimpsest-like dynamics of architectural thought. The line, the redrawn line and the superimposition of layers coalescing in a simultaneity of vector and plane are used to suggest an architecture. Stylistically the link between Hadid's work and Suprematism is obvious. This, again erroneously, reinforces the idea that the Revolutionary Russians and the Deconstructivists had something theoretical in common.

In his introduction to the catalogue of the 'Deconstructivist Architecture' exhibition, Mark Wigley picked up on the vein of Constructivist compositional protocol in this work: 'Russian Constructivism constituted a critical turning point where the architectural tradition was bent so radically that a fissure opened up through which certain disturbing architectural possibilities first became visible. Traditional thinking about the nature of the architectural object was placed in doubt. But the radical possibility was not then taken up. The wound in the tradition soon closed leaving but a faint scar. These projects reopen the wound.'[10]

Many historians interested in the Constructivists find it difficult to see why their motifs were adopted seventy or eighty years later to describe a late twentieth-century condition. Deconstruction was about the death of social unification. It was ambivalent; all it had left was the assumption that the uniform was disjunctive. It was this that led its practitioners back to the Constructivist protocols. To create their architecture, the Deconstructivists exploded the frequently simple and staid Constructivist placements into a hailstorm of sharpened fragments.

Twisting the Void

The other great Deconstructivist competition, for Hong Kong's Peak, focused on an expensive private health club. Zaha Hadid won it. Although her La Villette and Peak schemes were virtually simultaneous conceptions, the Peak bears a much more audacious concept than the Park (figs 238, 249–53). The former was configured around four huge accommodation beams artfully arranged in semi-excavated and bermed landscapes perched high on the Peak itself. The space was choreographed by the varying conditions created by the beams and their insertion into the landscape. These conditions were numerous, and therefore a sense of difference from one space to another could be generated relatively easily. The spaces between beams created cavernous voids within which Hadid 'floated' architectural elements, also using flimsy suspensions or emaciated props. The Peak concept displayed the same Suprematist hyperscripting as the La Villette proposal. The drawings showed a constellation of flying parts. Kenneth Frampton captured the floating awe of it all: 'This evocation of a hedonistic "world within a world", this immortal other place, has always been implicit in Hadid's work, and it is this

which emerges as the underlying poetic theme in her recent winning design for the Hong Kong Peak competition; the erotic implication, for instance, of being suspended in a vast, luxurious, starlit void at night, high above the distant panorama of the city and the sea.'[11]

Peter Cook and his then architectural partner, Christine Hawley, also entered the Peak competition. Their scheme was a very English take on the layering of space and the relationship of landscape to building. Not for them the nihilism of the loss of meaning, of time or of place; theirs was very much an architecture of genius loci, of specialness of place, of delicate view and verdant vista. The Cook-and-Hawley scheme was also a microcosm of many of the thoughts and projects that concerned these two architects then and later. Their entry centred on the dining area, which became a focal point within a series of strata, nets,

pavilions, water cascades and meshes. Like much of their early work, this project was highly romanticized, rejoicing in light and shadow; wayward, almost Art Nouveau balustrades; and carefully set episodes of experience as one travelled through the building. Stylistically it was an example of what Cook called 'Lyrical Mechanism'; its aesthetic was machined but deviant. The machined forms were often corrupted by billows and errant curves that acted against the tyranny and monotony of economies of scale and architectonic detail.

Melting Walls and Dripping Façades

After Archigram, Cook's work flirted with ideas of metamorphosis, of playful, fluctuating translucence and of abundant Arcadian landscape providing

260
Skywaft City
Peter Cook, 1985

the biological impetus for change: 'Veggies', as he called them. As Archigram was in its final stages of fracture in 1972, he produced the vividly coloured Urban Mark. This was a portion of a city – or indeed an entire pert city – programmed to be a complete, responsive environment. The project was represented by a set of metamorphic time-based drawings. Cook's agents of metamorphosis in this and many other projects to follow were communications and plant growth. As he put it, 'I have long been fascinated by the intermixing of vegetation with man-made substances, and most attractive is a reiterative idea about a chamber that will change slowly from solidarity – even integrity – with the ground (at the base) which gradually becomes translucent and thinner and then gradually becomes transparent and gossamer thin. You realize that the natural objects are there in a series of overlays and that their form and their extent is a mixture of the natural and the humanly contrived and you begin to be attracted by the notion that the environment is not only full of paradoxes, but of layers.'[12]

Cook also developed another legacy of the Archigram days – the narrative. His narratives concerned the users of a particular Cookian scheme, or the specific growth patterns of the landscape, or the sudden, unconsidered event or situation, and they ran hand-in-hand and indeed were the grist for Cook's metamorphic mill.

Arcadian City (1978) contained elements of Plug-in City and Urban Mark. At certain points it was conditioned by the cohabitation and dynamics of various social groupings which, one suspects, had been wryly noticed by Cook on his exhaustive international travels. These late twentieth-century fashionable idio-syncrasies and political machinations started to condition Cook's visionary city. He knew the importance of the millions of lives and their rich tapestry to the vitality of the city and its constituent forms.

Layer City (figs 254–5) made use of fashionable ideas of disjunctive composition. Its diagonal geometries were mitigated by maverick domed forms that had been eschewed by the architec-tural avant-garde for many decades. The Outriders of Layer City had a much more complex arrangement than the more conventional, slightly offset grid and undergrowth of the main urban set pieces at the centre of Cook's imaginary urbanity (fig. 258). Cook is well known for how he mistrusts the exclusion of any aspect of architecture's full language. Good taste, especially in the hands of the avant-garde, can be limited by adhering to a very few combinations of materials and the geometries of jointing. Cook never falls into this trap. The Outriders were composed of both recognizable and previ-ously unseen architectural elements. They were at once an integrated circuit and a domed, glistening utopia governed by a bejewelled potentate. Façades glinted in the sun and dropped into each other. Perhaps this was not a utopia but a dystopia, a New Babylon freshly estab-lishing itself like so much ivy after a particularly severe attack of weed killer? Was this a picture of the cyberpunk city yet to come, a city that lived on the treacly, unresponsive husk of the old city, rewiring it and fostering highly connected crepus-cular growths? The centre of Layer City, with its skewed grids, created a different vision. It was part theatre-in-the-park, part prince's palace, part Venetian

ceremonial marquee with roped VIP handrail/barrier. Layers and meshes of various frequencies enforced or liberated the central notion, which was that the character of any successful city is an eclectic mix of aspirations, districts and financial securities, and the aesthetic predispositions that go with them.

Many of Cook's projects of the 1980s were concerned with the ramifica-tions of the city master-plan. Many of his contemporaries left the complexities of full-blown master-planning to others, and therefore there is a lack of visionary thought in this area. These master-plans are often about the city's esoteric dynamics, the desires of city dwellers and their delight in the theatrical. These dynamics, desires and stages are mediated by armatures and information systems that facilitate flow, movement, expansion and elbow-room.

Skywaft City (figs 260–1) also contributed to contemporary debates about Constructivist compositional strategies and the role of natural vegeta-tive systems and ideas of growth in the city, as well as a preoccupation with skewed grids and the inclined beam, its support structure, habitation and change. As we have seen and will see later, with Daniel Libeskind's City Edge project in Berlin (fig. 266), the big beam began to become an obsession among the avant-garde. Cook's proposition maintained his eccentric English take on the warring geometries of Deconstruction and once again had a rather romantic, Arcadian patina to it, like an old steel cable attracting the green strands of seaweed on a muddy beach. The project itself seemed neither fully urban nor fully rural – it was both. One of Cook's particular fortes has been his invention of lyrical ideas of architecture that sit firmly astride the erroneous dichotomy of urban and rural. His quirky take evokes a musty smell of peaty decay, or the strangely sour smell of the less accessible parts of a wood or copse. None of his Deconstructivist contemporaries could contemplate an architecture that conjured with anything other than the pristine, visually driven shapes of fashion. Christine Hawley

261
Electric garden behind culture strip in Skywaft City
Peter Cook, 1985

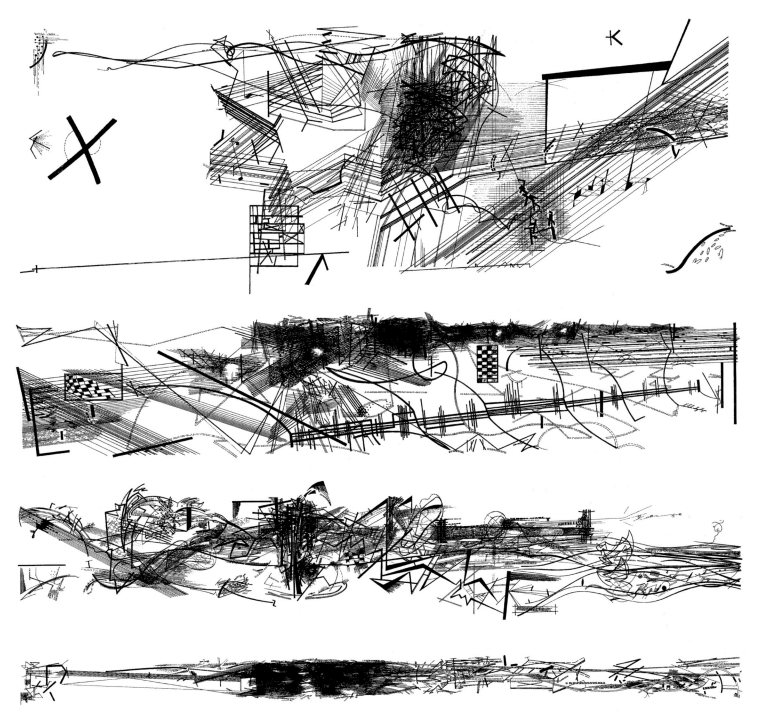

262
**'Chamberworks', III –
Horizontal; IX –
Horizontal; VI –
Horizontal; VII –
Horizontal**
Daniel Libeskind,
1983

described Cook's work this way: 'There is a continuous search not for answers but for clues; the folds, crevices, surfaces of organic composition are obviously now beginning to be a point of reference. Despite the drama and the often random appearance of his vegetable icons there is an underlying hierarchy, an order that suits the architectural mind well …'[13]

The melting of the wall, the changing translucency between inside and outside or between one space and another, is often at the root of Cook's projects. Sometimes this is declared; at other times it is implicit. His projects are closer to the lusty dream-journey of Poliphilo than to his peers. For Cook is at once eccentric and exuberant. Like Poliphilo his child-like naïveté disguises a steely heart throbbing with red-blooded wonder. He has always been an advocate of the use of humour. His witty optimism unfortunately wasn't imported by his contemporaries, and this fact can make the '80s seem a tad turgid. Cook created fictional worlds beautifully crafted to seduce his friends and inspire his peers. Like Poliphilo, he could evoke a wider lyrical world from mere fragments.

Between Zero and Infinity

In full 'Pataphysical mode, Alfred Jarry defined God as 'the shortest distance between zero and infinity in either direction'. *Between Zero and Infinity* became, almost a hundred years later, the title of Daniel Libeskind's first book.[14] At the time, Libeskind was head of the department of architecture at the Cranbrook Academy of Art. He had studied music in Poland and Israel before turning to architecture in New York and completing an MA in History and Theory of Architecture in the UK.

Between Zero and Infinity is interesting because it is a genetic blueprint for much of Libeskind's subsequent work. In it he posits his *oeuvre* in the context of the history of Modernism. He was influenced by the struggles of Modernist philosophers, writers, artists and musicians as well as architects. The maelstrom of

references includes Duchamp, Roussel, Jarry of course, James Joyce, El Lissitzky, Tatlin, Giordano Bruno, Henri Bergson, John Cage, Jiri Kolar and Edmund Husserl. The sources – some quoted, some implicit – are mashed, intertwined and augmented by Libeskind's idiosyncratic intelligence.

Before Libeskind was seduced into attempting to build facsimiles of his ideas, he laid down a foundation of concepts, formal articulations and graphic gambits that consisted of the *prima materia* of his architectural lexicon. From the late '70s to the mid-'80s he concocted four highly influential and iconic projects. 'Micromegas' (1979), 'Chamberworks' (1983) and 'Threatrum Mundi' (1985) were folios of drawings; 'Three Lessons in Architecture' (1985) was an installation of three machines at the Venice Biennale.

Libeskind perceived these works as a search by means of which to carry the Constructivist project to its ultimate conclusion. However, his quest to locate the boundaries of architecture and its discourse far exceeded the rather limited formal posturings of the Russian Revolutionaries. He was seeking an architecture that existed in time, that was vectorial and aware of its history, symbolism and syntax. During this period Libeskind created some of the most important architectural theory and drawings of the century. His synthesis brought a new vitality to architectural debate and illustrated a way forward from the then current battles between the historicists and the avant-garde. As he put it, '[T]here is an approach which is not as simple or clear to define as [the binary opposition of these stylistic battles] but which attempts nevertheless to deal with the poetic complexity of Architecture in time. It seeks to explore the deeper order rooted not only in visible forms, but in the invisible and hidden sources which nourish culture itself, in its thought, art, literature, song and movement. It considers history and tradition as a body whose memories and dreams cannot be simply reconstructed. Such an approach does not wish to reduce the visible to a thought, and architecture to a mere construction. An

orientation such as this admits in its methods and testifies in its intentions to the intensity of experience, to its "opaque transparency", and by its deferred expectations continually calls its own presumptions into question.'[15]

So Libeskind saw the embedded stylistic wrangles of the late twentieth century as the manifestations of two opposed imperatives. Architecture was being demeaned by the consumption, quantification and supposed rationalization brought about by industrial mass production. Also architecture's self-referential and constant reappraisal within its own limited frameworks was diluting its theoretical basis and leading it away from the centre of social discourse, thus assuring its marginalization.

Libeskind's notion was that approaches could be developed that linked contemporary architecture into the cross-disciplinary history of ideas yet were firmly Modernist and not in thrall to hyper-consumption and its associated avarice. This was a language of architecture that remembered yet explored the primacy and efficacy of space over words. It referenced Classical epistemology and sought contemporary ideas of Beauty. *Between Zero and Infinity*, the first Libeskindian take on these notions, sought to develop some kind of architectural notation for them in book form. This work and its ambitions also formed the basis for students' work at Cranbrook. Libeskind was a tenacious and inspiring teacher, and the legacy of his Cranbrook years continues to resonate around the architectural community. He gave formative licence and tuition to Ben Nicholson, Hani Rashid and Raoul Bunschoten, among others.

Between Zero and Infinity is a seminal document. It charts Libeskind's metamorphosis from normative Constructivist protocols of space-making and material juxtaposition through to a more acute polemical series of collages inspired by Kurt Schwitters and Jiri Kolar. The journey continues towards formal representations of contorted juxtaposed spaces apparently subject to a terrible mutant architectonic fecundity

('Micromegas: The Architecture of Endspace'). The spaces depicted in these drawings are highly complex feats of sheer obsession and have an insane quality lurking within them. Their language is still Constructivist, and one can imagine them having Malevich's and Tatlin's dynamic reliefs clustered on every available surface. One is enchanted yet uneasy about the loss of traditional architectonic signs and indicators that would reveal whether these works are representations of real space. They seem real, but they are also unreal; they inhabit the ethereal world of 'betweenness'. Glancing across them, the parched architectural mind thirsts for a clue, a little moisture in this symbol-less desert. There is a sense of spatial butchery; the limbs and torsos of the body of architectural discourse are dissected and mounted for all to see in post-Diderotian, post-apocalyptic tableaux. The drawings are palimpsests of the form-work architecture has heaped on itself, over time: 'That fateful and remarkable encounter between the "sewing machine and the umbrella on the operating table" has given birth to a whole bestiary of creatures and monsters – and not only in the mind. (The use of the word *monster* in this context refers to its etymology, that is, a portentous revelation or demonstration). The process whereby the making of architecture comes to resemble a laboratory experiment reflects the general secularization of culture, whose symptoms include the relativizing of meaning, the devaluation of tradition and the virulent attack on all forms of symbolic, emblematic and mythical experience.'[16]

One of the drawings within the 'Micromegas' folio is entitled *Moldoror's Equation*. Umbrellas and their opening arcs and loci can be discerned deep within the compositional structure (frontis). The umbrella's conical form contrasts with Libeskind's emblematic, manic and artful Constuctivist stick-debris. These drawings are generally ascalar, infinite, compact and complex, a synthesis between sign and element – a Proun for the new millennium. Each vista opens into other arrangements of self-similar

but forever variable, slightly askew alignments. Architecture and its comprehension become conditioned by multiple perspective points. Nothing is given preference; nothing has precedence. Here architecture and its trabeated genetics are stripped bare of artifice. A new artifice resides in the intense labour of representing the puzzle of space.

By 1983 Libeskind had further developed his excoriating vision of the architectural future. These thoughts erupted into another folio of works entitled 'Chamberworks: Architectural Mediations on the Themes of Heraclitus'. This series consisted of twenty-eight drawings, each composed of varying breadths and lengths of black lines (fig. 262). These works dispense totally with any allusions to architectural forms or elements: they are merely constellations of lines hemmed in by an invisible frame. The script for architecture has become just that; the words of architecture have been replaced by the sounds of its letters, and these sounds are the atonal symphonies of its clashing and the meanderings of its spatial vectors – always having speed, duration and direction. These striations of space are recognizable only by their vertical or horizontal event horizons and the frequency of their cutting or action. Architecture has become the trace and memory of particles in space and time that implode and therefore cease to register in this or that spatial realm. Here truly is the hypodermic scratch of Lautréamont's sewing-machine needle and the stiletto at the umbrella's apex. Here is their dance, their ecstatic embrace, their lustful, disappointed *petit mort*. These drawings, the architectural notations of their frightful union, seem to fit simultaneously within a tradition of avant-garde musical notation characterized and defined by the likes of John Cage, Tom Phillips and Cornelius Cardew during the 1960s.

'Micromegas' and 'Chamberworks' were still inscribed with the black ink of the architect's draughting pen, the last vestige of the bondage of architectonic protocol. This too Libeskind was to ditch in his next folio of work, 'Theatrum

Mundi: Through the Green Membranes of Space'. 'Theatrum Mundi' anticipated the re-emergence of biological symbolism in architectural theoretical discourse in the last ten years of the twentieth century. It also actively represented the destructive, insidious power of the virus and anticipated ideas of architecture as self-replicating growth patterns and the smearing of space. The accuracy and definition of the draughted line were replaced by the ambiguity of the sketched line and the painted wash. Constructivist

263
Lesson A: Reading Architecture, 'Three Lessons in Architecture'
Studio Daniel Libeskind, 1985

264
Lesson C: Writing Architecture, 'Three Lessons in Architecture'
Studio Daniel Libeskind, 1985

protocols also disappeared. This was the architecture of stain and smudge. The twelve works were labelled, beginning with '2' and ending with '1', perhaps to suggest that they should be viewed as a cyclical process, akin to the months and seasons of the year. Libeskind suggested that the *theatrum mundi* of the future would 'probably no longer have anything to do with the celebration of the dead or the living: with memory or imagination. The premonition of the future – the sense of Theatrum Mundi – is presented here in the form of a city besieged by an unknown infection, an action taking place within the nucleic medium that flows in the bloodstream of architectural thought'.[17]

Diverse and Ingenious Machines

Libeskind and his colleagues constructed three remarkable machines for the 1985 Venice Biennale. As with his previous work, they were steeped in enigma and open to interpretation. 'Lesson A: Reading Architecture', 'Lesson B: Remembering Architecture' and 'Lesson C: Writing Architecture' were their themes (figs 263–5). The Reading machine (meant to reveal 'the tautological reality of the architectural text'[18]) was influenced by those sometimes contained in medieval monasteries. In particular it bore more than a passing resemblance to the book wheel featured in Agostino Ramelli's *Various and Ingenious Machines* (1588).

The Remembering machine acted as a memory theatre and was composed of iconic bits of architecture's past. It had fragments of Diderot and evoked the spectacle of Renaissance set design. In its complex interior was an epistemology of architectural symbol and thought, yet it was merely a projection machine. The construction of new architecture happened outside it, while at its centre was a void contained in a blood-red metal box.

The Writing machine alluded to a mechanism created in Jonathan Swift's *Gulliver's Travels* (1726). Swift described a phrase-making machine invented by a wise man that concocted chance combinations of words. The mechanism consisted of an array of cubes and the turning of handles around its perimeter created permutations of sentences hitherto unwritten. These were then examined for their intellectual insight. Swift's machine has long been cited as a precursor to the 'Pataphysical machinations of Jarry and the combinatorial 'bachelor machines' of Duchamp. Libeskind's Writing machine 'processes both memory and reading material … the random mosaic of knowledge is gathered together into seven times seven faces [an important Libeskindian cabbalistic motif]…'[19]

With these four seminal projects, Libeskind did not forget the rich discourse of architectural history, but neither did he get caught up in its semiotic tangles. Cunningly he rearticulated the history of art, architecture and the machine's polemical imperative – as well as its absurdity and its speed – into an architecture that was both fertile and ripe

265 (opposite)
Lesson B: Remembering Architecture, 'Three Lessons in Architecture'
Studio Daniel Libeskind, 1985

266 (above)
City Edge model
Studio Daniel Libeskind, 1987

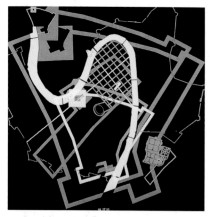

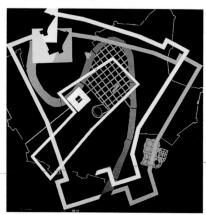

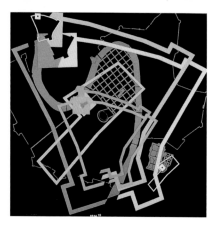

267
'Moving Arrows, Eros and Other Errors', Individual layers and ascalar resonances
Peter Eisenman, 1985

268
'Moving Arrows, Eros and Other Errors', Axonometric juxtapositions
Peter Eisenman, 1985

for its time. These initial researches would form the conceptual bedrock for his first real building: the Jewish Museum in Berlin.

Libeskind's more theoretical essays and drawings had allowed him to develop an architectural language which now needed to be honed against the specifics of a real site. He was to find a worthy city in Berlin, with its dramatic Cold War slicing, its cauterized infrastructure and its history of tyrannical oppression. In 1987 the IBA City Edge competition provided an arena for his investigations and a focus for his favoured geometries. The City Edge site was in the Tiergarten district, adjacent to the severe truncation of urban life that was the Berlin Wall. Libeskind's proposition was inspired by and yet in opposition to the notion of the Wall (fig. 266). This symbol of the division of space was subverted into a language of reconciliation, the Wall itself evoked by a huge inclined beam which 'exploits the logic of that wall, the violent slicing up of territory. The bar is an abstraction of the wall, slicing through the city, breaking fragments off the old city structure. But then it subverts the logic of the wall by lifting itself up and creating a new public space below: it becomes a device for breaking down divisions rather than establishing them'.[20]

A cacophony of vectors, divisions, striations and bars of material was collaged to create a patchwork of partial systems, rhythms and mappings. The aesthetic dressing of the scheme was highly reminiscent of Jiri Kolar's collages of the 1960s. Kolar wrote about his own work thusly: 'What I was referring to was the cross breeding of innumerable relationships in large cities, as Baudelaire writes about in his introduction to the *Petits poemes en prose*: "Which of us has ever imagined in his more ambitious moments the miracle of poetic prose, musical though rhythmless, flexible yet strong enough to identify with the lyrical impulses of the soul, the ebbs and flows of reverie, the pangs of conscience?" This notion of such an obsessive ideal has its origins above all in our experience of the life of great cities, the confluence and interactions of countless relationships within them.'[21]

The presentation of Libeskind's museum proposal was mainly based on extraordinary models; an actual hammer and open book were collaged into one of them. The models flirted with the allegorical and the analogical as well as the possible. Along with the drawings, they had deep associations with the 'Chamberworks' series (fig. 262). Could this very complex proposal have been built? It is difficult to say what exactly it would have looked like. The simple tactic of mixing the proposal with its allegorical patina and conceptual ambience led to a highly enigmatic concept. Also addressed was the functioning of spaces and their relationship to their forms. This was the abstracted world of Schwitters's *Merzbau* turned against itself. This landscape was flayed. The fragment was not honoured and given relic status; it was twisted into itself, ubiquitized, shown to be part of a total equity of vectors, one of trillions of fleeting importance or none at all. The swarm was more important than the individual, the cascade of limit and boundary solidified and cast into a bar, an ingot of compacted detritus. This was an architecture for a time at the End of Words.

Messianic Fervour

In the autumn of 1985 Bernard Tschumi asked Peter Eisenman and Jacques Derrida to collaborate on a project for the cinematic promenade of the Parc de La Villette. At the same time, Eisenman was working on a special folio project for the Architectural Association in London. The folio was called 'Moving Arrows, Eros and Other Errors – An Architecture of Absence' (figs 267–70). Both projects used the ideas of scaling, superimposition and displacement to build up layers of architectural fictions upon architectural fictions. In the Paris-based work, Eisenman intended to make analogies between La Villette in 1867, when an abattoir occupied the site of the park; Paris in 1848, before the abattoir, when

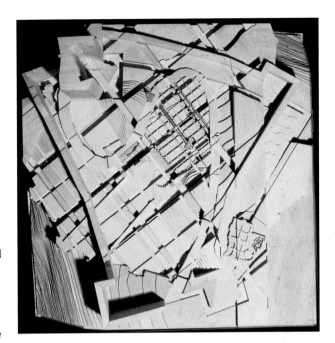

269
Model for 'Moving Arrows, Eros and Other Errors'
Peter Eisenman, 1985

270
Axonometric juxtapositions for 'Moving Arrows, Eros and Other Errors'
Peter Eisenman, 1985

the city walls occupied the site; and Paris in the time of Tschumi's La Villette project. Also superimposed were aspects of Italian projects which involved an abattoir and city walls.[22] All of these traces were artfully arranged at varying scales on the site, and this built up a composition that embodied nuances of other placements and histories, some specific to the site and others suggesting typological similarities. Eisenman likened the process to Freud's dreamwork.

'Moving Arrows' was created from some of the same protocols of disjunctive synthesis. In effect it was a palimpsest of fictions that could be read as a virtual memory theatre evoking a fictional past. An architecture of absence. A not truthful architecture that recognized discontinuity, 'that aspect of scaling which disrupts and thus criticises the status of the presence. In scaling, discontinuity differentiates absence from void. Absence is either the trace of a previous presence, it contains memory; or the trace of a possible presence, it contains an immanence'.[23] Here Eisenman took three versions of the story of Romeo and Juliet and collaged and collided the architectural symbols of sad love: 'Each narrative is characterized by three structural relationships each having its own physical analogue: division (the separation of the lovers symbolized in physical form by the balcony of Juliet's house); union (the marriage of the lovers symbolized by the church); and their dialectical relationship (the togetherness and apartness of the lovers as symbolized in Juliet's tomb.)'[24] Combined with other features of the site in Verona that might be construed to reflect any of these three conditions, Eisenman created a layered, multi-scaled proposition that could be rearticulated by the viewer because each layer was on a different transparent leaf. He even escaped from the compositional conceit of deciding where a layer was positioned in relation to its peers, perhaps the final dislocation or ecstasy of decomposition. No ending, no closure. Only fleeting satisfaction – no stable relationships, no architectural truth. Just lies, damned lies, and lines.

Reading between the Lines

In 'Deconstructivist Architecture', the exhibition curated by Philip Johnson and Mark Wigley, the two organizers were careful not to grant Deconstruction the epithet of a 'movement'. The exhibition consisted of Frank Gehry's Gehry House in Santa Monica; Libeskind's City Edge project; Koolhaas's and OMA's Apartment Building and Observation Tower in Rotterdam; Eisenman's Biocenter for the University of Frankfurt; Hadid's project for the Hong Kong Peak; Coop Himmelb(l)au's Rooftop Remodelling, Vienna, Apartment Building, Vienna and Skyline, Hamburg; and Tschumi's proposal for La Villette. This exhibition was the signal that the Deconstructivists were the new wave of architecture's glitterati. None of them ever looked back.

The zenith of the Deconstructivist era was invoked by a competition win. This time the winner was Libeskind; the project was his Jewish Museum for Berlin. The competition was held in 1988; the building was completed in 1999. It was with this building and its representations that Libeskind's previous researches, aspirations and points of departure were distilled. The site is on Lindenstrasse adjacent to the Kollegienhaus, the old Prussian courthouse. Libeskind wanted 'to create a new architecture for a time that would reflect an understanding of history, a new understanding of museums, and a new realization of the relationship between programme and architectural space. Therefore, this museum is not only a response to a particular program but an emblem of hope'.[25] He preferred to call this project 'Between the Lines', as the organizational concept was essentially two lines, one straight but broken and the other 'tortuous'. Like the City Edge project, these were both geographical and metaphorical lines of connection.

Libeskind composed what he called an 'Architectural Alphabet', a taxonomy of junctions, voids and masses. His language for the museum was essentially the same as in 'Chamberworks' or City Edge, but here this distinct aesthetic was bent to the service of the iconography of Jewish history. Libeskind not only appropriated and reinterpreted the 'found' symbolism of the Jewish community in Berlin; he also invented other symbolic set pieces to augment this epistemology.

The museum has four parts; in effect it could be construed as a musical score consisting of the variable choreography of four elements. Libeskind summarized these structures as follows: 'The first is the invisible and irrationally connected star that shines with absent light of individual address. The second is the cut-off of Act 2 of Moses and Aaron (Schönberg's opera), which culminates with the not-musical fulfilment of the word. The third is the ever-present dimension of the deported and missing Berliners; the fourth is Walter Benjamin's urban apocalypse along the One-Way Street'.[26]

The museum is also planned around three underground routes or 'roads': 'The first and longest "road" leads to the main stair, to the continuation of Berlin's history, to the exhibition spaces in the Jewish Museum. The second leads outdoors to the E.T.A. Hoffman Garden and represents the exile and emigration of Jews from Germany. The third axis leads to the dead-end Holocaust void. Cutting through the form of the Jewish Museum is a void, a straight line whose impenetrability forms the central focus around which the exhibitions are organized. In order to cross from one space of the museum to the other, the visitors transverse sixty bridges that open into the void space – the embodiment of absence'.[27]

In a sense Libeskind is the high priest of the supposed style of Deconstruction. It is paradoxical that the Jewish Museum was born out of discussions and projects that sought not to use architecture as a means of favouring any one philosophical idea about space, time, body and measurement. Deconstruction seemed to be expounding a notion of the city in which nothing was privileged. The Jewish Museum, however, is not about this ubiquitous value of no value. It is

that cosseted recreational uses. At times of hurricane and storm surge, the whole wall was meant to tilt to provide an effective coastal-defence system. Another project was for a Meta-Institute in Havana. Its aim was 'to devise principles, practices, and "rules" by which institutions (social, political, cultural) can continually revise and reform themselves. But the institute proposed for Havana … is devoted to the analysis and heuristic modelling of both stable and fluid terrains, the paradoxical landscapes of the contemporary city that embody human and natural forces of change.'[17]

In March 1995, Kobe, in Japan, suffered a massive earthquake. By association Woods was inspired to consider the city of San Francisco and to create a series

290
Injections, Planes
Lebbeus Woods,
1992–3

291
Injections, Scab
Lebbeus Woods,
1992–3

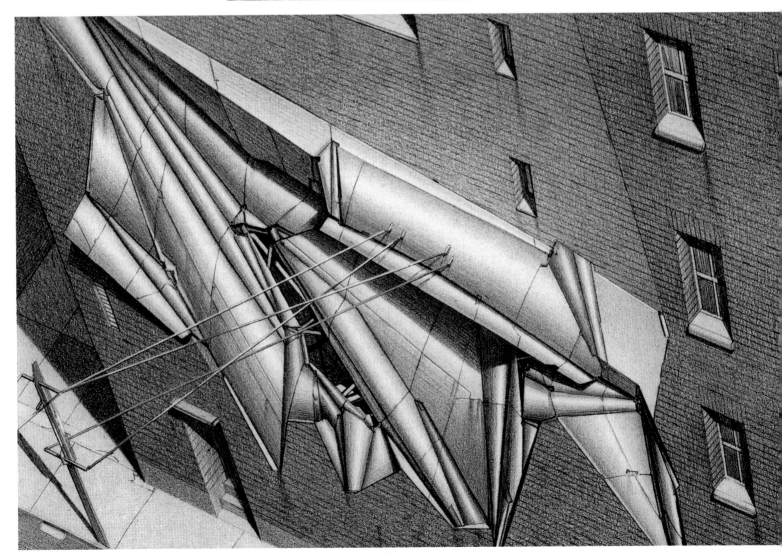

**Quake City/Shared
Houses**

Lebbeus Woods, San
Francisco Bay, 1995

of projects that sought to mitigate the destructive power of earthquakes. 'Seismicity' was the collective name given to these clusters of propositions. Seismicity included Shard Houses (fig. 283), Slip Houses, Fault Houses, Quake City, Wave Houses and Horizon Houses. Shard Houses were positioned '[o]n the stable pilings of piers that once served the shipping industry on the west side of San Francisco … [they] are built of scavenged shards of the industrial wasteland, but are also shards themselves, of a now scattered

cultural whole … Their community comes together, if at all, almost by chance. When the quake comes, the landfill known as Bay Mud, on which the houses rest, liquifies, floating the houses closer together or farther apart.'[18]

Slip Houses sit 'on a nearly frictionless surface, inertia keeps Slip Houses immobile even as the quake literally, violently oscillates the earth beneath it. The earth moves, the house does not'.[19] Quake City (fig. 292) consists of 'decisive edges of spaces without names, rooms,

zones of rooms, sites for a clarity of action that need no enforcement',[20] while Fault Houses 'cut [the quake] precisely turning within the new space to carve in geometric progressions, releasing energy that may trigger microquakes that effectively unlock the fault'.[21] Finally, as we have seen, Wave Houses' frames flex and re-flex in the quake,[22] while Horizon Houses 'turn, reorienting their forms and fixed interior spaces relative to the horizon, hence "changing" them, in the experiential sense'.[23]

In more recent years Woods has turned his enviable draughting skills towards a preoccupation with landscapes of fluid patched plates and an ecology of skating architectures that might inhabit them. This metallic turbulence again posits a new phenomenological condition consisting of a mediating ground of shifting production, culture and vector. Of course, the cataclysm of 11 September 2001 attracted the Woodsian sensibility, and he created a design for an existential stairway of remembrance on the World Trade Centre site.

Temple of Webbed Light

A beautiful relativistic architecture of memory, mechanics, light, journey and the spaces between normal representations was created by ex-Archigrammer Michael Webb beginning in the late '70s and early '80s. It remains a beacon for a whole generation of architects who are interested in the notions of technological and personal architectures of memory and their possible impact on the rereading of landscape. Here again is our high-tech Poliphilo in the Arcadian landscape of dream and iconography.

Webb's Temple Island Project is one of the great speculative works of architecture from the twentieth century (figs 294–6). This project comes nearest of all to being architectural theory's *Large Glass*. It is set on the Thames at Henley, just outside Greater London. Henley – Webb's boyhood roaming ground – is the site of the Henley Regatta, one of the crucial events of the English aristocracy's 'season'. To the uninitiated, Webb created an architecture that seems wholly invisible. However, with patient exploration, deep thought and a familiarity with the protocols of imagined worlds, one starts to see its gorgeous beauty and massive ramifications.

Webb used the form of a small Classical temple on a little island in the Thames as his spatial laboratory. His calibratory devices were the Classicism of the temple, the markers of the Regatta and the velocity of speeding objects, in

particular a Webbian submarine: 'But upon the clothes hanger of Temple Island are hung some notions which intrigue me … One is the notion of a building existing in the form intended only as a result of speeding towards it, or into it, or past it (a shift from early Archigram, where it was the building itself that moved, or at least, bits of it). And this means the observer occupies a position, albeit fixed; thus perspective projection reasserts itself. In axonometric projection, the observer is everywhere (almost) and nowhere. Perspective emphasizes the presence of the STATION POINT.'[24]

Webb's friend Lebbeus Woods immediately hit on the difficulty of reading the work: 'Webb is taking us … on a journey through laborious geometrical projections, curious abstractions and formulations that would seem to be an elementary story of stimulus – response. Except for the drawings. They assert themselves with a hermetic power transcending their role as Pavlovian apparatus.'[25] Woods saw his friend as an alchemist-adept engaged in a magnum opus, its discoveries, protocols and aspirations only fully recognizable to initiates who have studied and been inducted into some of the secrets of relativistic spatiality and discussions of second-order cybernetics. What then, Woods asked, are we to think? Has Webb, like the old alchemists, given us a false lead in his analytical labyrinth? There is some evidence to support this possibility. Webb's mind and his productions have a medieval cast to them: they are complex to the point of mystification – hardly modern in a reductive or scientific sense. His analysis reveals more questions than answers and the deeper it goes the less cause and effect it reveals. Why, for example, does the temple appear to us through the submarine periscope dot matrix, as if on a TV screen?[26]

Like Woods's Epicyclaruim (figs 287–8), the temple on Temple Island was transformed by Webb into his personal Tempietto, a clothes-horse for his notions of architectural order and epistemology. This epistemological odyssey began with a beam from an electric floodlight as it

shone across a spherical surface. Points of view, velocities and projections were tracked and traced, augmented and transcribed into drawings, some of which depicted a verdant Arcadia. Others were highly abstracted as they dealt with the protocols of exactitude within technical drawing, and still others were almost those of a naval architect, streamlined and double-curved. No single type of architectural drawing was sufficient to delineate this type of project, which dealt with many more than three dimensions.

Michael Sorkin recognized that Webb's project was highly contemporary yet deeply enmeshed within the English scene during and just after the last world war, when the long-socked, short-trousered Webb traversed the site with the boyish wonder of a young swallow: 'Certain persistent originating images emerge over and over. St Paul's (not St Peter's), the Spitfire (not the Hurricane), the London Bus (the old RT type, not its boxy successor). To be sure, these are objects

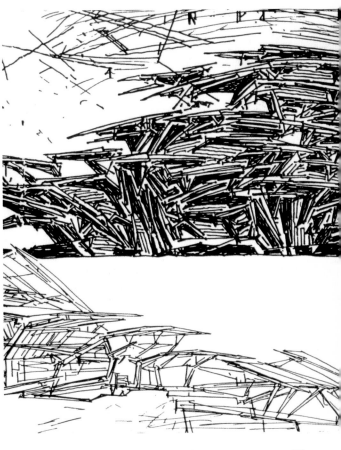

united in their Englishness, but that's not so central. More crucial is the studied perfection of their compound curvature.'[27]

Webb constructed a highly complex memory theatre of views, events and parallaxed secret gardens. A new *Hypnerotomachia* for the late twentieth century seen through the dreaming of a speeding eye. He utilized relativistic notions of Place and geometry and collided them with the axis of Time. The fundamental enigma of Webb is his ability to be highly controlled and conditioned by exact method and his odd propensity to create worlds that bow with pregnant poetics. He is the architectural poet of temporal arithmetic. His Thames trip alluded to another such journey, that taken by Lewis Carroll and the Reverend Robinson Duckworth in the company of the three Liddell sisters on 4 July 1862.[28] Alice, like Webb's viewers, often experiences the paradox of relativistic motion whilst in Wonderland.

294
Speed Bleed
Michael Webb,
Temple Island,
Henley–on–Thames,
1970–

295
Speed of object as a percentage of the speed of light
Michael Webb,
Temple Island,
Henley–on–Thames,
1970–

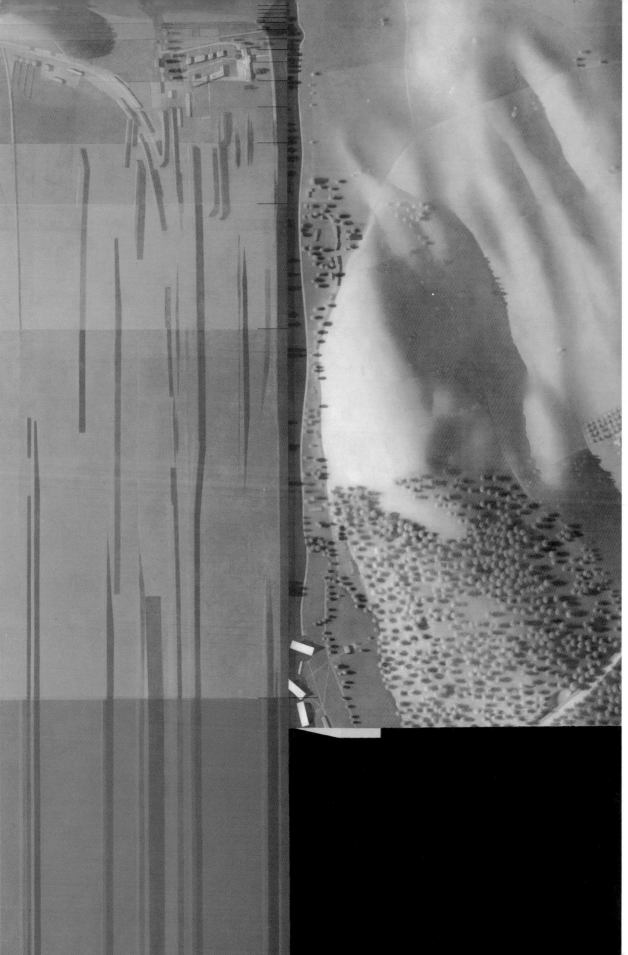

296
Speed Bleed
Michael Webb,
Temple Island,
Henley–on–Thames,
1970–

Adverting Absurdities

Felix Robbins

Felix Robbins explores the notions of memorialization in a different way from Webb, Woods, Hejduk and Libeskind. Adverting Absurdities was produced at midnight on the Millennium. Robbins's architecture has a melancholy, dynamic sadness yet also rejoices in formal combinations. The fecund space of immanent poetic possibility is the stuff of his work. To reveal this fast-breeding space, he must use the memories of computers. His architectural search is conducted within four spatial arenas: the space of programmable computer script, the Modernist poetic lexicon of Samuel Beckett and others, cybernetic notation and modality, and, finally, algorithmic formalism: 'This work seeks to disturb a language of production and creation within contemporary architectural practice, by outlining an intensive and multiple conception of the imminent possibilities of a tectonic, poetic and theoretical manifestation formed through an integration and differentiation of disparate structures of potential.'[29]

Robbins rejects the simple formal expediency of contemporary practice and replaces it with a 'pre-existing' architecture. Architects have long been aware that before a building is built or a design created, a variety of constraints

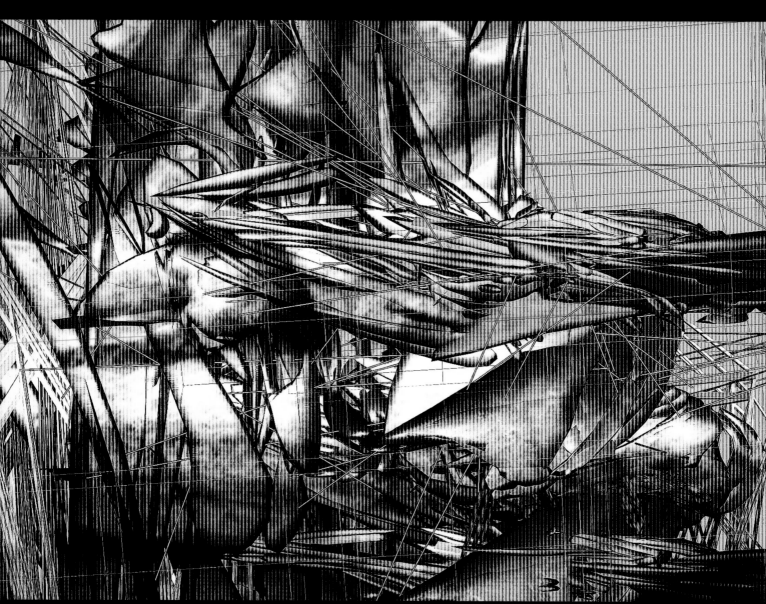

intensity, and escapes the death of architecture by collaborating with its already present absence.[30]

Robbins's contribution is his revealing of the microscopic resonances of architectural potential. But it is ultimately a lost terrain; its brooding presence and complexity are merely representations of what exists in architectural ether, billions of bifurcating alternative realities cascading into infinity. Robbins's world is as unique as yours or mine; it all depends on the shifting poetics and priorities of his algorithms, when they make space and for how long. Robbins enjoys the paradox of architecture and plays with madness.

301–5
Adverting Absurdities, possibilities of formal expression
2003–4

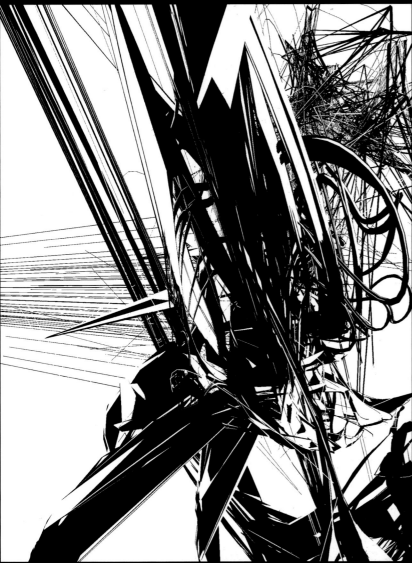

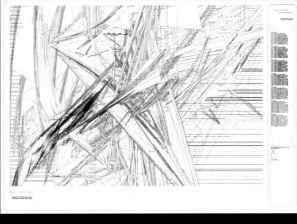

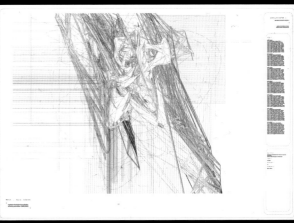

The Poetry of Small Things

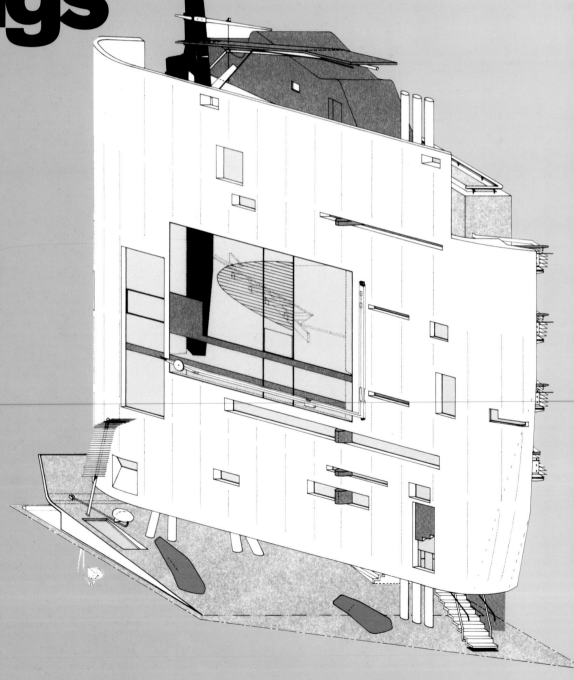

Visionary architecture also can be provoked by an interest in small things – for example, how metal can be jointed and fabricated, how figurative elements can be woven into buildings, how certain shapes have a creative resonance, how architecture might mediate its junction with the ground, or how design might respond to the hidden world of electromagnetic radiation. The architects featured in this chapter have such preoccupations. Peter Wilson's ship shapes and bridge-building, as well as his later Eastern Fields work with Julia Bolles; Peter Salter's work with Chris Macdonald; Raoul Bunschoten's phenomenological work; and, finally, Dunne and Raby's proxemics and Placebo projects are all referenced and illustrated.

Exterior of Cosmos
Commercial Building
Bolles and Wilson,
Tokyo, Japan, 1989

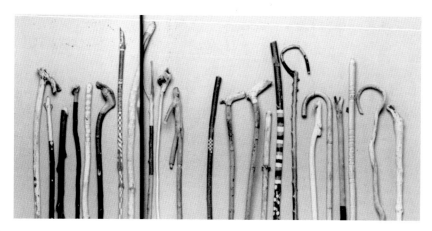

'But now methods of analysis and of action have modified cultural anthropology, the investigation of man and his mental and material productions, conscious attempts to modify our surroundings and ourselves, are all parts of a process of permanent education that involves us completely. The visible traces of this work are very few, because it is not transmitted through images, drawings and projects but through one's engagement in daily routine and slowly but surely it shapes up as the coincidence (identity) between history and project, work and school, one's personal and physical life.'
Superstudio

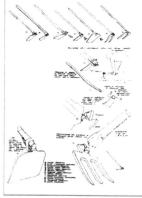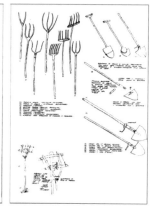

'In the corner, opposite the bed, a stool with a highly polished stainless steel plate is plugged into the wall. The switch is on. The plug has only one pin. When naked flesh and cold steel join, excess electricity accumulated in the body during the day is drained away. Left on the floor are a pair of pyjamas made from metallicized rip stock fabric, altered to cover hands, feet and head. Although uncomfortable against the skin, they provide the sleeper with a different kind of comfort.'
Anthony Dunne and Fiona Raby

Following the '60s heyday of the speculative, polemical and hedonistic architectural project, it was difficult for many to discern an avant-garde trajectory that would bear the same level of breathtaking images yet move the debate on to embrace the political reality of the '70s. The hangover after the hubris provoked many avant-gardists to reassess the content of their work and to find it wanting in a decade that was to yield the oil crisis, three-day working weeks and economic depression. In 1973 Superstudio started to move away from the ubiquitous, continuous grid, from machine buildings and from young, hippie, funky furniture, moving on to develop a series of studies of simple objects. These objects often seemed to be on the verge of disappearing; they were traditional things honed by hand and use, threatened by the crushing

power of the ubiquitous, anonymous, factory-produced product. Superstudio felt that if they could develop a cogent methodology to analyse things such as walking sticks, hoes, rakes and forks, they could excavate an architecture that was dependent not on the rarefied practices of the Academy and the profession but on the fundamental relationships of human survival and spatial cultivation (figs 307–9). As Peter Lang and Bill Menkin put it, 'Extra-Urban material cultures are studied and subjected to experiments like some enormous encyclopaedia (which is neither Diderot's nor The Whole Earth Catalogue). For two years Superstudio studied utensils and their connection with work and with the transformation of the environment.'[1]

Superstudio's researches were conducted as seminars and lectures within an architecture school. The school, they believed, like the factory or the city, was a primary situation in which change could be wrought. They knew that architectural education vicariously promotes the power

appropriate the ambience of the place and project a useful vision of the future, balancing private, public, and institutional requirements'.[10] Wilson contributed an Endless Bridge, the First Clandeboye Bridge and a Gate House (all 1984). Bridge-building was still a powerful preoccupation: 'The bridge for us, perhaps because of Heidegger's wonderful "Building, Dwelling, Thinking" – has long been an iconic convergence of material and existential issues. The object which brings its location into existence, the logical and sometimes purposefully less than efficient collaboration of materials and a moment of suspension snatched from the continuity of everyday experience.'[11] In the second half of the 1980s, Wilson's confidence grew. Larger buildings were attempted and more complex spatial compositions posited. This later tranche of works included Forum of Sand (fig. 330), ZKM Centre for Art and Technology (1989), Tokyo Opera (1985), Paradise Bridge Amsterdam (fig. 327) and the iconic Cosmos Street Commercial Building (figs 328–9) and competition entry Comfort in the Metropolis (1988).

The Ninja and the Antenna

In 1990 Wilson wrote about the Japanese capital, Tokyo, where places and events had equal importance – in contrast to a more hierarchical Western system of urbanism: 'For Tokyo, the menu of component events is different. Though the density factor is greater, the model of an endless non-hierarchical field nevertheless describes the Eurolandscaft better than the now floundering apparatus of Western city planning.'[12] These ideas of the ubiquitous, dense spaces of sometimes strange non-Western events caused Wilson to speculate on and develop other ways of instigating a design. One might be termed creating and then inhabiting an 'electronic shadow' and the other 'biographical chance'.

Tokyo, like any modern city, is an invisible field of pulsing electronic data. This ephemerality of convenient

mediating technologies and ubiquitous access to data has become more vital to the contemporary city than direct road systems or functional buildings. Equally, however, respite from these invisible rays of communication and shelter from relentless telecommunication intrusion and digital surveillance are becoming increasing concerns. Wilson's project for

the Comfort in the Metropolis competition involved creating electronic-radiation shields that cosseted shadowy, silent, still spaces: 'Things are becoming invisible. The house is a black hole, an electronic shadow. "Ninja" architecture. As yet, the architecture has not fully come to terms with this contemporary condition (the Tokyo condition). Comfort is therefore

319–20
Water House – Intersection House
Peter Wilson, 1976

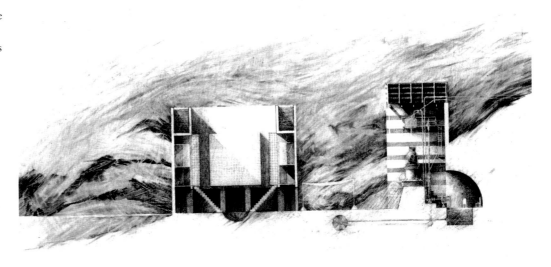

defined as a respite, as a "cone of minimum electronic interference" (mu).'[13] The Japanese architect Toyo Ito, judge of the competition and architect of the well-known Tower of Winds opposite Wilson's proposal, described the latter's proposition: 'An object called a Mechanical Mask crouches at the base of the Tower of Winds and opposes it through the mediation of a filter that is like a shield reacting to light. Behind it is a shelter for a bedroom, called a Glove, with a membrane which appears to be supported by something that resembles human ribs but which floats like a strip of cloth and bulges in the wind.'[14] This project introduced the 'Ninja' to Wilson's work; it became a motif in his next project, Cosmos Street. The Ninja was reminiscent of a black shark's or ray's egg sack: 'A lot of people have said the shape is diabolical. That was not my intention. It was simply a linguistic gesture, an experiment.'[15]

Wilson was introduced to a client who was commissioning projects from unusual architects to be located along Cosmos Street in Tokyo. The client even wanted to change the street's name to 'Architects' Street'. Oddly, he was not concerned with programme or function. He wanted a design that was different and interesting and that would encourage the value of his property portfolio to rise. Such buildings have been called 'Antenna' buildings as they attract interest and debate and catalyze development around them. Wilson had the tricky problem of attempting to design an intentionally vacuous building that took its cues from the tumult and idiosyncrasies of the Japanese city. He used the Ninja motif, this time structurally, to form the supporting sculptural spine of the building (fig. 306). Only glimpses of the brooding, black shape manifested themselves inside. The façade wrapped around the Ninja core was fenestrated and composed by taking inspiration from a newspaper article about Wilson's client. Wilson started to design his façade by punctuating it in the same positions as the gaps in the article's text. The client's photograph became a large rectangular

321–3
Views and walkway detail of Pont des Arts
Peter Wilson, 1983

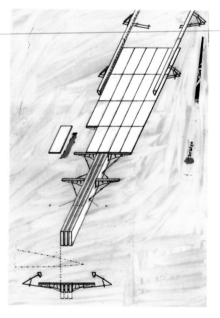

by an intricacy of draughting, yet the drawings still maintain the hand-crafted expediency of architects constantly refining, constantly searching. At certain times the work reminds us of Art Nouveau architecture and at others it suggests the Archigram pod, a scrapyard and a trellised pergola.

Macdonald and Salter's proposition for the Accademia Bridge exhibited many of their preoccupations at the time: 'The proposal suggests the provision of two bridges, distinct in scale, construction and the means by which they reach the ground. Enclosures at either side are developed as ante-spaces to both the bridges and the incidents of the city beyond. Both bridges are intended to achieve an unusually rich surface texture.'[17] The bridges were resolved by two enclosures with a particular urban context at each end. Their intertwined, sinuous plan form – each operating at different levels, one affording more intimate sensations of the water's surface – were metamorphosed at either end into a series of eloquent cellular spaces. The project, whilst being highly specific, courted enigma with its unannotated drawings and the clashing forms of aircraft fuselages positioned along the landing platform by the Accademia.

This work skilfully sat astride the divide between mechanical and biological form. By 1990 Macdonald and Salter were working on a Folly for the Osaka Expo. Here, repeated at various scales, was one of the staple spatial tactics of the partnership: the container/vessel enclosed by a filigree of trellises. The architectural game between the void/container and porous box was played out with considerable dexterity. The project also involved the viewer in its construction process. Walls were made of clay and earth: 'The territory of the Osaka Folly was described by a series of rammed earth walls and plugs, navigation markers in a shallow excavated landscape. The process of making the walls required the contractor to lay 7 cubic metres of clay each day over a period of nineteen days. The contractor could choose to add five walls or to proceed with only one – in either case,

each day of construction was registered by a new thickness and colour of the clay layer. However, as the work proceeded, the clay ran out and the contractor resorted to using the various earths of the site. Caught in the process of construction the visitor was encouraged to linger.'[18] The building weathered and eroded in unforeseen ways and was also colonized by moss and the new shoots of plants. Architectural growth and form dynamically changed in front of visitors' eyes.

Hertzian Tales and Design Noir

During the mid-1990s designers and architects became interested in another type of lithe green shoots and moss-like agglomerations – those of the swiftly evolving electrosphere. Based at London's Royal College of Art, Anthony Dunne and Fiona Raby started to explore the netherworld of invisible radiation. The spatial opportunities of this virtual material have many ramifications. Their first project illustrating these preoccupations was called Fields and Thresholds (1994). In their work the conceptualization of telecommunications as 'networks and terminals' was replaced by this 'fields and thresholds' image. Screens, keyboards and desks were replaced by continuous fields of telecommunicative possibility zoned into pockets of responsive space. These zones could be at the scale of desk-top objects, furniture or environments, their variable sensitivity coming through the use of ultrasonic fields, which provide a form 'in-between space'. Ultrasonic rangefinders from cameras, infrared intruder alarms for the home, and optical switches for monitoring factory production lines could all be utilized to articulate variable thresholds between physical and telematic spaces. The 'grapevine' is probably a more appropriate metaphor than the 'conference' to describe the forms of communication this system could support. Informality, chance meetings, coincidence and so on could all find expression here. The designs were speculative proposals that approached

telecommunications through the material culture of objects and spaces in an effort to pull technology out of its narrow technical field.

Fields and Thresholds spawned a series of interventions that included The Balcony, The Cabinet and The Torso. Each intervention was a piece of 'furniture' designed to encourage chance encounters, coincidence, synaesthetic moments and surreal juxtapositions. Such spatial structures illustrated ideas about what the architects called 'tele-proxemics'. Most verbal communication is supported by informal uses of space operating at almost subliminal levels. Space and distance are used to define and negotiate the interface between private and public, particularly during moments leading up to contact. This sense of distance is not only visual but also acoustic, thermal and olfactory, and forms a sensory envelope of kinaesthetic sensitivity that varies from person to person and culture to culture. Architecture and furniture design have always allowed this human sensitivity to the social use of space to find material and spatial expression. Dunne and Raby concerned themselves with exploring the possibilities of linking this to telecommunications.

The Balcony was a large padded surface for leaning that had a sensitive zone defined by a ringed boundary. This sensitive zone could be tuned in to a selection of remote sources by the casual user's hand movements. This information was translated into varying degrees of aesthetically distorted sound, the source of which was either live environmental sound from the immediate location or perhaps an ambient mix of live local radio broadcasts. If someone was nearby and relaxing next to the object, it was hoped that the sound filtering through would attract attention and draw in yet another person who might be passing. The Cabinet reminded one of a shamanistic artist who would rush out onto the moors to catch and box up the foggy dawn in an attempt to contain a place. The place, however, was mediated by technology, and only a few would have been aware of its

331–3 (opposite top, left and middle)
Accademia Bridge
MacDonald and Salter, 1985

334 (opposite right)
ICI Trade Pavilion
MacDonald and Salter, 1983

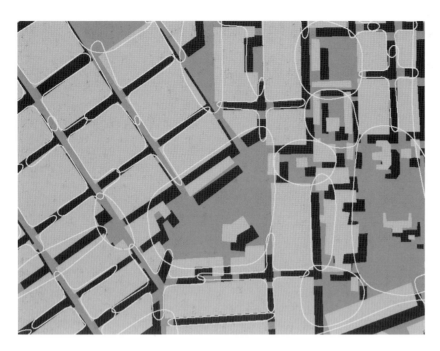

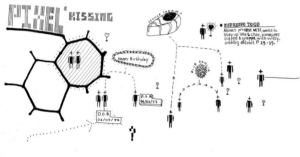

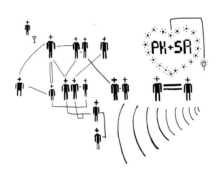

existence because it would have been placed in a semi-private space. This object offered the privilege of privacy, perhaps being used by a very small number of people. It was an object for keeping in touch. Projected into it and filling The Cabinet was the colour of a distant sky. The time of day and weather condition of the remote location were constantly part of the activities within the space. The object was ambiguous. It did suggest a cabinet made of wood with a large volume and glass doors. However, with no shelves and an awkward sloping base, it was not really effective for storing 'things'. The holes cut in the doors allowed someone to sit inside.

Finally, The Torso was a waltzing object that needed to be constantly danced around a tele-locality to enable it to maintain a radio link with other remote sources. It eavesdropped, catching snippets of conversation. Some might worry about these fields of remote sensing and playful surveillance. This modesty would be ill founded, as we are bodies among almost infinite invisible but observable fields.

Placebo Furniture

Dunne and Raby have created numerous projects that flirt with such invisible worlds. There is always a healthy surrealism in their work and a wry wink or nod. Dunne also completed a PhD during the '80s, as well as a book entitled *Hertzian Tales*.[19] This book is a highly enjoyable, well-researched text on the histories and future possibilities of electromagnetic objects. It is critical reading for those architects who are interested in the unseen, surreal landscapes of tomorrow.

At the end of the '90s Dunne and Raby created a project that would provide the creative backbone of their 2001 book *Design Noir: The Secret Life of Electronic Objects*.[20] This was called the Placebo Project. As usual Dunne and Raby were exploring a world where electronic objects leaked radiation of various types and of various intensities. Radio waves are part of the electromagnetic spectrum; electrical wiring, computers and mobile phones generate electromagnetic fields. This hidden electro-scape is made visible by all manner of sensors and meters, and these are Dunne and Raby's bricks and mortar, their *prima materia*, their playground. Their world is populated by people who sleep behind weird egg-crate squares of electromagnetic shielding just to give their internal organs a rest, people who own vibrating 'Nipple Chairs', and gilded angels that conceal mobile-phone antennas.

Design Noir is a funky concoction of user surveys, stories from the electromagnetic edge, statements of intent and descriptions of phenomena. It is also highly serious and academically rigorous. The Placebo Project is illustrated by photographs of normal people using the prototypes. These photographs are not normative, however; they have a strange subversive power. Are these models mad? Are they drugged? This way of representing designs rams home the idea that these are 'everyday' objects, not the form-pornography of superstar designers. The photographs have the eerie quality of the Hypnosis record covers of the '70s. Dunne and Raby's collection of objects are at once 'flared' and 'straight'. By 'flared', I mean 'baroque' as they surf their energy carpets. By 'straight', I mean that Dunne and Raby seem to go out of their way to design objects in a simple, almost childlike way. The Nipple Chair, for example, has four straight legs, a square seat and a square back – the back of course features two vibrating nipples. These embedded nodules indicate when radiation passes through the sitter's upper body. The Placebo objects also include a GPS Table (this piece is both a table and a global positioning device), an Electro-draught Excluder (a strategic positioning device that helps to deflect electromagnetic draughts), a Nipple Chair 'Electricity Drain' (sitting naked on the contact points of the plug-in chair causes a person's accumulation of electricity to drain from his or her body through the special earth pin) and the Phone Table (its ring is silenced, but the top glows gently green when someone calls) (figs 337–42).

Dunne and Raby expose the normative protocols that some designers use to create their work; these protocols are often myopic. Dunne and Raby also open our eyes to an invisible, surreal, fun and beautiful world that exists under all of our noses.

339 (above left)
GPS Table
Dunne and Raby,
Placebo, 2000–1

340 (left)
Nipple Chair
Dunne and Raby,
Placebo, 2000–1

341 (top)
Compass Table
Dunne and Raby,
Placebo, 2000–1

342 (above)
Electro-draught Excluder
Dunne and Raby,
Placebo, 2000–1

The Land of Scattered Seeds

John Puttick

John Puttick's work rejoices in the poetry of small things: seeds and the growth of plants over time. He weaves modern-day tales to create self-contained realities that reflect our own. All the complex relationships of life – be they social, ecological or economic – are studied and developed in miniature. These relationships are then played out through space and structure, revealing surprising connections between the most disparate things. No hierarchy of scale exists in the work, the smallest detail providing as many possibilities as the city and proving equally moving.

The Land of Scattered Seeds investigates relationships between Humanity and Nature – the efforts of human beings to control the natural world, and the cold indifference of Nature – and also relationships between individuals as they attempt to find their places in the modern city. Beginning with the desperation of two brothers, the inhabitants of a street in the centre of Graz in Austria incrementally convert their environment into a patchwork of farms, vineyards and gardens. The ambitions of each character lead to conflicts and collaborations which evolve through the development of exquisite new constructions and the growth of plants. Nature – with ambitions of its own – constantly threatens to overwhelm them. The teeming life that results is microscopically documented in the book and manifests itself in an intricate model concealed within the drinks cabinet of one of the leading characters.

Utilizing the only space they have available – the exterior of their apartment buildings – Franz establishes a vineyard, while Jorg grows pumpkins to refine into Kurbisol. The two compete maniacally. Across the street live Olga and Florian, retired from the civil service. Horrified by the vegetal chaos erupting in the area, the couple cultivate formal gardens on the façade of their building as an act of floral defence. Lola, owner of the local hairdressing salon, proves more enter-

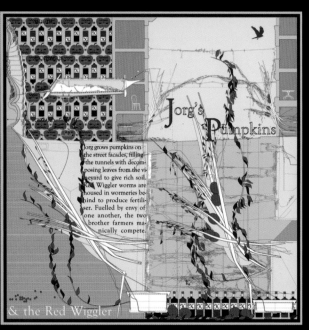

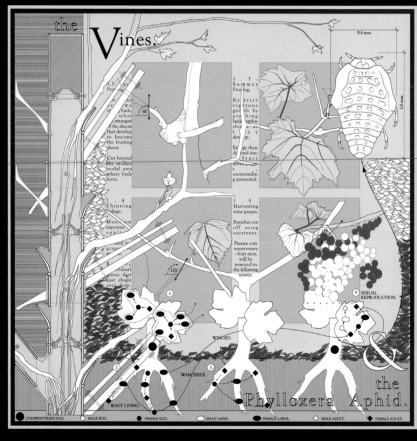

During the 1970s and '80s, a very small number of architects started to see the potential for integrating the computer into architectural design. These included the cybernetician Gordon Pask, Cedric Price with John Frazer (in London), and Nicholas Negroponte at MIT. These individuals represented the paradigm for a later generation inspired by the rapid genesis of cyberspace during the 1990s. Architects such as Marcos Novak, Greg Lynn and others began to explore new technologies and push visionary architecture onto the knife-edge between the virtual and the actual. Nanotechnology and biotechnology further blurred the distinction between the animate and the inanimate – as it continues to do today.

352
**Hot Desk – Prototype
Nanotechnological
Vat/Desk**
Neil Spiller with
Sixteen Makers, 1994

'By "augmenting human intellect" we mean increasing the capability of a man to approach a complex problem situation, to gain comprehension to suit his particular needs, and to derive solutions to problems. Increased capability in this respect is taken to mean a mixture of the following: more rapid comprehension, better comprehension, the possibility of gaining a useful degree of comprehension in a situation that previously was too complex, speedier solutions, better solutions, and the possibility of finding solutions to problems that before seemed insoluble'.
Douglas Engelbart

'Cyberspace is liquid, liquid cyberspace, liquid architecture, liquid cities. Liquid architecture is more than kinetic architecture, robotic architecture, an architecture of fixed parts and variable links. Liquid architecture is an architecture that breathes, pulses, leaps as one form and lands as another. Liquid architecture is an architecture whose form is contingent on the interests of the beholder'.
Marcos Novak

On the cusp of the twentieth and twenty-first centuries, the ontological changes first anticipated by the Futurists, the Surrealists and the Situationists – and even the Symbolists of the 1880s – are coming to pass. In some ways this book has been about the harbingers of a new age of architecture that is relational, responsive, computational and metamorphic. This chapter will chart the final shifts in architectural theory as the twentieth century drew to a close.

As with many of the previous chapters, our Renaissance journeyman Poliphilo would understand its basic premises. Diderot and Dalí would also find resonances with their work. Poliphilo's dream-world oscillated from one mythic reality to another. He stood at once outside and inside his dream; he drifted from one encrusted iconic and mythic system to another. He met gods, chimeras and other non-human spirits, and his memory distorted and collapsed

his perception of geographical distance. These complex, cornucopic neo-mythologies created an only partially understood world view that would require a faster, more omnipotent intelligence to perceive its full integration and entwined meanings. Poliphilo's dream jump-cut space as he was drawn into others' spaces of lust, aesthetic impression, hope, awe and loss. These paraspaces with their heightened rhetoric were used as epiphanic, carthartic and pedagogical depth-charges in the sleep-swathed, befuddled mind of Poliphilo. His dream was a Learning Machine: it showed, it told, and it criticised.

Poliphilo's world, computer programmers would recognize, was algorithmic. It consisted of a set of problem-solving instructions which worked towards solutions. The input and output data could vary accordingly. Poliphilo's psychological state and his reading of these 'instructions' in many languages, each with varying codes, protocols and interfaces, conditioned the results he perceived.

As we have seen, Poliphilo's world was a memory theatre. Memory theatres were a Renaissance prelude to the initial computation machines designed by Charles Babbage. Like Raymond Lull's combinatorial wheels, Babbage's machines were dependent on cyclical rotation. Poliphilo's polytheistic world and modern-day computers are strangely similar. The computer writer Erik Davis has discussed this similarity: 'While the dominant mystical images of cyberspace today stress its unity as a global electronic mind, [William] Gibson cannily suggests that the dynamics of polytheism may be a more appropriate religious metaphor for the chaos of the new environment.'[1]

Diderot would understand the cyberspatial urge to fully define everything, the desire to make sense of the complex relations between organic and inorganic cybernetic systems and their integration with human and non-human users. Dalí would recognize paradigms of genetic replication and cybernetics and the incredibly Surreal world that the interaction of the virtual and the actual with soft and hard technologies can produce.

Communication and Control

As we have seen, the twentieth century was often about seeing the synthesis between various branches of science and the arts. The history of cybernetics was also multidisciplinary, inclusive and relativistic. The Second World War was the catalyst for the evolution of cybernetic ideas. Norbert Wiener and his colleague Julian Bigelow developed a theory of prediction that redefined the mathematics of ballistics utilizing notions of systems feedback and revolutionized the accuracy of anti-aircraft fire. Wiener had previously spent many a happy hour in the company of Arturo Rosenblueth whilst the former was Professor of Mathematics at Massachusetts Institute of Technology and the latter Professor of Physiology at Harvard's Medical School. In 1943 Rosenblueth, Wiener and Bigelow published a paper entitled 'Behaviour, Purpose and Teleology'. This paper was about various ways to classify behaviour relative to ideas of 'purpose'. An object's behaviour was influenced by the systems around it. This idea is fundamental to cybernetic systems, and this paper was the first to recognize this critical relationship. Wiener and his colleagues developed many cybernetic theories and published many papers, and it became clear that cybernetics was the up-and-coming science of control and communication.

As we have seen, the evocation of cybernetics and its use in architectural terms were apparent in Constant's later pieces for his New Babylon (figs 76–81), in some of Archigram's work and in Cedric Price's Fun Palace (figs 82–4). Others also attempted to create cybernetic architectures. In 1960 the Neo-Constructivist artist Nicholas Schoffer produced a manifesto entitled 'Spatiodynamism, Luminodynamism and Chronodynamism'. Schoffer moved from the sculptural to the architectonic scale as he became more inspired by the electronic devices he could design into his work. These experiments led him to write his manifesto proclaiming a dynamic and electronic Constructivism. His most successful architectural pieces were Cysp 1

– a hybrid expression of cybernetics and spatiodynamism, part of a spectacle at the Théâtre Sarah-Bernhardt, Paris, in May 1956 – and two large cybernetic towers, the first of which was erected in the Parc de Saint Cloud in 1954 and the second of which has stood in the Parc de Saint Bouverie in Liège since 1961.[2] In 1969 Schoffer designed an urban plan called *La Ville Cybernetic*.

Schoffer's work centred around feedback loops, the effect of chance and human interference (fig. 353). Chance can be 'directed' by the action of different natural agents, which 'choose' rhythms having variations predetermined by virtue of cybernetics or by the direct action of an interpreter. For Schoffer it followed: 1. that the rigorous construction of a work is qualitatively determined by its basic structure and determines it in turn; 2. that the temporal multiplication of the work is effected by the reciprocal action of the component factors, without these being transformed in isolation as in the principle of catalysis; 3. that the organization of the component factors determines its functioning.[3] Like John Cage and others, Schoffer started to see the designing of space as an open-ended system dependent on a second order of aesthetics connected with the definition of cause-and-effect algorithms: 'The artist no longer creates one or several works. he creates creation.'[4]

The Architectural Relevance of Cybernetics

During the years 1968–76 it became clear that traditional cybernetics was neglecting something: the role of the observer. The observer is part of the system being observed and therefore needs to be considered in any attempted cybernetic definition. As we have seen, this notion is known as second-order cybernetics. Gordon Pask was one of the thinkers central to the development of this second order. Pask's huge contribution was to the notion of humanity as a learning machine and the idea that conversations between observing systems were epistemological and therefore personal and subjective.

Pask was also the bridgehead between architectural avant-garde-ism and cybernetic and computer systems. We have already noted his contribution to Cedric Price's Fun Palace. Pask could see many issues within architectural problem-solving and its discussions about aesthetics where a cybernetic point of view might be helpful. To this end he contributed an essay to *Architectural Design* on 'The Architectural Relevance of Cybernetics' in 1969. This essay, which had a considerable impact, posited that rapid advances would be made in at least five areas guided by cybernetic theory: 'Various computer-assisted (or even computer directed) design procedures will be developed into useful instruments.

Concepts in very different disciplines (notably social anthropology, psychology, sociology, ecology and economics) will be unified with the concepts of architecture to yield an adequately broad view of such entities as "civilization", "city" or "education system".

There will be a proper and systematic formulation of the sense in which architecture acts as a social control) i.e. the germ of an idea, mentioned as "holism", will be elaborated).

The high point of functionalism is the concept of a house as a "machine for living in". But the bias is towards a machine that acts as a tool serving an inhabitant. This notion will, I believe, be refined in the concept with which the inhabitant co-operates and in which he can externalize his mental processes, i.e. mutualism will be emphasized as compared with mere functionalism. For example, the machine for living in will relieve the inhabitant of the need to store information in memory and the need to perform calculations as well as helping out with more obvious chores like garbage disposal and washing up dishes. Further, it will elicit his interest as well as simply answering his enquiries.

Gaudí (intentionally or not) achieved a dialogue between his environment and its inhabitants. He did so using physically static structures (the dynamic processes depending on the movement of people or shifts of attention). The

353
Sans Titre Sculpture
Nicholas Schoffer,
1953

dialogue can be refined and extended with the aid of modern techniques which allow us to weave the same pattern in terms of a reactive environment. If, in addition, the environment is malleable and adaptive the results can be very potent indeed.'[5]

In this essay Pask also introduced the notion that the architectural profession might start to use computers as surrogate assistants: 'One final manoeuvre will indicate the flavour of a cybernetic theory. Let us turn the design paradigm in upon itself; let us apply it to the interaction between the designer and the system he designs, rather than the interaction between a system and the people who inhabit it. The glove fits, almost perfectly in the case when a designer uses a computer as his assistant. In other words, the relation "controller/controlled entity" is preserved when these omnibus words are replaced by "designer/system being designed" or by "systematic environment/inhabitants" or by "urban plan/city". But notice the trick, the designer is controlling the construction of control systems and consequently

design is control of control, i.e. the designer does much the same job as his system, but he operates at a higher level in the organization hierarchy.'[6]

In 1964, the Architectural Association gained a particularly difficult student: Ranulph Glanville. His student work illustrated Glanville's ability to speculate on the future of computation and its architectural ramifications. During the 1967–8 academic year he designed a supermarket. This is how he met Gordon Pask. In fact Glanville designed a shopping system in place of a supermarket. The shopper had a catalogue, phoned up and then dialled in codes for the items he wanted. The items were kept in an automated warehouse. The collected stuff was delivered. To avoid traffic congestion, Glanville wanted to use balloons with homing devices: when you emptied the (possibly personalized) containers of their contents, the reduction in weight allowed the balloons to ascend again and return home.

Glanville was told there had to be a building. So he designed a vast parking lot with elevations made of clip-on panels which could be moulded from anything you liked. Near all parking spaces were delivery chutes. You went upstairs to a vast showroom with display cabinets, putting a magnetic card (the BarclayCard had recently appeared) into slots of the cabinets containing what you wanted. The cabinets rotated and could be moved: they were actually placed by throwing darts across a room at the plans. When you left to return to your car, you put the card into a reader, and your shopping was collected from the warehouse above. (Glanville's tutor Richard Rogers remarked that the warehouse could be made of solid gold, considering the cost of the computing.) You took your car to a chute, put your card in again, and the goods came down right into your boot.

Further into Glanville's student career (1972) he produced a series of projects that used computation. The Talking Wall was a series of microphones built into walls in terraced houses that sent signals to a bank of tape recorders. These sampled the various inputs, randomly

playing back a mix through the same walls. The social benefit was that secrets, especially those related to domestic violence, wouldn't remain secrets for very long. Another project that anticipated the consumer electronics of over thirty years later was Cell video: a response to the spinning of the news coverage of the Vietnam War. Texas had just produced a wrist-watch TV based on lines of diodes. Glanville proposed a TV camera with an etched light-sensitive chip (essentially the technology for image-collecting in today's cameras) that would be given to everyone in the world. The manufacturing cost would be the same as that of an aspirin tablet. These cameras would fit into a buttonhole. They had three states: private, public and off. Private was just that: like a mobile phone today. Public meant others could hitchhike on your camera to see what you were seeing (and hearing, of course). Off meant just that. You could watch on your TV, or on an improved wrist-watch TV. Transmission would be by a cellular network of receivers. Compression would be achieved by only transmitting the differences in image – again a novel idea that is common now.

Concurrent with Pask's cybernetic thoughts at this time, the architect Nicholas Negroponte was developing research at MIT into the construction of what he called an 'Architecture Machine'. This was to be the concrete embodiment of Pask's virtual architectural assistant. In 1970 Negroponte published his team's research to date. The Architecture Machine was of course an aspiration that has still to be fully realized. Negroponte's book is much better at specifying the problem inherent in designing a designing machine than at delivering a solution: 'Architecture, unlike a game of chequers with fixed rules and a number of fixed pieces, and much like a joke, determined by context, is the croquet game in Alice in Wonderland, where the Queen of Hearts (society, technology, economics) keeps changing the rules'.[7] Negroponte went on to speculate on the internal workings of the Machine: 'Surely some constraint and consideration [are] necessary if components are to converge on solutions in

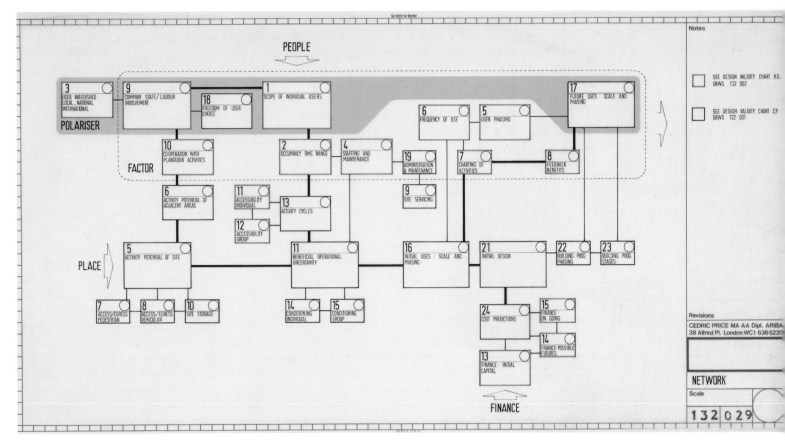

NETWORK

Scale

132 029

"reasonable" time. Components must assume some original commitment, five particular sub assemblies should be part of an architecture machine: (1) a heuristic mechanism, (2) a rote apparatus, (3) a conditioning device, (4) a reward selector, and (5) a forgetting convenience … These five items are only pieces of an architecture machine; the entire body will be an ever-changing group of mechanisms that will undergo structural mutations, bear offspring, and evolve, all under the direction of a cybernetic device.'[8]

By 1975 Negroponte's preoccupations had digressed from the symbiotic hardware and software hybrids of the Architecture Machine era to the fertile ground of what he termed 'Soft Architectural Machines'. This again resulted in an MIT Press publication. The work drew heavily on Pask's 'Conversation Theory'. Indeed Pask contributed the introduction to Negroponte's book, a piece entitled 'Aspects of Machine Intelligence'. Pask's description of an overview of his theory is instructive: 'Intelligence is a property that is ascribed by an external observer to a conversation between participants if, and only if, their dialogue manifests understanding.'[9] Therefore Negroponte's work on artificial architectural assistants had to address the notion of understanding and creative conversation. This dialogue is at the core of architectural design and its effective delivery, and in Negroponte's work it was predicated on his optimism about artificial intelligence being the key to his machines. This conversational dynamic is also at the core of much of the other work featured in this chapter.

Evolutionary Architecture

Pask was also a mentor of John Frezer Frazer was inspired by living things to attempt to develop architectures that also lived and evolved in some way. This was not an imperative that sought to standardize architectural production but an attempt to diversify and strengthen design processes (fig. 355). The main tool in these experiments was the computer.

356
Generator network
Cedric Price, 1979–84

357
Working electronic model of the Generator project
John and Julia Frazer, computer consultants to Cedric Price, 1980

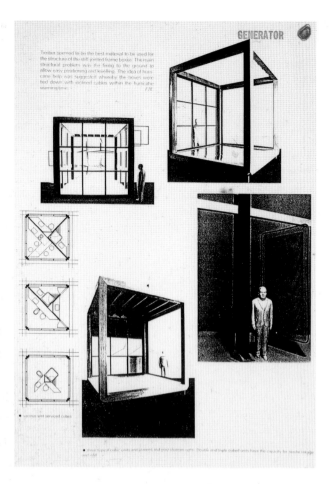

GENERATOR

Timber seemed to be the best material to be used for the structure of the staff-garden frame boxes. The main structural problem was the fixing to the ground to allow easy positioning and levelling. The idea of hurricane help has been suggested whereby the boxes were tied down with inclined cables within the hurricane warning time. FN

• various unit serviced cubes

• these type of cubic units and screens and post shadow units. Double and triple cubed units have the capacity for double image and roll

In 1995 Frazer produced a book, *An Evolutionary Architecture*. Again it had an introduction by Gordon Pask. Pask declared that if one agreed that information transfer was becoming more important, one had to admire Frazer's work. The first paragraph of Frazer's own text leaves no doubt about his concerns: '*An Evolutionary Architecture* investigates the fundamental form-generating processes in architecture, parallelling a wider scientific search for a theory of morphogenesis in the natural world. It proposes the model of nature as the generating force for architectural form. The profligate prototyping and awesome creative power of natural evolution are emulated by creating virtual architectural models which respond to changing environments. Successful developments are encouraged and evolved. Architecture is considered as a form of artificial life, subject, like the natural world, to principles of morphogenesis, genetic coding, replication and selection. The

aim of an evolutionary architecture is to achieve in the built environment the symbiotic behaviour and metabolic balance that are characteristic of the natural environment.'[10]

An Evolutionary Architecture documents Frazer's research aimed at establishing the processes, techniques and algorithms that would create many aspects of evolutionary spatial practice. From 1966 onwards he developed a 'Reptile' structural folding-plate system (originally intended for a gymnasium roof) that could be generated from a single seed. Self-replication, changes of morphology and spanning capability could be determined and drafted by computer. Frazer enlisted the help of the Cambridge University Mathematical Laboratory, where he worked alongside John Horton Conway, who himself was working on his theories of 'The Game of Life'. Conway was to become one of the founding fathers of the creation and study of cellular automata, a very important computational paradigm. Frazer offered a definition of cellular automata in the glossary of *An Evolutionary Architecture* as 'A regular array of cells whose state at any time is dependent upon the state of the individual and its neighbours at the previous instant, under the operation of transition rules'.[11] The two men didn't collaborate but eyed each other curiously.

In 1979 it was Frazer and his colleagues, like Pask before him, who worked with Cedric Price, and the result of their collaboration was hailed as the first truly cybernetic building. The project

was called 'Generator'. Generator was built for the employees of the Gilman Paper Corporation in Florida (figs 356–9). Price was not given a brief, but he wanted the project to be a system that was proactive and full of 'delight', a system that fostered and cosseted creativity. Price designed a system of roughly 13-by-13-foot structural volumes and a series of smaller infill panels, combinations of which could be used to construct all manner of varied architectures. What made Generator different was that it had some rudimentary self-awareness and knowledge. Its architecture was machine-readable. Frazer explained the project's simple but revolutionary cybernetic rationale: 'Price's proposal for the Gilman Corporation was a series of relocatable structures on a permanent grid of foundation pads … We produced a computer program to organize the layout of the site in response to changing requirements, and in addition suggested that a single-chip microprocessor should be embedded in every component of the building, to make it the controlling processor. This would have created an "intelligent" building which controlled its own organization in response to use. If not changed, the building would have become 'bored' and proposed alternative arrangements for evaluation, learning how to improve its own organization on the basis of this experience.'[12] Price represented this astounding building system with a series of cartoon-like descriptive diagrams that depict his and his client's architectural and political optimism.

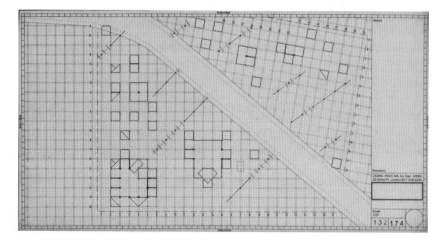

During the 1970s, as well as further developing the Reptile system, Frazer became inspired by the idea of cellular automata, which were being heralded as the mechanisms with which scientists and mathematicians might be able to create artificial intelligence. Conway's 'Life Game' was claimed to be a universal computer and could demonstrate emergent behaviour not originally conceived or programmed by its creators. In 1979 John and his brother Peter created a working model of a self-replicating cellular-automata computer: 'Each cell of the system had sufficient integral electronics for it to know the rules of self replication, to be aware of its neighbours, and to display with LEDs the addition point of the next cell. Application of the rules results in the pattern of replicating cells, giving a working model of a simple array processor which is capable of reproducing itself. Lights indicate where cells are added by human intervention or by robotic arms controlled by the system.'[13]

In 1990 Frazer's design unit at the AA designed and made the Universal Constructor (figs 354, 360–2). This was a three-dimensional structure built of transparent plastic cubes, each simply self-aware like previous two-dimensional experiments. Inside each cubic module were the necessary electronics to allow it to have 256 possible states. The state of each cube was displayed on eight internal LED's. The Universal Constructor could be used for numerous applications involving the design of space. These included the creating of unique dance choreography in which each state was symbolic of a position in Laban dance notation. An architectural evolutionary model was also attempted.

Evolutionary experiments were continued by Frazer through the '90s. The penultimate paragraph of *An Evolutionary Architecture* defined the developmental imperative of much that was to come later, both in his work and in the work of others: 'An evolutionary architecture … will conserve information while using the processes of autopoiesis, auto catalysis and emergent behaviour to generate new forms and structures. It will

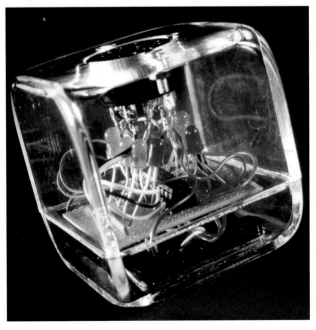

360–1
Universal Constructor, a working model of a self-organizing interactive environment
Group project, 1990

be involved with readjusting points of disjuncture in the socio-economic system by the operation of positive feedback. This will result in significant technological advances in our ability to intervene in the environment. Not a static picture of being, but a dynamic picture of becoming and unfolding – a direct analogy with a description of the natural world.'[14]

Stepping the Light Fantastic

At the beginning of the 1990s, this revolutionary and evolutionary experimentation was being all but ignored by the architectural cognoscenti. But something was beginning to stir – electrotecture was starting to hit America, or at least the avant-garde centres of New York and Los Angeles.

In contemporary computer design there is a rule called Moore's Law, which states that computation power will double every fourteen to eighteen months for the same amount of money. Therefore cheaply available computational power was increasing at a furious rate. The '90s were characterized by the effects of this exponential rise in the dexterity and calculating ability of computers. It is extraordinary that at the beginning of the decade the architectural profession was inertly embedded in traditional protocols of design that had changed very little from much earlier in the century. At the end of the '90s everyone was using computers to design, manufacture and represent architectural creations. The more theoretically minded members of the profession likewise changed direction (fig. 363).

In the beginning, fiction, particularly science fiction, was far ahead of the architects. William Gibson, inspired by the virtual space that exists behind the screen of video arcade games, and by video-game users' belief in the reality of that space, constructed an imaginary electronic space that could be 'entered'. At the same time, the MIT Media Lab was founded, with Nicholas Negroponte becoming its Director. And the first Macintosh computer was being readied for shipping.

362
Underside of Universal Constructor during assembly
AA Diploma Unit 11, 1990

363
Experimental neural-network computer
Miles Dobson, 1991

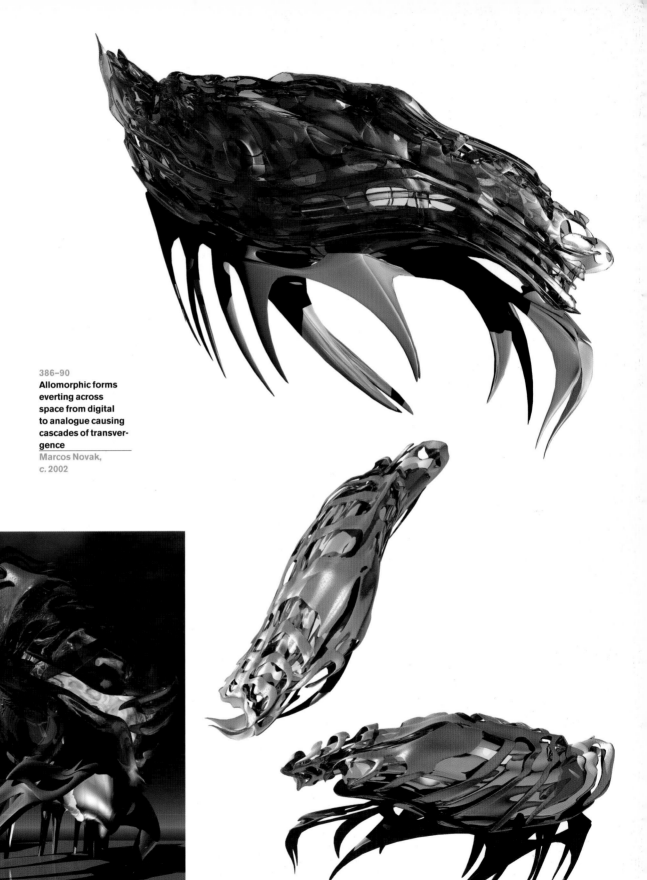

386–90
Allomorphic forms everting across space from digital to analogue causing cascades of transvergence
Marcos Novak,
c. 2002

Variance, Alliance and Deviance

Neil Spiller

With a combination of virtual, cyber-space and real-world architectural notions, is it possible to embroider space so that activities elsewhere, at whatever scale, can condition the formation and growth of an architecture? Such an idea is capable of producing a sublime space that grows and decays, changes and rearranges, that speaks of human beings as the actors in a series of linear, non-linear and quantum events. Small expansions, minute stresses, strains and stains, both virtual and actual, all can be utilized. I have created my Communicating Vessels project to illustrate this potential. The project has many pieces, and the following describes only one subset of the whole.

The piece has two input-generating machines, the first of which is at the heart of the project. It is called the Velásquez Machine and is situated in the Orangerie of the Jardin des Tuileries in Paris. These elliptical galleries contain Monet's *Water Lilies*. Like Monet, my preoccupation is compositionally to straddle the virtual and the actual, art and matter. Velásquez was the first artist to depict himself at work. The Velásquez Machine vibrates in tune with the narcissism of artists linked (as it is) to the amount of material self-published by them on the Web. Over time its vibrations will become more and more pronounced. The Machine holds a frying pan with a perforated bottom; two fish lie in the pan. Inside the clasped centre of the machine along with the fish and the frying pan are nine Roo-Objects. These are jumping hydrochloric-acid innoculators, similar to mechanical fleas. Underneath the Machine is the Oncological Couch on which lies a highly sensitive 'tongue'. As the fish decompose, pieces fall onto the tongue. These small impacts are then recorded and transmitted, becoming the planting plan for a vista many miles away on a site in Fordwich, near Canterbury in England.

The second site is Bramante's Tempietto at S. Pietro in Montorio, Rome. This building has come to be

391 (below)
Interior perspective showing Dee Stools – Pataphysical Laboratory
2004

392 (bottom left)
Plan of Dee Stools – Pataphysical Laboratory
2004

393 (below right)
External perspective of Dee Stools – Pataphysical Laboratory
2004

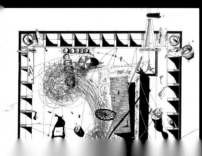

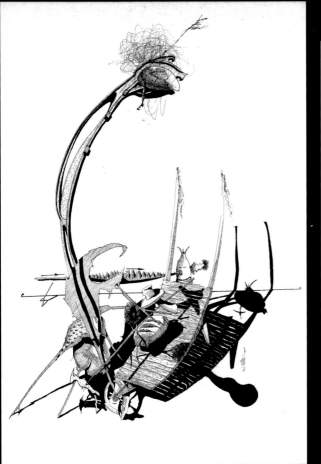

394 (above left)
**Wheelbarrow with
Expanding Bread**
2002

395 (left)
Holey Hedge
1998

396 (above right)
Spacetime Bee-gate
2001

understood as a perfect piece of the architectural Sublime. The courtyard was originally planned and designed by Bramante but, alas, not built to his circular and radial design. I have designed a measuring stick that 'lives' in this area; this is my second input machine. The stick is programmed with a little memory that remembers the exact proportions and idealized dimensions of Bramante's Tempietto and its surrounding courtyard and compares them with what it finds. The Tempietto itself yields minor differences, while the courtyard geometries yield larger discrepancies.

The Ever-Changing Vista is the receiver of some of the input information gleaned from the Velásquez Machine. It is characterized by a symbiotic relationship between its position and the vista that forms around it. Attached to the side of the Machine is a suspended plumb-line terminating in a fried egg. The vectors created by the suspended egg as the Machine vibrates condition the overall movement of the Wheel Barrow sculpture around the landscape. (The fried egg is a reference to Spanish vernacular painting in Velásquez's own time and, vicariously, Dalí's Velásquez-inspired infatuation.) The Metro-light is an homage to Hector Guimard's Paris Metro stations and Dalí's paranoid critical interpretation of them. In this project the lights attract moths and insects at night. Their random bumpings determine the activation of the Roo-Objects, while the speed of planting and growth are conditioned by the Bramante stick. So a complex system of cause and effect is built up around a set of semiotically charged objects to deliver a contextual, glocal, ascalar yet cybernetically beautiful architectonic ecology: an ecology somewhere between building and landscape. These landscape pieces and their relationship to one another are highly 'Pataphysical. Their formal logistics are conditioned by notions of variance, alliance and deviance.

397
Velásquez Machine over Oncological Couch
2002

398
Sculpture and Vista Dynamics showing momentary viewing of parallax shadows, Fordwich, Kent, England
2002

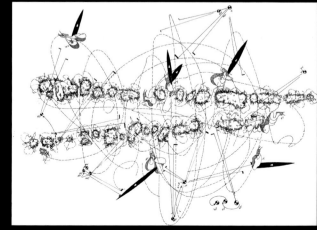

Indexical Glossary

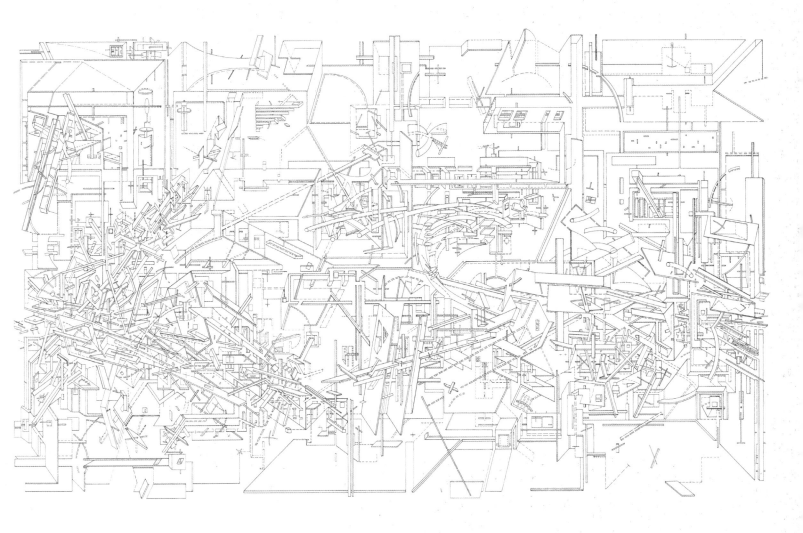

399
Dance Sounds from
'Micromegas'
Daniel Libeskind,
1979

Alberti [8]

Leon Battista Alberti (1404–1472) was the first Renaissance man, accomplished in mathematics, athletics, painting, and architectural design and theory. A true visionary architect, he had little interest in actually constructing his designs but was obsessed with divining a true, perfect architecture. Probably born in Genoa, Alberti was educated in Padua, and in 1431 went to Rome to join the Papal service. He believed that architectural beauty was defined by the harmonious juxtaposition of form, proportion and decoration so that any subtraction or addition would destroy this beauty. This striving for optimized beauty was, he believed, the architect's fundamental task.

Alchemy [9, 120–21, 133]

Alchemy is the art of transforming material both spiritual and actual. The alchemist sees his transformations as a way of refining the basest of materials into progressively purified form. His aim is to attain the 'philosopher's stone': gold. However, this is merely a physical manifestation of a spiritual quest. The alchemist works on himself as well as on external materials; his 'art' involves processes of solution, distillation, condensation, heating and cooling, as well as a whole host of cyclical processes. Alchemists were often persecuted as heretics, and their art was always secret. A complex poetic literature evolved to cryptically describe its processes.

Apollinaire [24, 28–9]

Guillaume Apollinaire (1880–1918) was an apologist for his generation of the European avant-garde in art and poetry. A journalist, poet and art and theatre critic, he invented the term *surrealism*. In 1913 his collection of literary work, *Alcools*, was published, thus establishing his poetic reputation. His friends included Picasso among others. Having enlisted in the French army as soon as he could, his wartime pleasures ended in March 1916 when he was hit in the head by shrapnel. Back in Paris Apollinaire was instrumental in introducing three of the main Surrealist writers to each other: Breton, Soupault and Aragon. He was as well the first critic to attempt to define the various types of Cubism.

Aragon

Louis Aragon (1896–1966) was a medical student in a Paris hospital, which is where he first met André Breton. As a Surrealist poet, Aragon's work explored the sexualized city, a city of change, intoxication, desire and illusion. He often flipped between types of literary and scientific prose, for example describing a journey or scene using contrasting styles. This created the effect of 'jump-cutting' the narrative. Aragon also sought to chart the burning emotions and ecstasy of love. The desiring body traversing space was a common Surrealist preoccupation.

400
Plan of Bâtiment du Graduation Saline at Chaux
Claude-Nicholas Ledoux, 1741

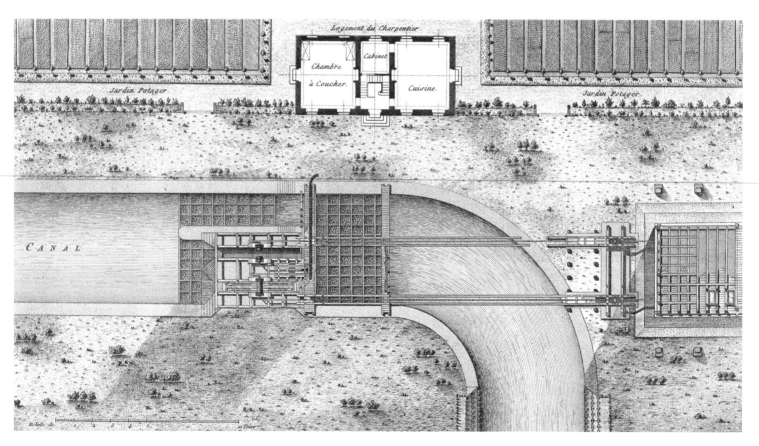

Archigram 10, 14, 61–3, 65, 71, 75–8, 80–86, 88, *91*, 93–4, 100, 102, 104–5, 111, 127, 148–50, 175, 195, 204, 211, *227, 232, 242*

Lodged as it was in the 1960s, the Archigram group failed to anticipate the dominant importance of certain technical developments, in particular biotechnology, nanotechnology and environmental issues. Archigram's work was about the possibilities for architecture, not only with regard to speculation about language and form but also in terms of the widening of the site of conceptual interest that projects might occupy and the ways in which drawings could be tools of speculation.

Archizoom 85, 87

The avant-garde Italian architectural group Archizoom was founded in 1966; its membership consisted of Andrea Branzi, Gilberto Corretti, Paolo Deganello and Massimo Morozzi. The group took their name from the *Zoom* issue of Archigram's magazine. Along with Superstudio, Archizoom was part of the 'radical architecture' movement. This movement rejected prevailing Modernist dogma and replaced it with projects consisting of non-centred, non-hierarchical cities. For these architects, landscape was a field of potential waiting to be colonized both technologically and spatially.

Art of Memory 9

The art of memory is implicitly related to the evolution of the hermetic tradition. This tradition's primary historian was Frances Yates, who seminal book *The Art of Memory* traces its history and development. The art requires an adept to create a mental architecture or landscape populated by forms, people and symbols which can evoke memories once the psychic terrain has been imagined. Renaissance magi such as Raymond Lull and Giordano Bruno were experts in this method of ordering their terrestrial and religious worlds. Both were also advocates of moving memory theatres based on concentric rings that could operate to accommodate changes in time and scale.

Asymptote 66–9, *228*

Asymptote, which consists of Hani Rashid (1958–) and Lise-Anne Couture (1959–), has an office in New York. In 1989 they won awards in the Los Angeles Gateway competition. This project hangs over a freeway and was intended to be a catalytic cultural centre dedicated to speed, production, images, technology and the ephemeral. It was planned to be seen in the anamorphic gaze of the speeding car, truck or motorcycle. Latterly the pair have been experimenting with new computational technologies and have made a continuing and valuable contribution to debates about the impact of such advances on architecture.

Baroque Architecture 104

The main characteristic of Baroque architecture – built mostly during the seventeenth and early part of the eighteenth centuries – is a flamboyant display of swollen forms kept in order by Classical motifs. The style's formal and spatial compositions are extremely complex. Concave and convex space and detail are juxtaposed to create a voluptuous architecture. Borromini's built work in Rome is a well-known example of the mature Italian Baroque. Circles are often intertwined with elliptical plan-geometry to create spaces that seem constantly to be metamorphosing from simple into complex forms. Details often appear to billow across walls.

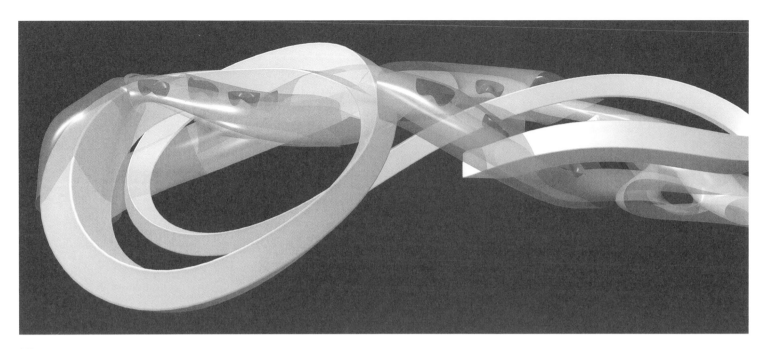

Boullée 171, 187

Etienne-Louis Boullée (1728–1799) was, like Ledoux, an influential Neo-Classical architect. He is best known for his visionary project for a monument to Isaac Newton featuring a 500-foot-high dome. Boullée's designs reached the apogee of their visionary zeal between 1780 and 1790. Characterized by their reliance on simple Platonic forms, they often depended on the uncanny feeling induced by familiar shapes raised to huge, magical scales.

Breton 29, 43–4

André Breton (1896–1966) was the instigator, founder-member and chief censor of the Surrealist movement. In 1930, defining much of what would become known as Surrealist work, Breton wrote the following in his 'Second Manifesto': 'Everything tends to make us believe that there exists a certain point of the mind at which life and death, the real and the imagined, past and future, the communicable and the incommunicable, high and low, cease to be perceived as contradictions. Search as one may, one will never find any other motivating force in the activities of the surrealists than the hope of finding and fixing this point.'

Bruno 17, 145, 152

Giordano Bruno (1548–1600) was a magus remembered primarily for his hermetic texts and his mnemonic systems. In her book *Giordano Bruno and the Hermetic Tradition*, Frances Yates describes his world view this way: 'The earth moves because it is alive around a sun of Egyptian magic; the planets as living stars perform their courses with her; innumerable other worlds, moving and alive like great animals, people an infinite universe.' This was essentially a Newtonian universe powered not by gravity and momentum but by animism, and the interrelationships within it could be recalled via a set of memory wheels.

Buckminster Fuller 49, 61, 72, 75, 77, 101–2, 105, 112

Richard Buckminster Fuller (1895–1983) made his first real impact on architecture with the Dymaxion House in 1927. His dream was to create low-cost prefabricated housing which was light, not dependent on large foundations and quickly assembled. Fuller was a twentieth-century Renaissance man, a philosopher, an architect and an engineer. He is remembered for his geodesic structures, some meant to be projected over entire cities. These domes had great structural strength, economy of materials and standardized detailing. Buckminster Fuller was also

a great teacher as well as being concerned about the damage buildings can do to the planet.

Bunschoten 152, 183, 185–7, *188, 228–9*

Like Ben Nicholson, Raoul Bunschoten (1955–) was a student of Daniel Libeskind at the Cranbrook Academy of Art. In his early work he tried to get close to the underlying essence of architecture – its ontological nature. This resulted in a series of highly idiosyncratic projects from Spinoza's Garden to The Skin of the Earth. The cut, the ground, the scar, the artfully placed and an archaeology of detritus are all linked in Bunschoten's architectural lexicon. In more recent years he has concerned himself with developing proactive and analytical notational design tools which aid him in positing urban design propositions.

Burry *22, 31–2, 35, 230–31, 240*

Mark Burry (1957–) is a practising architect as well as Professor of Innovation (Spatial Information Architecture) at RMIT University, Melbourne. Since 1979 he has been a consultant to the foundation that commissioned Gaudí to design the Sagrada Família in Barcelona in 1882. Burry's role has been to unravel the mysteries of Gaudí's use of second-order geometry for the design of

404
Model for Spinoza's Garden seen from above
Raoul Bunschoten, 1985–6

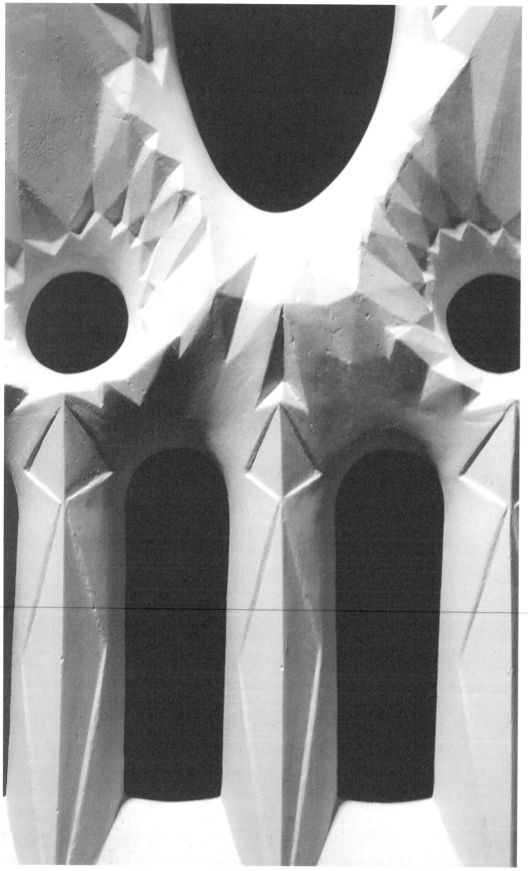

the cathedral's nave. Burry also is interested in the broader issues of design and construction and the use of computers in design theory and practice.

Chard 18, *19*, 20, *21*

Nat Chard (1959–) is a professor at the Royal Danish Academy School of Architecture, Copenhagen. Previously he taught in London at the Bartlett and elsewhere. Chard has worked in a number of London practices and on his own projects, and he has also lectured widely in Europe, Asia and North America. His current project is called 'drawing indeterminate architecture, indeterminate drawings of architecture'.

Cheval 29

Ferdinand Cheval (1836–1924) captured the essence of Surrealism in building. He did this unawares, however. As a postman, he would collect stones in a wheelbarrow and then toil into the night creating an amazing Dream Palace out of them. At its highest, this building reaches to 30 feet; it is about 88 feet long. André Breton felt it to be one of the great examples of what Surrealist architecture might be and allowed himself to be photographed in front of it more than once. The nobbly aesthetic of the Dream Palace crops up time and time again in Surrealist attempts at architecture; Dalí's *Dream of Venus* (1939) is but one example.

De Chirico 10, 25, 166, 167

One of the most influential painters of the twentieth century, Giorgio de Chirico's (1888–1978) 'metaphysical' paintings depict strange, silent, hard landscapes full of foreboding and enigmatic associations. The Surrealists were inspired by his early works; he can be seen to have influenced Dalí, Ernst and Tanguy among others. De Chirico rebuked the Surrealists' advances, however, and they in response failed to recognize the achievement of his later paintings, which were more classically inspired. In his metaphysical work, the

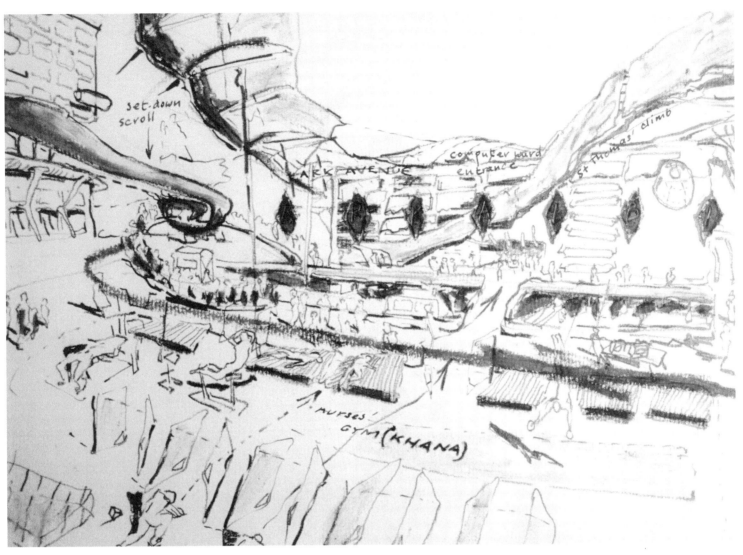

juxtaposition of unrelated forms in a non-unified perspectival space created uncanny compositions which seemed to be founded on a type of psychic automatism.

Clear 119, 130, *131*

Nic Clear (1963–) studied at the Polytechnic of Central London, completing his thesis project under Robin Evans. After graduating he worked with Kevin Rhowbotham under the name Non-Specific Urbanism (NSU) and invented the acronym FAT, meaning Fashion Architecture Taste. Clear ran his own company Clear Space for many years before setting up the now defunct General Lighting and Power, whose work covered everything from pop promos to architecture and

from advertising campaigns to art installations. Clear has been teaching at the Bartlett since 1990. Having abandoned the 'corporate architectural complex', he divides his time between writing fiction, performance, and making drawings and films.

Coates 126–7, *128*, 130, 185, *231*

Nigel Coates (1949–) is Professor of Architecture at the Royal College of Arts, London. He has also taught at the Architectural Association. In 1979 he became Unit Master of Diploma Unit 10. In 1983 he formed NATO (Narrative Architecture Today) with eight Unit 10 students. Coates's work has been exhibited internationally. In recent years he has been in partnership with Doug Branson, practising as Branson Coates.

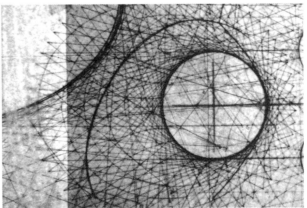

405 (opposite)
Façade model of Sagrada Família
Mark Burry, 1979–

406 (top)
Ark Albion
Nigel Coates/NATO

407 (above)
Computer wire-frame detail, Sagrada Família
Mark Burry, 1979–

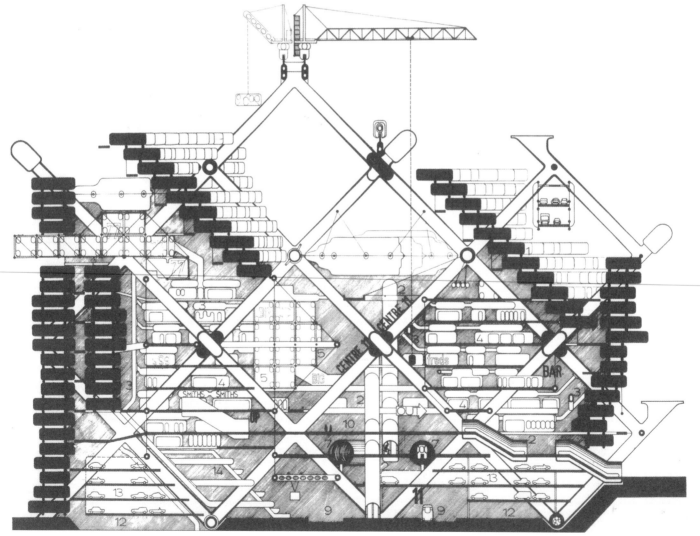

Constant *17, 40,* 41, 44–53, 72, 204, 211, *232*

The artist Constant Niewenhuys (1920–2005) was the first person to define the curious characters that inhabited the theoretical megastructures of the 1960s. These characters did not have to work; they indulged in play, space-forming, sex or education for the fun of it. During the '50s, '60s and early '70s Constant created a grand polemical project called New Babylon. As the only Situationist to consider architecture as part of that movement's political concerns, he used Situationist tactics of space-forming and evaluation as the primary ways to question the pervading economic and functional justifications of city planning. He was later expelled from the movement.

Constructivism 23, 34–5, 47, 62, 141, 145, 148–9, 150, 152–3, 155, 159, 204

To quote Stephen Bann's book *The Tradition of Constructivism*, 'Constructivism, like the Bolshevik Revolution, may have been centrally concerned with clear and logical reasoning, with the perfection of human institutions, and with the establishment of general laws based on scientific fact. Yet the foremost constructivist artists were those who saw the world through the "prism" of their own technique.'

Cook *11,* 72, 75–9, *80,* 82, 84, 88, *91, 92, 93,* 94, 96, 146, 149, 150, 152, 170, 185, *232*

Peter Cook (1936–) studied for his diploma in Architecture at the Architectural Association, London; his teachers included Peter Smithson. In 1961 he created the first *Archigram* publication with David Greene. Archigram consolidated later on with more members. In 1973 Cook was appointed Director of London's Institute of Contemporary Arts. From 1975 to 1996 he worked on projects with Christine Hawley, and between 1990 and 2004 he was Chairman of University College London's Bartlett School of Architecture. He continues to write, design, teach and build. The idea of change, whether organic or inorganic, is essential to an understanding of his work.

Coop Himmelb(l)au 84, 106, *107, 140,* 143, 148, 158, *233*

Wolf Prix (1942–) and Helmut Swiczinsky (1944–) formed Coop Himmelb(l)au in 1968. Their early work was a mixture of polemic, performance and electronically augmented mobile spaces, sometimes motorized, sometimes inflated and sometimes burning. They became known internationally in the wake of the 'Deconstructivist Architecture' exhibition at the Museum of Modern Art, New York. Above all, they share a strong distaste for an eclectic and historicist tradition in Viennese architecture. This 'suffocating' backdrop represents the negative starting point of their determination to 'free' architecture from preconceived ideas about form, function, programme and context. Their later work is more concerned with an aesthetic of shards, angles and contorted structure.

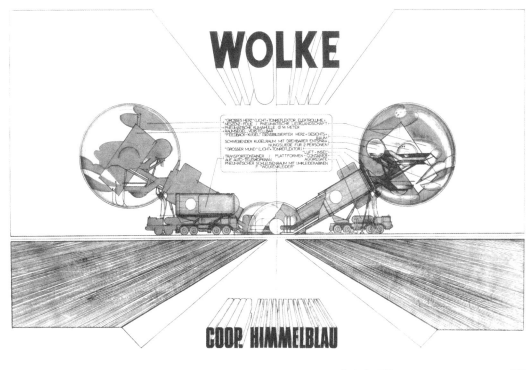

Cubism 23–4, 28–9, 34

Cubism is at the root of all abstract art forms created since the beginning of the twentieth century. Its founding fathers, Picasso and Braque, sought to replace traditional perspectival representation with the juxtaposition of views seen by moving or different viewers conditioned by their own cognitive presuppositions. This disintegration of the object or scene allowed a concentration on the partiality of views, the nature of paint and the substance of objects. Apollinaire was influential in establishing a taxonomy of Cubist aspirations in his *Les Peintres cubistes* (1913).

Cybernetics 48–50, 53, 59, 178, 180, 204–5

Cybernetics is a term invented by Norbert Wiener (1894–1964) to describe the analysis of the interaction between machines and biological systems. Any system can be studied in this way. Cybernetics' fundamental analytical paradigm is the feedback loop. A simple cybernetic device is the governor on a steam engine, which, being responsive to steam pressure, can moderate it accordingly. Cybernetics interests itself in how systems use information, modelling and controlled actions to achieve their intended outputs; second-order cybernetics further considers the role and impact of observation on systems, whether human or not. In this context the viewer is part of both the system and the study.

Cyberspace 34, 41, 203, 211, 222

Cyberspace consists of the many and varied spaces constructed within and in conjunction with, as well as augmented by, computers. These spaces are infinite. Some believe that the space the telephone user mentally and technologically constructs is a manifestation of cyberspace; others believe that only the full-body immersion of goggled virtual reality is cyberspace. Contemporary culture includes all manner of computer/human interfaces as cyberspatial. Cyberspace has changed and will radically rearticulate architecture; the implied movement of much of twentieth-century visionary architecture is now untenable.

Dada 10, 23, 29, 44, 64, 85, 108, 119–20, 125, 127

Dada's gestation commenced during 1916 in Zurich with the opening of Hugo Ball's Cabaret Voltaire. Dada was without political allegiance or artistic persuasion and did not believe in anything except that artistic creation meant nothing. It despised the methods, protocols and systems invented by society to categorize things. Dada preferred lunacy. Its advocates had been profoundly affected by the mass destruction of the First World War, by the stupid posturings of generals and politicians, and by the placidity of most of Europe's citizens. Dada attracted the attention of André Breton and in some respects was a precursor to Surrealism.

Dalí 31–2, 169, 204, 224

Salvador Dalí (1904–1989) was born in Figures in Catalonia. In 1921 he began studying at the School of Fine Arts, Madrid. He collaborated on the first Surreal fim, *Un Chien andalou* (1928); in the following year, after an introduction by Miró to the Parisian Surrealists, he participated in their exhibition at the Galerie Gocmans in Paris. In 1939 Dalí left Europe for America. A technically talented painter as well as an extremely learned artist, his displays of theatricality undermined his great contribution to twentieth-century art.

Debord 44–5, 52–3, 65, 120–21, 127, 145, 215

Guy Debord (1931–1994) was leader of the Situationist International. Debord, like Breton before him, had a very particular idea regarding the preoccupations his SI colleagues should have. This slightly blinkered attitude gives a coherence to their body of work but also cut off areas of

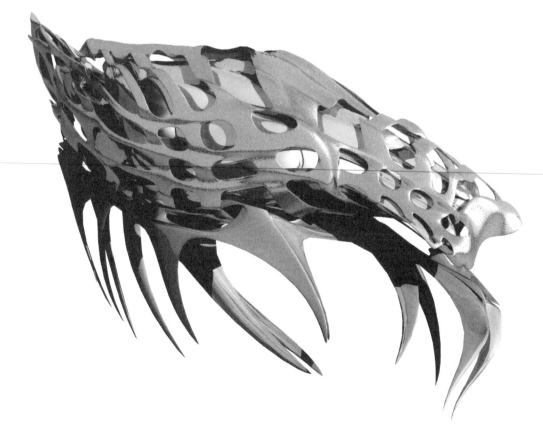

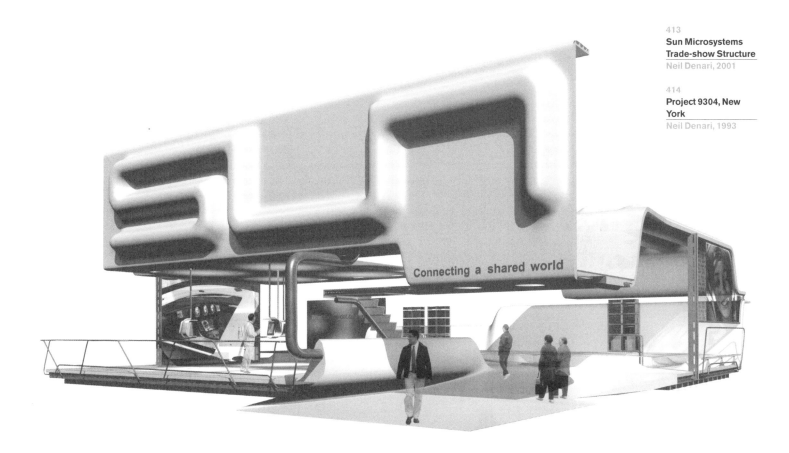

investigation. It also caused Debord to become disenfranchised from Constant's foray into architectural space. Debord's seminal text *The Society of the Spectacle* is a dissection of the protocols and tactics of exclusion of the capitalist 'Spectacle'.

Deconstruction 139, 141, 143, 145, 148–50, 158, 160, 211–12

Deconstruction is the name of a style of architecture that emerged during the late '70 s and early '80s. This sharded, angular and supposedly fractured architecture became characteristic of the output of the avant-garde particularly after the influential exhibition at MOMA, New York in 1988. Allegedly Deconstruction was founded on the literary theories of Jacques Derrida, who himself was fairly sure that his work could not be applied to architecture. The aesthetic of Deconstruction had a distinct formal affinity with that of the Russian Constructivists; some argued that this

was simply a language of change and experiment and therefore entirely appropriate, while others said that it was an antiquated language developed in entirely different cultural conditions and therefore entirely inappropriate.

Denari 111, 216, *235*

Neil Denari (1957–) studied at the University of Houston in the early 1980s, as well as at Harvard University. An inspiring teacher, he is a builder of highly engineered structures. He is influenced by the sleek skins of aeronautical objects, the notations and iconography of technology, and the philosophy of science. This hyper-machine aesthetic is at its best when it is let loose on the American or Japanese city. The hyper-real space of contemporary urban living accepts Denari's formal and spatial preoccupations without so much as a second look.

Diller + Scofidio 9, 36–9, 94, *108*, 109, 110, *236*

The practice of Diller + Scofidio consists of Elizabeth Diller (1954–) and Ricardo Scofidio (1935–) and dates from 1979. The two partners concern themselves with the interstitial relationships between architecture, art, theatre, everyday ritual and the choreography of ephemeral urban spaces. Their work has been performed and exhibited worldwide. They have been greatly influenced by Duchamp and his mechanization of desire. Their work questions the position of architecture in relation to cultural and social conventions, using an analytical method of reading behavioural patterns, leisure activities and spatial codification.

Domenig 88, *92, 102–3*, 104, *236*

Gunter Domenig (1934–) studied architecture at the Technical University,

Graz. From 1963 until 1973 he was in partnership with Eilfried Huft (1930–), together they were influential in the Megastructural movement. Since 1973 Domenig has been in practice on his own and has been Professor of Architecture at the Technical University, Graz. Amongst his most significant buildings are the Zentralsparkasse in Vienna and his own house in Steindorf, which he started in 1986 and which is still being constructed. This project is intensely autobiographical and operates as Domenig's four-dimensional test-rig and laboratory. Its wayward geometries and cacophony of materials and junctions illustrate a still-evolving personal and esoteric language of architecture.

Duchamp 9, 14, 25, 27–8, 36, 60, 63, 94, 152, 155

Marcel Duchamp (1887–1968) was born in Normandy. In 1912 he began a small series of paintings, the best known of which is *Nude Descending a Staircase* (1912). These compositions attempted to capture the movement of human bodies in space. His so-called *Large Glass: The Bride Stripped Bare by Her Bachelors, Even* (1915–23) is renowned as one of the great enigmatic art pieces of the twentieth century. In 1917 Duchamp bought his first 'ready-made' and created his first optical machine. He was interested in games, particularly those of chance (he was a very good international chess player), as well as in notions of

perspective and pictorial
representation. All of these
preoccupations can be traced
throughout his work.

Dunne & Raby 183, 195, *196–7*, 212, *237*

Anthony Dunne (1964–) and Fiona
Raby (1963–) use products and
services as a medium to stimulate
debate amongst designers, industry
and the public about the various
implications of emerging technologies.
Many of their projects are collaborative,
working with industrial-research labs,
academia and cultural institutions to
design speculative products and
services. Projects include a
combination of essays and design
proposals exploring the aesthetic
meanings of electronic objects; a
collection of psychological furniture for
home and garden; and a group of
electronic objects which explore mental
well-being in relation to domestic
electromagnetic fields.

Eisenman *100–1*, 104, 141, *156*, 157–8, 185, 211, *238*

Peter Eisenman (1932–) is both a
practitioner and a theoretician. He
studied architecture at Cambridge; this
is where his polemical approach
originated. His work is in opposition to
the traditional form/function equation
of Modernism, exposing this established

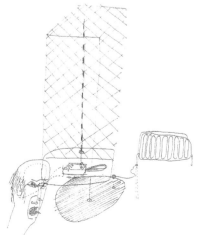

417 (left)
Conceptual sketch
Dunne and Raby,
c. 2000

418 (top)
**Draught Excluder
Hero**
Dunne and Raby,
2000

419 (above)
**Map of Helsinki,
Cellular City for FLIRT
project**
Dunne and Raby,
2000

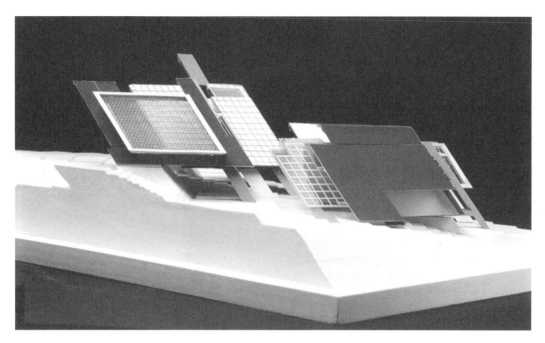

sophism for what it is. Eisenman has had a preoccupation with the house form, and much of his theoretical work has focused on its taxonomy. He sees his architecture as having a textural quality; the literature of drawing and building is revealed through repeated reading and with reference to his other literatures/architectures.

Ernst 9, 60–61, 120–21, 211
Max Ernst (1891–1976) studied philosophy at Bonn University. In 1919 he was the co-founder of the Cologne Dadaist group, moving three years later to Paris, where he became involved with the fledgling Surrealist movement. Ernst was interested in collage and invented the *frottage* technique in 1925. Early on, he produced collage-novels such as *La Femme 1000 têtes* and *Une Semaine de bonté*. Much of his work was also inspired by the alchemical opus. The resulting combination of real and psychic meanings in his work align it with that of the medieval magi.

Flusser 136
Born in Prague, Vilem Flusser

(1920–1991) emigrated to Brazil at the age of twenty. He was a lecturer, a writer and a philosopher of communication, design and language. Flusser was the author of a number of books, including *Language and Reality* (1963), *A History of the Devil* (1965) and *Towards a History of Photography* (1981). A posthumous collection of his essays entitled *The Shape of Things* was published in 1999.

Frazer 185, 203, *206*, 207–9, 212, *238–9*
John Frazer (*c.* 1940–) studied at the Architectural Association, London. He has worked in conjunction with architects such as Cedric Price and Walter Segal and on his own. Frazer specializes in developing intelligent evolutionary architecture which reconfigures itself utilizing computer technology. *An Evolutionary Architecture*, published in 1995 to coincide with an exhibition of the same name at the Architectural Association, investigates the form-generating processes in architecture, considering the discipline as a form of artificial life and proposing a genetic representation of it in the form of DNA-like code-script.

Friedman 49, 72–3
Yona Friedman (1928–) was one of the foremost Megastructural theorists, making designs for many examples of '*urbanisme spatiale*' (1960–62).

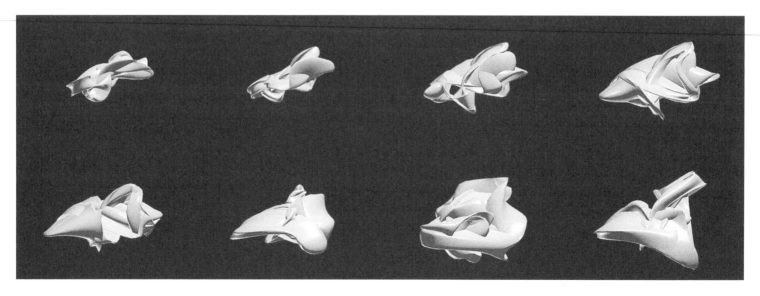

Friedman developed numerous spatial and mechanical techniques for structure, enclosure, service infrastructure and mobility, becoming interested in the importance of 'games' for human happiness. The making of space like a game allowed computers to be harnessed in the pursuit of new spatial configurations. Friedman's projects included aerial megastructural cities over New York, Paris and Algiers.

Future Systems 98, 105–6, *107, 239*

Future Systems was formed in 1979 by Jan Kaplicky (1937–), who had fled from Prague in 1968. The practice's projects were often small and mobile, and utilized high-technology components; this gave them an aesthetic of yachts and spaceships. Future Systems is predicated on the notion that the limited palette of traditional architectural materials can be augmented by transfer technologies from other disciplines, particularly aircraft design, boat-building and spacecraft design. In 1987 Future Systems were joined by Amanda Levete (1955); subsequent work became larger in scale.

Futurism 26–7, 34, 44, 72, 125, 127, 204

Futurism is the only art movement from the first half of the twentieth century that was mostly independent of Paris. The first publicity it received was

Parisian, however. In *Le Figaro* its founder-member Filippo Marinetti declared the existence of 'a new beauty' characterized by the speed of the machine. Futurism existed from 1909 to about 1915; though short-lived it was powerful, producing a number of manifestos concerning painting, sculpture, architecture – and lust. The architectural representative of Futurism was Sant'Elia, whose work – though not always in line with Futurist orthodoxy – inspired the Megastructure movement. Sant'Elia's work was exhumed and discussed by the architectural theorist and critic Reyner Banham.

Gaudí 22, 23, 29, 31–2, *33–5, 240*

Antoni Gaudí i Cornet (1852–1926) was born in Reus in Catalonia. At twenty-one he began to study architecture. He also worked as a master builder, which gave him a full understanding of the differing dynamic qualities of various materials. This understanding can be seen in his ability to create plastic, seemingly dripping architectural forms. Gaudí built a few masterpieces around the Barcelona area, one being the Sagrada Família. In 1914 he dedicated his effort exclusively to this as-yet-unfinished church. His work inspired the young Dalí to enthuse about the 'edible' nature of Art Nouveau.

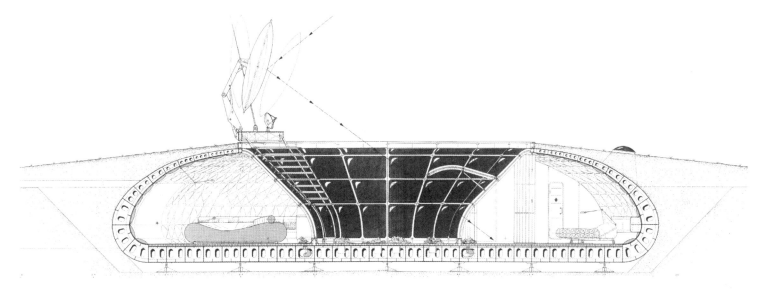

spent teaching architecture, design, art and cybernetics. He holds a number of posts around the world and is returning to the making of music.

Greene 72, 75, 80–83, 85, 88, 90, 92, *93*
David Greene (1937–) was Archigram's poet, a founding member along with Peter Cook. As well as Greene's poetic aspirations, which introduced narrative into Archigram's output, he was interested in the evolutionary path that technology would take towards invisibility. So he created projects in which the technology was embedded in familiar objects like logs or rocks. Or technology became almost anthropological as with his free-grazing lawnmowers. Another of Greene's contributions was to provide a forum for architectural investigation within the everyday world of picnics and garden sheds, an area that architects seldom considered at the time.

Hadid 94, *138*, 139, 143, *144–5*, 148–9, 158, 185
Zaha Hadid (1950–) studied architecture at the Architectural Association, London from 1972, graduating with honours in 1977. She worked with Office for Metropolitan Architecture and taught with Rem

Gibson 210–11
William Gibson (1948–) is the award-winnng author of science-fiction novels including *Neuromancer*, *Mona Lisa Overdrive*, *Count Zero*, *Virtual Light*, *Idoru* and *All Tomorrow's Parties*. He is the inventor of the word *cyberspace*, which he coined to describe the backdrop for *Neuromancer*.

Glanville 206, 211
Ranulph Glanville (1946–) studied at the Architectural Association, London, where he spent much of his time composing and performing electronic and acoustic music. Having been invited by Gordon Pask to undertake a PhD in cybernetics, the work he created has been described as follows: '[B]y an exercise in abstract cybernetic algebra, Glanville … cleared the primordial ground'. Then came a PhD in Human Learning, in the course of which Glanville explored how architects choose to experience and describe space. His professional life has been

Koolhaas and Elia Zenghelis. Her own unit at the AA terminated in 1987. Hadid's first major competition win was for The Peak Club, Hong Kong. Her work is instantly recognizable and has been called Suprematist in inspiration. Hadid's architectural lexicon is predicated on the juxtaposition of sinuous, shard-like or trapezoidal forms plaited over one another. Recently she has enjoyed much international success, and large examples of her work are beginning to be built.

Hamilton 59, 60–63, *64*
Richard Hamilton (1922–) is one of the original Pop artists. His 1956 collage *Just what is it that makes today's home so different, so appealing?* seemed to define an era as well as an artistic ideal. Hamilton was a member of London's Independent Group, which was focused around the Institute of Contemporary Arts during the 1950s. This group defined a generation, and its interest in the smooth factory aesthetic of cars; the advanced technologies of robotics; the aesthetics of populist comics, films and books; the rise of the television advert; and the ongoing mechanization of society caused it to create exhibitions, art, photographs and theoretical essays that changed the world of art for good.

Hawley 94, 96, *146* 149, 152

Christine Hawley (1948–) is Dean of the Bartlett School of Architecture, University College London. She studied architecture at the Architectural Association under Archigram's Ron Herron, later becoming the architectural partner of Peter Cook. Hawley's own early work was within the lyrical mechanist camp which she helped to define. It was Arcadian, slightly Classically inspired and romantic, consisting of mist, shadow, promenade and vista. Later, during the 1990s, it became more double-curved, sinuous and extruded, reaching out into the urban context with well-defined walkways. Route and function have equal emphasis in Hawley's work. Her sections are characterized by an almost Corbusian sensitivity to materiality and placement.

Hejduk 165–9, 178, 185, *241*

John Hejduk (1929–2000) was Dean of the Irwin S. Chanin School of Architecture at the Cooper Union for the Advancement of Science and Art, New York. He was a sensitive and poetic architect whose work and teaching greatly inspired other practitioners mentioned in this volume such as Daniel Libeskind and Elizabeth Diller. Hejduk studied architecture at Cooper Union, the University of Cincinnati and Harvard, from which he graduated in 1953. He published more than twenty books of poetry and polemical architecture, each a combination of hand-drawn work together with poetic spatial conditions and imagined narratives of use.

Herron 43, *58*, 61, *70*, 75, 78, 80, *81*, 82, 84, *85* , 87–8, 90, 92, 100, *227*

After completing his National Service in the RAF Herron joined London County Council Architects' Department in 1954. This is where he met Warren Chalk and Dennis Crompton and, through a mutual friend, Peter Cook, David Greene and Michael Webb. In 1962 they joined the Euston Project team under Theo Crosby. The

Archigram Group was formed in this period and combined to produce *Archigram* magazine. Herron commenced teaching at the Architectural Association in 1965, continuing until 1993. After the Archigram office closed in 1975 he joined Pentagram, forming Herron Associates in 1982. In 1993 Herron became Professor and Head of the School of Architecture at the University of East London. Herron Associates were the architects of the Imagination building in Store Street , London and in 1989 merged with Imagination for a time.

Jarry 10, 24–5, 29, 36, 152, 155, 219

Alfred Jarry's (1873–1907) life was short but extraordinary. Author of a unique series of plays, novels, poems and other literary forms, his work is often ignored because of its nonsensical Surrealism. However, it formed a critical bridge between the Symbolist poets of the 1890s and the avant-garde movements of the first half of the nineteenth century. Jarry is best known as the author of the play *Ubu Roi*. He was also the creator of 'Pataphysics, a cruel, satirical science that apes the bizarre self-importance of actual science, its discoveries and (in Jarry's opinion) its silly search for rules with no exceptions. Jarry was a master of describing the exceptional. Life and work, reality and fiction had no artificial boundaries for him.

Johnson 211

Philip Johnson (1906–) has been client, critic, author, historian, museum director and architect. In 1949, after a number of years as the first Director of the Museum of Modern Art's Architecture Department, Johnson designed a residence for himself in New Canaan, Connecticut for his master's thesis: the now-famous Glass House. He coined the phrase 'International School of Architecture' for an exhibition at New York's MOMA and collaborated with Mies on the Seagram Building in New York. Johnson

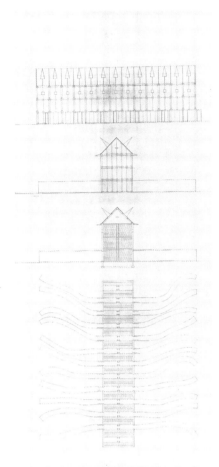

was a co-curator with Mark Wigley of MOMA's famous 'Deconstructivist Architecture' exhibition.

Jones 114–17

Wes Jones (1958–), who originally came to prominence as a design partner at Holt Hinshaw Pfau Jones, has always been interested in technology transfer and the mechanical as an inspiration for his architecture. After six years at Holt Hinshaw Pfau Jones, he formed his own practice, Jones, Partners: Architecture. The first five years of JPA work is detailed in *Instrumental Form*, a monograph published by Princeton Architectural Press. Jones has received the Rome Prize in Architecture and taught in the schools of architecture at Harvard, Princeton, Columbia, UCLA, Ohio State University and the Southern California Institute of Architecture.

ROBO HOUSE 2

427
Robo-House
Ron Herron, 1985

428
Interior of Endless House
Frederick Kiesler, 1959

Koolhaas 158, 185, 211

Rem Koolhaas (1944–) emerged during the late 1970s with the book *Delirious New York*, a celebration of the heterogeneous spaces of historic and contemporary New York City. The book sought to reveal the distorted psycho-geographical and programmatic diversity and hybridization of this exceptional city. It was an instant hit. Later completed projects included the Netherlands Dance Theatre in The Hague, an Educatorium (a factory for learning) in Utrecht, housing in Japan and proposals for such things as an Airport Island in the North Sea. Koolhaas's office, OMA, is one of the best-known architectural firms in the world today. He won the Pritzker Prize for Architecture in 2000.

Lautréamont 25

Isidore Ducasse, Comte de Lautréamont (1846–1870) is mainly remembered for his *Chants de Maldoror*, which was adopted by the Surrealists as one of their key reference texts. The famous expression used in the book, 'encounter on a dissecting table of a sewing machine and an umbrella', was employed by them as a basis for their search for a new aesthetic conditioned as much by the mind as by so-called reality.

Kiesler 42–3, 45, 47, 49, 54, 73, 75, 81, 130, *242, 244*

Fredrick Kiesler (1896–1966) was born in Vienna and studied there from 1910 to 1916. He was an architect, a sculptor and a stage designer, as well as a member of the De Stijl group. In 1932 Kiesler gained American citizenship, working as a theatre director at the Juilliard School of Music in New York from 1933 until 1957. His best-known built work was the short-lived Art of this Century Gallery (1942) and his building housing the Dead Sea Scrolls in Jerusalem, the Sanctuary of the Book (1961–5). Kiesler was on the periphery of the Surrealist movement and was a great friend of Duchamp.

Kolar 152, 157

The Czech Jiri Kolar (1914–1998) was the co-founder of Group 42. His early works comprise traditional poetry compositions. In the 1950s his poems began to reach out to the visual realm and incorporate various media; his work during the '60s was characterized by geometrical abstraction, visual poems and technical objects. Kolar developed a lexicon that pushed the boundaries of the hybridization of image and poetry, resulting in chiasmages, rollages and wrinklages. He went on to inspire architects such as Daniel Libeskind and others.

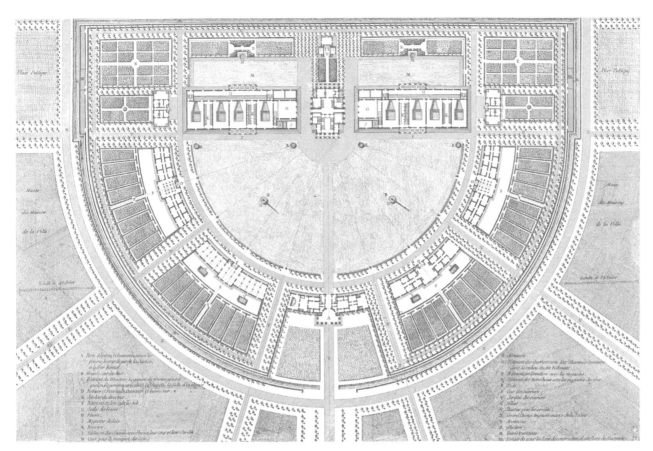

Le Corbusier (1887–1965), the great Swiss architect and city planner, was born Charles-Edouard Jeanneret in La Chaux-de-Fonds, a watch-making city in Switzerland. He pioneered functionalist architecture with the use of reinforced concrete and the concept of a house as a 'machine for living in'. He was also a Purist painter, and his work exhibits painterly concerns. Recently much research has been done to explore the connections between Le Corbusier's work and Surrealism. He was probably the greatest master architect of the twentieth century.

Claude-Nicolas Ledoux (1736–1806) started his career as an architect connected to the court of Louis XVI. Later he became inspired by the unbuildable visionary architecture of Piranesi. Ledoux's style was one of stripped-down Classicism, extreme yet highly ordered. His work for the city of Chaux is the most powerful product of his philosophy. Ledoux's elemental approach sought to reconcile the primeval and the Classical in an effort to determine, teach and enforce the moral character and work ethic of entire cities.

During the early 1980s, Daniel Libeskind (1946–) was Director of the Cranbrook Academy of Art's architecture depart-ment. It was there that he developed some of his important theoretical projects. Libeskind participated in the MOMA Deconstruction exhibition with a project situated in Berlin. Berlin, and latterly New York, comprise his ideal architectural canvas. Both are multi-cultural cities, have a Jewish component to their histories, and are the sites of great loss and grief as well as cultural and architectural resurrection. Libeskind's work is symbolic yet critically Modernist. His Jewish Museum in Berlin is one of the great buildings of the twentieth century.

Born in Ipoh, Malaysia, C. J. Lim (1964–) graduated from the Architectural Association, London in 1987. He is Director of the BSc Architecture Course and Diploma Unit Master at the Bartlett in London and has been Visiting Professor of Architecture at the Mackintosh School of Architecture in Glasgow, Technological University Lund, Städelschule Frankfurt and Curtin University, Perth. Lim represented the UK at the 2004 Venice Biennale.

El (Lazar Markovich) Lissitzky (1890–1941) was born in Polshinok, Russia. First he was trained as an engineer, then as an architect. His work became

distinctive during 1919, when he developed the notion of the 'Proun', an interstitial point between painting and architecture. During the 1920s Lissitzky was active in many fields of the creative arts, particularly graphic design, theatre design and architecture.

Lynn 203, 211–12, *213*, 215–16, *217–18, 245*

Greg Lynn (1964–) graduated in philosophy and environmental design as well as architecture. He has taught architectural design at Columbia University in New York and at UCLA, as well as in Amsterdam and Vienna. From 1989 until 1992, he was a member of *ANY* magazine's editorial board. Lynn was instrumental in establishing the so-called 'Blob-architectures' of the close of the twentieth century. His interest in computer design, emergent form and computer-aided manufacture gives his architecture an instantly recognizable aesthetic. He has done much to define some of the ideas, design protocols and formal fetishisms of current fashion.

Malevich 34, 94, 133, 153, 211

The Russian artist Kasimir Malevich (1878–1935) invented Suprematism. His *White Square on a White Ground* (1918) may have carried abstraction as far as it could go. Malevich's artistic epiphany came in Paris in 1912, when he started to subscribe to the Cubist world-view. Suprematism had to do with the establishment of a fifth dimension in painting. Much of old art should be destroyed, Malevich felt, as it failed to be of 'five' dimensions.

Marey 18, 26, *27*, 36

Etienne-Jules Marey (1830–1904) spent his life documenting the movement of objects and their relationship to time. He is remembered for his photographs of human and animal subjects in motion and is reputed to have inspired the Cubists and Marcel Duchamp. During the 1880s Marey developed many augmented cameras that enabled him to record movement. He was in contact with Thomas Alva Edison and Eadweard Muybridge,

among others who shared his interests. His work continues to be an inspiration today, particularly to such architects as Diller and Scofidio and Nat Chard.

Marinetti 26, 211

Filippo Marinetti (1876–1944) was a founder-member of the Futurist movement. His work includes poetry and polemical prose. In 1932 he produced a Futurist cookbook to coincide with his proposed revolution in food. Marinetti believed that Italian culture was stultified by its cuisine, so he concocted new recipes which he felt would benefit his country's cultural ambition. These included an 'heroic winter dinner', an 'extremist banquet' and an 'improvised dinner'. The mechanized squeal of machines was music to Marinetti's ears, as he saw mechanization as a way to attack entrenched conservatism.

McHale 60–61, 63–5, 72, 77, 101

During the 1950s John McHale (1922–1978) was a member of London's influential Independent Group. McHale was interested in the influence of film, mass production, consumerism and the mass media, and how they contributed to the ongoing revision of humanity's mental

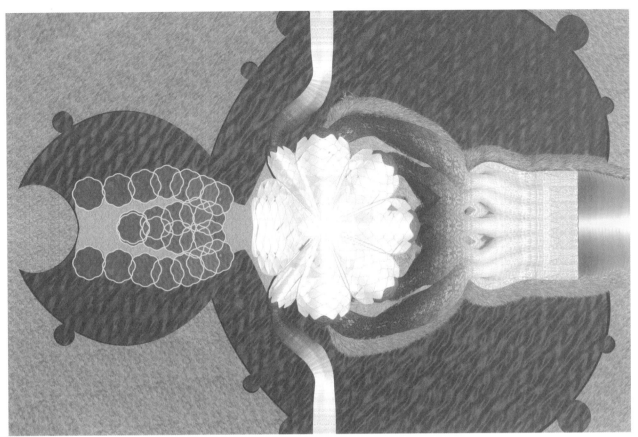

and physical state. Ultimately McHale was concerned with how we might accommodate such shifts architecturally and technologically. He was an artist, a demographer, a biographer and an architectural and urban futurologist, deeply influenced by Buckminster Fuller as well as cybernetics. McHale's work was always incisive, laterally inspired and technologically savvy.

Megastructure

Rayner Banham's influential book *Megastructure: Urban Futures of the Recent Past* (1976) gave a name to all manner of large, city-scale architectural systems that were developed during the 1960s. These included Constant's New Babylon, Archigram's Plug-in City, Yona Friedman's *urbanisme spatiale* and many more. Banham showed that these huge structures, so popular with the avant-garde of the time, could be traced back to work by Le Corbusier, to Basil Spence's Sea and Ships Pavillion at the 1951 Festival of Britain, to Pop

art and to the old London Bridge. Megastructure aimed to create a liberating urbanism conditioned by user choice, spatial hybridization and technological intelligence.

Metabolism

Metabolism, a subset of Megastructural ideas, was a peculiarly Japanese take on '60 s and '70s high-density urbanism. As Kenzo Tange put it, 'Everyday people come into the centre of the city, and then must return in the evening to their homes outside the city. For the average man the time required for this trip is an hour. In this [Metabolist] project the architect is thinking of the future of the city. He has divided it into two elements, one permanent and one temporary. The structural element is thought of as a tree – permanent element, with the dwelling unit as leaves – temporary elements which fall down and are renewed according to the needs of the moment. The buildings can grow within

this structure and die and grow again – but the structure remains.'

Mies van der Rohe 102, 130, 134

Ludwig Mies van der Rohe (1886–1969) was born in Aachen, Germany and spent his early years as an architect in the studio of Peter Behrens. His seminal projects included the Barcelona Pavilion (1929) and the Seagram Building in New York (1958). Mies coined the expression 'Less is more', which became an architectural litany during the second half of the twentieth century. Mies was one of the great so-called Modern masters along with Wright and Le Corbusier. He also established himself as a teacher at the Illinois Institute of Technology, Chicago. His architecture is characterized by walls and roofs that define space and create varying degrees of enclosure and scale. These spaces are often materially sumptuous but simply detailed and true to their materiality, which is expressed simply and carefully.

Morphosis 160–63, *246*

Morphosis was formed in the late 1970s by Thom Mayne (1944–) and Michael Rotondi (1949–), who became known during the Deconstructed '80s. Their work, characterized by their drawings more than their buildings, mixed scales of presentation: a detail might be artfully collaged with an elevation or an axonometric; elements always projected lengthy shadows. The practice was instrumental in consolidating the Deconstructivist approach by developing protocols of representation, form-making and the juxtaposition of disparate materials.

Muybridge 18, 26, 36, 61

Eadweard Muybridge (1830–1904) was one of the most important photographers and analysts of human and animal movement. Born in Kingston-upon-Thames in England, he moved to America in 1852. He later worked for the US War Department and was instrumental in recording large areas of the American West Coast on film. During 1872 one of his first attempts to capture animal locomotion was made in order to settle a bet on the exact position of a horse's legs and how they differed from trot to gallop. Muybridge developed a series of augmented cameras which gave him the ability to capture movement, amongst them the zoopraxiscope.

Negroponte 203, 206–7, 211

Nicholas Negroponte (1943–) is Wiesner Professor of Media Technology at the Massachusetts Institute of Technology and founding Chairman of MIT's Media Laboratory. Negroponte has served as Chairman of Media Lab Europe, the Lab's sister institution in Ireland. He studied at MIT and has been a faculty member since 1966; he also founded MIT's pioneering Architecture Machine Group, a combination lab and think-tank responsible for radically new approaches to the human/computer interface. In 1995 he published the *New York Times* bestseller *Being Digital*, which has been translated into over forty languages. He is a founder of and writer for *Wired* magazine.

Nicholson 108–9, 111, *112–13*, 119, 120–22, *123*, 152, 185, *247*

Ben Nicholson (1954–) is one of the truly extraordinary architects of his time. His work is beautifully presented, artfully constructed and intellectually fecund. Nicholson's formative years were spent as a student of Daniel Libeskind at Cranbrook. His work is not rooted in a sophistic understanding of history, as is true of many contemporary architects; rather it is embedded in architecture's symbolic geometries. Whilst this historical knowledge is always present, Nicholson is a great observer of contemporary society. His design activities are often concerned with the everyday and the domestic in a consumer economy, and his output can be a polemic against this invisible Spectacle.

Novak 50–51, *52–3*, 203–4, 211–12, 215–16, *219–21, 234, 247–8*

Marcos Novak is a 'transarchitect', artist and theorist investigating the emerging tectonics of technologically augmented space, and a leading proponent of virtual environments as autonomous and fully architectural spaces. Currently a Professor at the University of California, Santa Barbara, Novak has developed what he calls an 'everted' architecture, a small series of projects which cast the virtual onto the actual and vice versa. He has written extensively on the relationship between fluid digital spaces, music, sculpture and architectural theory.

Paolozzi 59, 60–61

Eduardo Paolozzi (1924–2005) was the son of Scottish and Italian parents. An important member of the Independent Group and involved in its subsequent instigation of Pop art, he was interested in making collages from contemporary catalogues and

magazines in the 1950s. These works had a contemporary mosaic aesthetic of machines, blocks of colour, metal and piping. Paolozzi was domiciled from 1947 until 1950 in Paris, where he was influenced by the work of Klee and Giacometti.

Pask 49, 50, 53, 203, 205–6, 208

Gordon Pask (1928–1996) was an extraordinary man, a cybernetician par excellence. Pask's major contribution to cybernetics was Conversation Theory. As his obituary in the *Guardian* described it, 'When Pask built his machines and his theory, his philosophical view was at odds with artificial intelligence, which arose from the seeds of cybernetics but presumes that knowledge is a commodity to pluck from the environment and stick in a cubbyhole. Pask's learning environments, whether for entertainment or touch-typing or statistics, viewed the human as part of a resonance that looped from the human, through the environment or apparatus, back through the human and around again.'

'Pataphysics 23, 25, 27, 155, 216, 219, 224

In the words of its inventor, Alfred Jarry, "Pataphysics will be, above all, the science of the particular, despite the common opinion that the only science is that of the general. 'Pataphysics will examine the laws governing exceptions, and will explain the universe supplementary to this one; or, less ambitiously, will describe a universe which can be – and perhaps should be – envisaged in the place of the traditional one, since the laws that are supposed to have been discovered in the traditional universe are also correlations of exceptions, albeit more frequent ones, but in any case accidental data which, reduced to the status of unexceptional exceptions, possess no longer even the virtue of originality.'

Piranesi 7, 10–13, 44, 125, 169, 170, *248*

Giovanni Battista Piranesi (1720–1778) was an Italian graphic artist famous for his engravings and etchings. He created more than two thousand prints

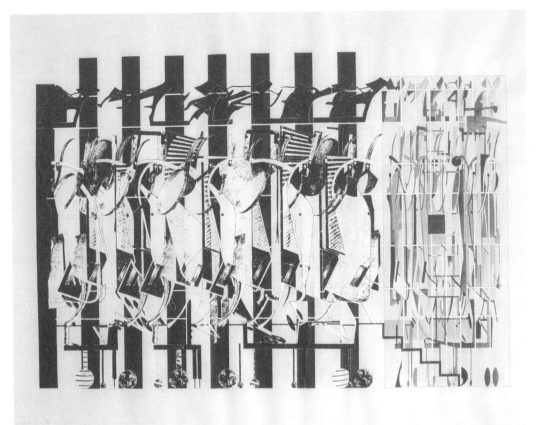

The work has been exhibited in Coimbra, Munich and London, and a copy of Puttick's book *The Land of Scattered Seeds* was purchased by the Museum of Modern Art, New York.

Jesse Reiser (1958–) and his partner Nanako Umemoto (1959–) are New York-based architects. Reiser's architectural education included a stint at Cranbrook Academy under Daniel Libeskind during the 1980s. The partners' early work concentrated on finding new contextual relationships with 'site'. Later their work began to focus on the potential of geodesic structures. The geodesics of Buckminster Fuller, with their often Platonic geometry, do not inhabit the same world as Reiser and Umemoto's, whose conceptualization allows for an open-ended play of function, context and structure. Their architecture shifts and turns, cossets and cushions.

Peter Reyner Banham (1922–1988) was Professor of History of Architecture at University College London and, later, Professor of History and Theory of Architecture at the State University of New York at Buffalo. Still later he moved to the University of California, Santa Cruz. He was a convenor of the Independent Group,

436
Liquid Architecture Cyberspatial Structure
Marcos Novak, 1991

437
Exterior view from *Carceri*
Giovanni Battista Piranesi, 1761

of real and imaginary buildings, statues and ornaments. His enthusiastic renderings of ancient Roman monuments include accurate portrayals of existing ruins as well as imaginary reconstructions of buildings in which alterations of scale and juxtaposition of elements enhanced a sense of grandeur. Piranesi is chiefly remembered for his *Carceri*, etchings which depict the imaginary interiors of prisons. His work was highly influential on the twentieth-century avant-garde.

Cedric Price (1934–2003) was born in Staffordshire, England. He studied architecture at Cambridge from 1952 until 1955, becoming President of the Cambridge University Society of Arts in 1954 and then attending the Architectural Association from 1955 to 1957. Price worked for Fry, Drew and Partners as well as on exhibition projects with Erno Goldfinger before setting up Cedric Price Architects. He was life President of the Hot Stuff Club. Price's philosophy of design was one of calculated uncertainty, of enabling and of the accommodation of changes in spatial priorities over time.

John Puttick (1976–) studied architecture at the University of Nottingham and the Bartlett. His diploma project was awarded a commendation in the RIBA Silver Medal student award. He worked at Acumen, a design studio in Houston, Texas and for David Chipperfield Architects in London, and is currently working at Make Architects. His work is concerned with the weaving of contemporary stories through narrative, structure and space. The tales and drawings present complex, self-contained realities that reflect our own. Social, economic and ecological relationships are examined in miniature.

confidant of Archigram and many of their contemporaries, and theoretical apologist for a whole generation of visionary architects in the 1960s. Reyner Banham was an inspiring and insightful architectural critic, polemicist and thinker.

Rhowbotham 119, 130, *131–3, 250*

Kevin Rhowbotham (1953–) was formerly Visiting Professor of Urbanism at the Technical University, Berlin; Distinguished Professor of Architectural Design at the University of Illinois at Chicago; and Unit Master at the Bartlett and at the Architectural Association, London. He was a founder-member of Fashion Architecture Taste, Alphaville, Big Open Box and the Field Organization, and has instigated and organized over forty exhibitions in the UK, Europe and the US. Rhowbotham has practised architecture since 1982, privately since 1992, and has published three books and numerous articles in a variety of journals.

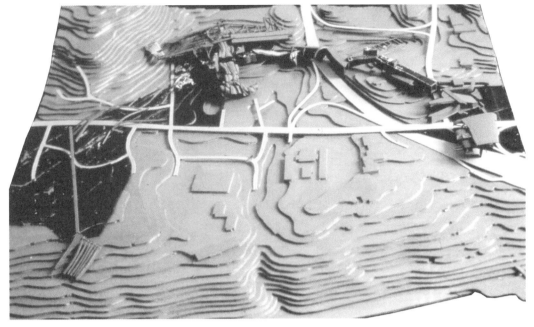

Robbins 178–81

Felix Robbins (1971–) studied architectural design at the University of Edinburgh and the Bartlett in London. For several years he has worked on and researched methods

of advanced digital design which seek to incorporate an intensive poetic and mathematical language into a depth of architectural manifestation and formation. Robbins has worked for the design studios of dECOi in Paris and oceanD in London.

Roussel 10, 25, 27, 36, 76, 152

Raymond Roussel (1877–1933) was born in Padua. He developed a way of writing that allowed him to create highly descriptive yet precise prose which could describe the most extraordinary scenarios. He is mostly known for his novels *Impressions d'Afrique* (1910) and *Locus Solus* (1914). Roussel's novels often include yearning machines which are hybrid mechanical/organic systems. It is said that his work influenced Duchamp and inspired the construction of the *Large Glass*. Like Lautréamont, Roussel was a core reference for Breton and the Surrealists.

Salter 183, 185, 192–3, *194*, 195, *250–51*

Peter Salter was greatly influenced by the Smithsons' way of brutally expressing the materiality of architectural elements. This combined with a particular type of structural

438 (above)
Master plan for Croton Aqueduct
RAA Um, 1993

439 (left)
Hermann the birdman, from The Land of Scattered Seeds
John Puttick, 2002

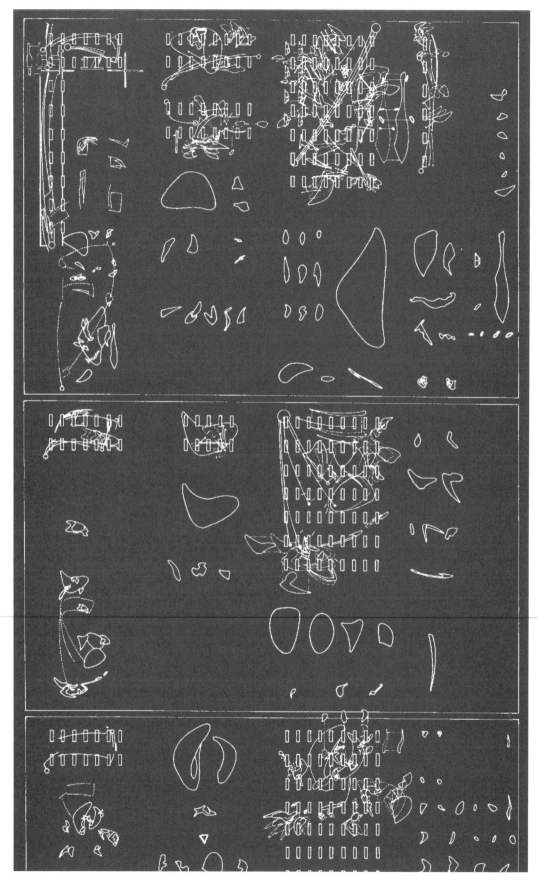

expressionism has resulted in his immediately recognizable architectural language. Salter taught for many years in the Architectural Association's Intermediate and Diploma schools. His unbuilt work is characterized by an obsessive attention to detail; every flange, weld and bolt is drawn, celebrated and considered. His projects have a natural, sensitive feeling to them; they are almost magical yet very hard-edged, substantial and tactile.

Sant'Elia 27, 28–29, 211

The Italian architect Antonio Sant' Elia (1888–1916), associated with the movement known as Futurism, wrote the movement's architecture manifesto. He created visionary drawings of buildings, often transport interchanges which he likened to gigantic machines. His projects for these nodes seemed almost Gothic with their mechanized finials and lattice columns. Sant' Elia died on a First World War battlefield. In the 1970s Reyner Banham rehabilitated his reputation and cited him as an influence on 1960s avant-garde groups such as Archigram.

Schein 73, 74

Ionel Schein (1927–) designed the first all-plastic house in 1956. An alumnus of Bucharest University, he graduated in 1948. Schein worked in Le Corbusier's office for six months in 1953. Schein's view of architectural practice was overtly multidisciplinary, and his office had members of many disparate disciplines. In London his plastic houses were an inspiration for the Smithsons and various members of Archigram. Schein helped to design the architectural zeitgeist of the Pop art-fuelled '50s and '60s; his presence is even now felt in the more speculative architectural schools.

Schwitters 120–22, 152

Kurt Schwitters (1887–1948) loved the Dadaists' love of nonsense. His own contribution to Dada was called 'Merz'. On the face of it Merz was just about collecting rubbish. These art pieces could take the form of collages, reliefs or room-sized installations. Schwitters collected discarded material from all manner of uses and pieced it together to create unlikely juxtapositions, postcards of the reality that exists beneath perceived reality. This surreal underpinning of reality was Schwitters's playground.

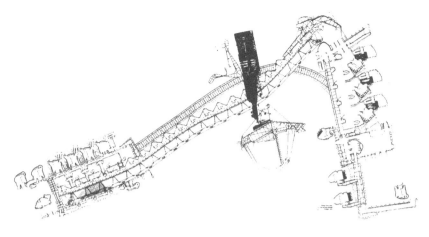

Situationism 13, 14, 17, 41, 44–5, 48, 50–51, 53, 125, 127, 129–30, 204

The Situationists formed themselves from a group of avant-garde artists and intellectuals influenced by Dada, Surrealism and Lettrism. The Situationists were concerned with the unleashing of society's collective imagination as well as its individual perspectives. They developed tactics to subvert space and art. Their chief orator and writer was Guy Debord, whose *Society of the Spectacle* was a major influence on architects who sought to destabilize the politically legislated production of space and its subsequent protection. The '60s group Superstudio shared much of the Situationists' politics and spatial practice. The artist Constant produced the group's most coherent architectural work.

Smithsons 59, 61–2, 72, 102, 143, 192

Alison (1928–1993) and Peter (1923–2003) Smithson were members of the Independent Group and Team 10, equally well known for the theoretical formulation of New Brutalism and for their built work, which includes the Economist Building in London. They were hugely important both as teachers of architecture and as designers of buildings, influencing Archigram's members as well as more recent architects.

Soane 13

Sir John Soane (1753–1837) was a highly original architect who developed an extremely personal style that was at once Neo-Classical and intensely romantic. Soane was influenced by Piranesi and Ledoux, and his work is seen at its most esoteric in his own house, 13 Lincolns Inn Fields, in London (1812–13). The house, planned as a memory theatre with mirrors and top-lighting, is stylistically eclectic but succeeds in being living space, store of inspirations and autobiographical essay all at the same time. Soane was knighted in 1831. His largest works were done as Surveyor to the Bank of England beginning in 1788.

Spiller 30, 202, 216, 222–5, 252

Neil Spiller (1961–) formed Spiller Farmer Architects in 1986, becoming Neil Spiller Architects from 1993. His work is often characterized by an interest in the conjoining of advanced technology (cyberspace, augmented reality, nanotechnology) with arcane, often forgotten notions such as 'Pataphysics, alchemy, Surrealism and cybernetics. This creates architectures that escape the simple categories of Modernism and posit more reflexive ideas of space. Spiller is Professor of Architecture and Digital Theory at the Bartlett School of Architecture, University College London.

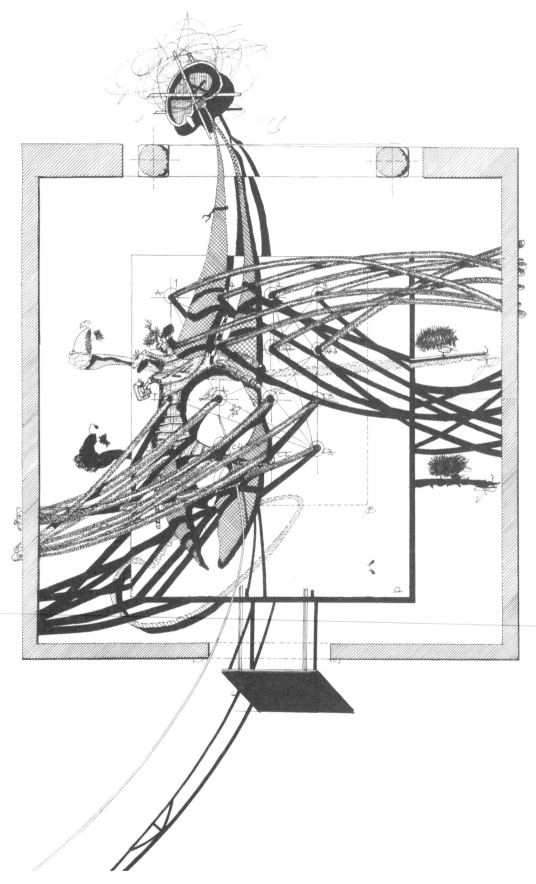

Spuybroek 54–7, 216, *253*

Lars Spuybroek (1959–) is the principal of NOX, an architecture office in Rotterdam. Since the early 1990s he has been involved in researching the relationship between architecture and media, often more specifically between architecture and computing. He was the editor-publisher of one of the first magazines in a book format (*NOX*, and later also *Forum*) and made video and interactive electronic artworks, in the last five years focusing more on architecture. Spuybroek's work has won several prizes and has been exhibited all over the world, including presentations at the Venice Biennale in 2000 and 2002.

Superstudio 71, 85–7, *89–90*, 184–5, *253–4*

The Italian radical group Superstudio and their frequent co-conspirators Archizoom were formed between two exhibitions during the winter of 1966–7. Superstudio included Adolfo Natalini (1941–), Cristiano Toraldo di Francia (1941–), Piero Frassinelli (1939–), Roberto Magris (1935–) and Alessandro Magris (1941–). The group is known mostly for its series of polemical collage projects for the Continuous Monument. Their work encompassed many scales from furniture to city. Latterly some of the group became interested in the relationship between humankind, its simple tools and transmutation of the land. This the groups' members perceived as the fundamental act of architecture.

Suprematism 34, 94, 133, 148

Suprematism, a version of Cubism, was invented by Kasimir Malevich, who conceived of it as a pure act of painterly geometry. The style consisted of planes of colour juxtaposed with other coloured shapes, figure and ground being of equal importance. The resonance between form and void, between colour and non-colour, all had the same aesthetic significance. Suprematicism is often cited as one of the main influences on the work of Zaha Hadid.

Surrealism 10, 13, 25, 29, 43–4, 60, 77, 108, 120, 125, 127, 204, 219

Surrealism, as described by André Breton, was 'Psychic automatism in its pure state, by which one proposes to express – verbally, by means of the written word, or in any other manner – the actual function of thought. Dictated by thought, in the absence of any control exercised by reason, exempt from any aesthetic or moral concern, Surrealism is based on the belief in the superior reality of certain forms of previously neglected associations, in the omnipotence of dream, in the disinterested play of thought'.

Tatlin 34, 152–3

Vladimir Tatlin (1885–1953) first became noticed when he contributed to exhibitions between 1911 and

1913. In 1913 he radically changed his views on art after a journey to Paris during which he saw some of Picasso's Cubist reliefs. By 1918 he was head of the Visual Arts Department of Narkompros. In 1920 Tatlin created his best-known work, *Monument to the Third International*. His last work was the Letatlin flying machine, an object that he believed was the most dynamic and utilitarian of its time.

Tschumi 10, *11*, 119, 125–6, 139–41, 143, 145, 157–9, 185, 212

Bernard Tschumi's (1944–) first constructed work, the Parc de La Villette complex in Paris, showed him to be a pioneer of '80s Deconstruction; its layering of formal systems and the iconography of the red *folie*-points grid are instantly recognizable. Before this,

however, Tshumi had been an Architectural Association Unit Master and had produced the polemical project *The Manhattan Transcripts*, which concerned itself with how event, narrative and time-line in film theory might posit an architecture of movement in which 'programme' lost its prestige to the vicissitudes of 'event'. Tschumi was Dean of the Architecture Faculty of Columbia University in New York until 2003.

Webb 43, 72–5, 83–4, 111, 165, 175–8, *258–9*

As a member of Archigram, Michael Webb (1937–) produced some of their most technically considered and visionary architecture. A very talented draughtsman, Webb uses this skill to seduce the viewer into his world of

443 (opposite)
Plan, Genetic Gazebo drawing, Communicating Vessels
Neil Spiller, 2005

444 (above)
Continuous Monument
Superstudio, 1969

445 (left)
World Trade Centre Competition
Lars Spuybroek/ NOX, 2003

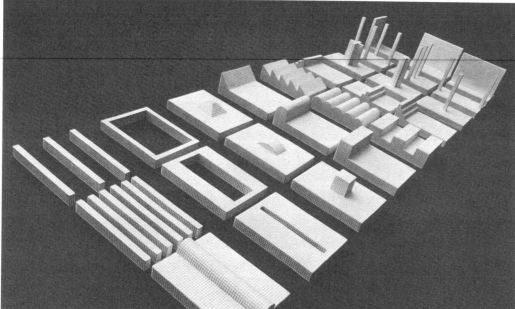

gliding cars/suits/submersibles, car-park fun palaces and watery memory theatres. This he always does with a deep sense of Englishness. He is not a great self-promoter, and therefore his work, particularly since Archigram, is little known except by grateful cognoscenti, who are very influenced by it. Much of it has been concerned with the house in motion and the vehicle as home.

Wigley 140, 148
Since 2004 Mark Wigley has been Dean of the Architecture School of Columbia University in New York. He has served as guest curator for widely attended exhibitions at the Museum of Modern Art; The Drawing Center, New York; the Canadian Centre for

Architecture, Montreal; and the Witte de With Museum, Rotterdam. Webb is an accomplished scholar and design teacher, having written extensively on the theory and practice of architecture, and is the author of several books, including *Constant's New Babylon* (1998) and *The Architecture of Deconstruction* (1993). In 1990 he received the International Committee of Architectural Critics' Triennial Award for Architectural Criticism.

Wilson and Bolles-Wilson *182*, 183, 185, 187–92, *193*, *255–6*

Peter Wilson (1950–) was born in Melbourne, Australia. In 1972 he began to study architecture at the Architectural Association, London, graduating two years later with honours and the Diploma Prize. From 1974 to 1975 he was assistant to Elia Zenghelis and Rem Koolhaas; he subsequently became an Intermediate Unit Master and a Diploma Unit Master. From 1994 until 1996 Wilson was a guest professor at the Kunsthochschule Weißensee/Berlin. In 1980 he formed Bolles+Wilson with Julia Bolles–Wilson (1948–). Since then all projects have been jointly authored. Bolles-Wilson was a student of Koolhaas and Zenghelis at the AA, graduating in 1979. She is currently Professor of Architectural Design at the University of Applied Science, Münster.

Woods 13, *16*, *109*, 110–11, *164*, 165, 169–75, 178, 211, *257*

Lebbeus Woods (1940–) was born in Michigan. He was trained as an engineer as well as an architect. In 1964 he left university to work for a succession of well-known practices including Eero Saarinen and Associates. Since 1976 he has lived largely in New York and has created a body of visionary architectural work that has been hugely inspirational to generations of students. Woods's work has the illustrative power of Piranesi and the free-thinking aspirations of Constant. His architecture is humanitarian in a way that forsakes neither the scientific nor the aesthetic.

446 (opposite top)
***Architettura Ripflessa*, Golden Gate Bridge**
Superstudio, San Francisco, 1971

447 (opposite bottom)
Istogrammi
Superstudio, 1969

448 (below)
Perspective of Pont des Arts
Peter Wilson, 1983

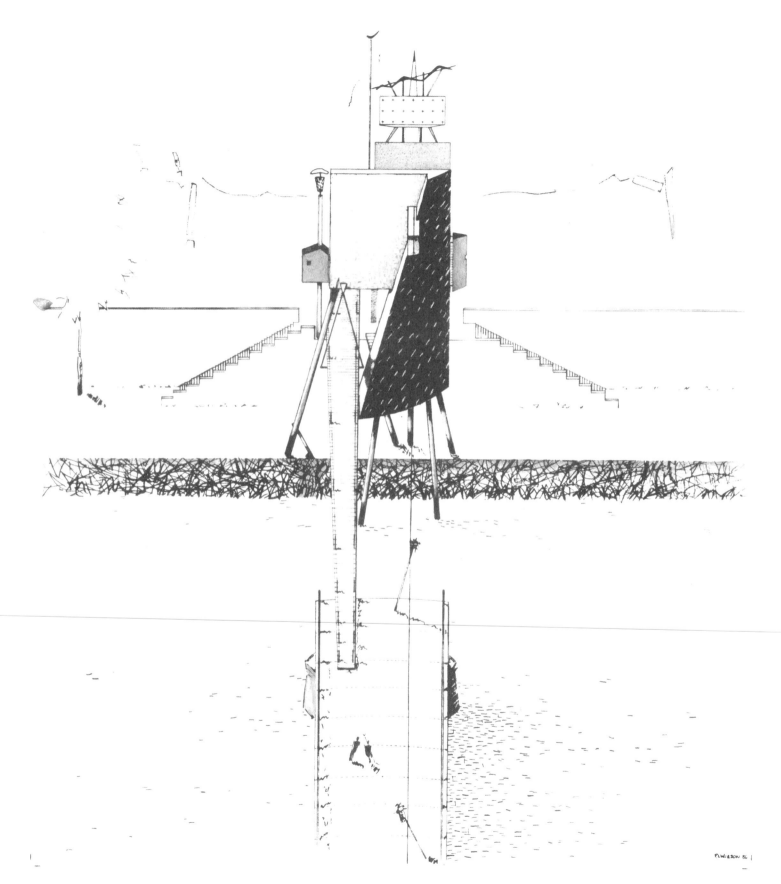

Wright 100–101, 112, 130

Frank Lloyd Wright (1869–1959) is thought by many to be the greatest architect America has produced to date. Wright first worked for Louis Sullivan. He developed house designs that seemed to be of the landscape; they were low and welcomed the outdoors inside. From 1937 to 1939 he designed Falling Water, a house of horizonal slabs which cantilever over a waterfall. Wright produced many iconic works during his long life, his designs becoming more otherworldly as he got older. He inspired many architects who came after him, particularly Bruce Goff.

449
Pont des Arts
Peter Wilson, 1983

450
City of Air
Lebbeus Woods, 1984

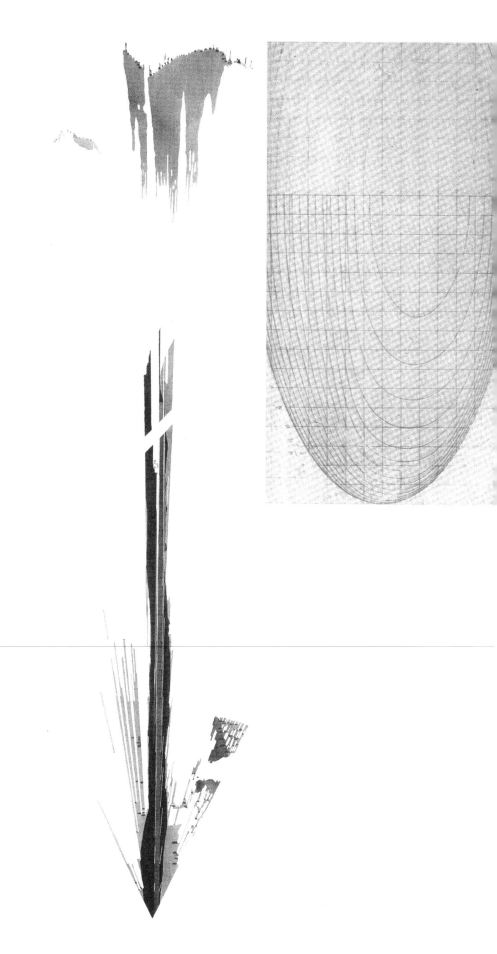

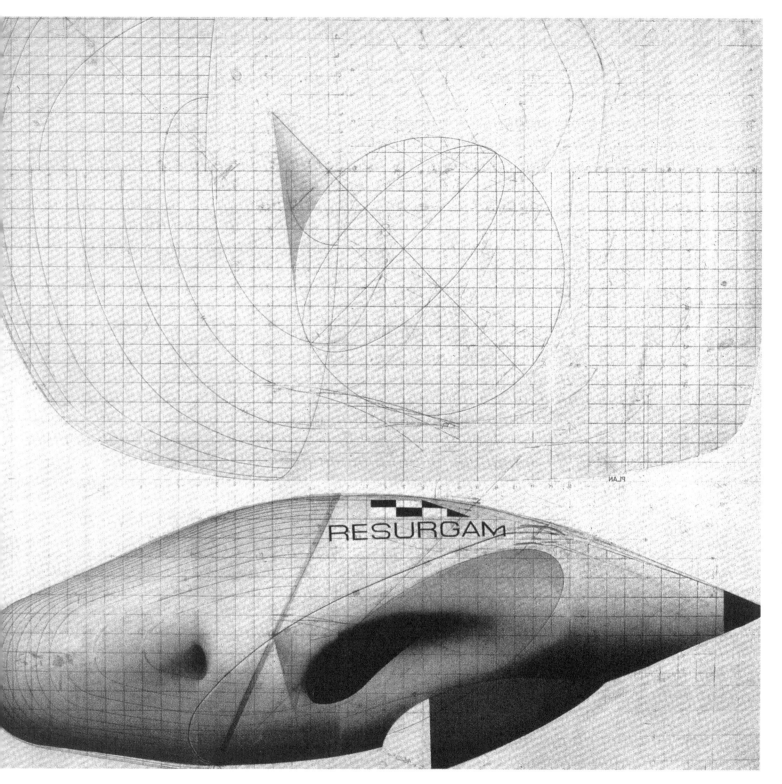

RESURGAM

451 (opposite)
**Parallox Temple
Island, Space Bleed**
Michael Webb, 1980s

452 (above)
**Temple Island
Resurgam**
Michael Webb, 1980–

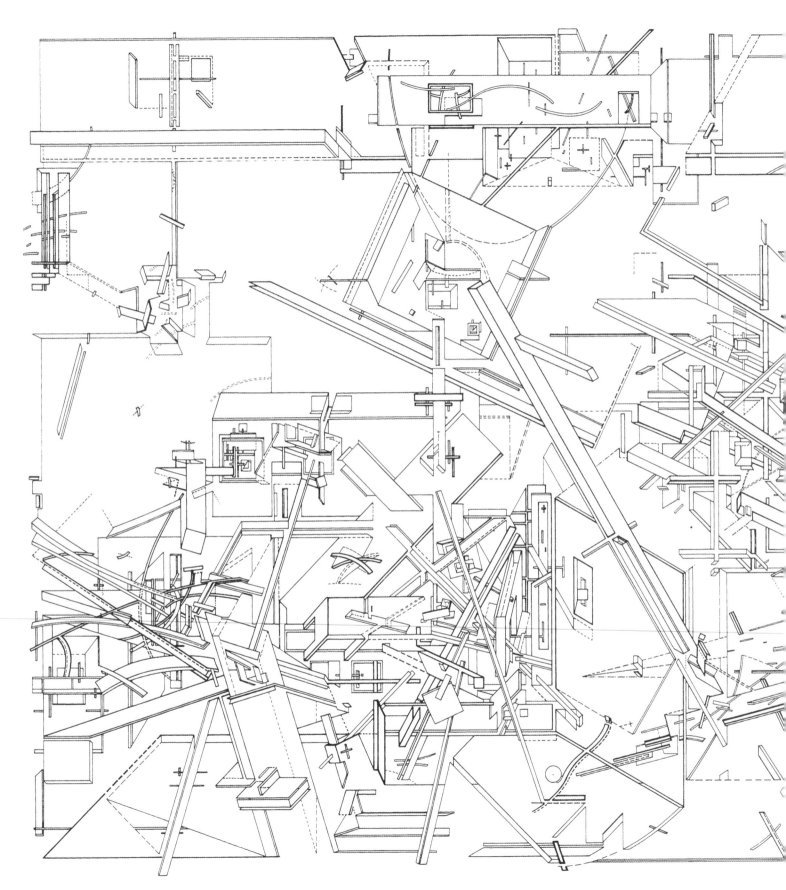

Indexical Glossary

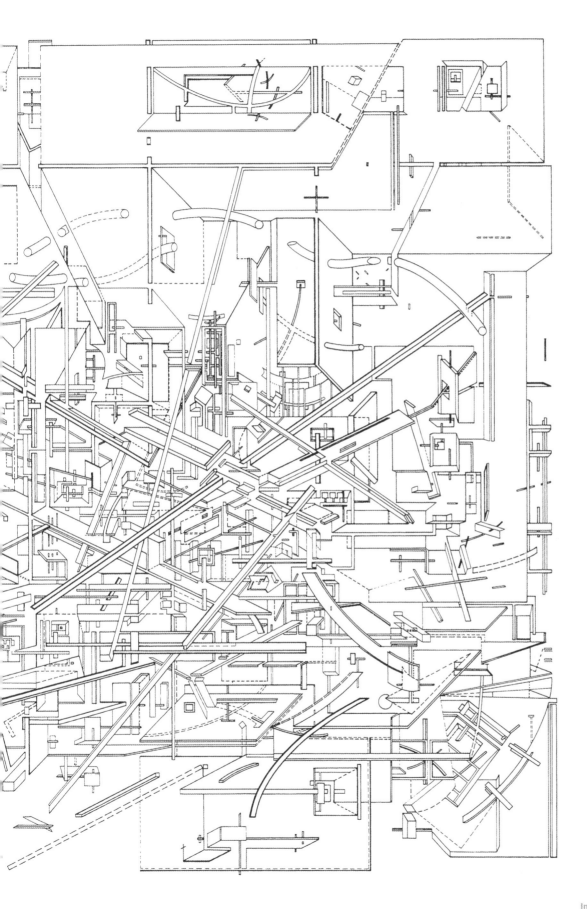

References

Arcadia, Alchemy, Antiquity and Machines

1. Francesco Colonna, *Hypnerotomachia Poliphili*, trans. Joscelyn Godwin (London: Thames & Hudson, 1999), p. x.
2. Robert Harbison, *Eccentric Spaces* (New York: Alfred A. Knopf, 1977), p. 78.
3. Frances A. Yates, *The Art of Memory* (Chicago: Chicago University Press, 1966), p. 123.
4. Colonna (note 1), p. 292.
5. *Ibid.*, p. 116.
6. Peter Reyner Banham, 'A Home is Not a House', *Art in America* (April 1965).
7. Colonna (note 1), p. 14.
8. John Wilton-Ely, *Piranesi as Architect and Designer* (New Haven: Yale University Press, 1993), p. 4.
9. Colonna (note 1), p. 1.
10. Harbison (note 2), p. 83.
11. Anthony Vidler, *The Writing on the Walls* (New York: Princeton Architectural Press, 1987). A wider discussion of the context of Ledoux's work is featured in this book.
12. Jules Assezat and Maurice Tourneux, eds, *Oeuvres complètes de Diderot* (Paris: Garnier, 1873), vol. XIII, p. 369.
13. *Ibid.*
14. Guy Debord, 'De l'architecture sauvage', introduction to Asger Jørn, *Le Jardin d'Albisola* (Turin: Posso, 1974).
15. Colonna (note 1), p. 311.
16. Yates (note 3), pp. 224–5.
17. 'Nat Chard, Architecture of Our Interior', in Neil Spiller, ed., *AD Integrating Architecture* (London: Academy, 1996), p. 79.
18. *Ibid.*, p. 77.
19. *Ibid.*, p. 81.

Absurd Speeding Objects and the Cabaret of Science and Dreams

1. Roger Shattuck, *The Banquet Years: The Origins of the Avant-garde in France 1885 to World War I* (London: Vintage, 1955), p. 30.
2. *Ibid.*, p. 33.
3. *Ibid.*, p. 302.
4. *Ibid.*, p. 208.
5. Alfred Jarry, *Exploits and Opinions of Doctor Faustroll, 'Pataphysician: A Scientific Novel*, trans. Simon Watson Taylor (London: Grove Press, 1965), p. 6.
6. Michel Carrouges, in *Le Macchine célibi*, ed. Harald Szeeman (New York: Rizzoli, 1975), p. 31.
7. Comte de Lautréamont, *Chants de Maldoror*, Chant VI, in *Oeuvres complètes* (Paris, Gallimard, 1970).
8. Carrouges (note 6), p. 31.
9. F. T. Marinetti, 'The Founding and Manifesto of Futurism 1909', in Umbro Apollonio, *The Documents of 20th Century Art: Futurist Manifestos* (New York: Viking, 1973), p. 21.
10. *Ibid.*
11. Anton Giulio Bragaglia, 'Futurist Photodynamism 1911', in Apollonio (note 9), p. 40.
12. Bruno Corradini and Emilio Settemelli, 'Weights and Measures and Prices of Artistic Genius – Futurist Manifesto 1914', in Apollonio (note 9), p. 135.
13. Antonio Sant'Elia, 'Manifesto of Futurist Architecture 1914', in Apollonio (note 9), p.1608.
14. *Ibid.*
15. Valentine de Saint-Point, 'Futurist Manifesto of Lust 1913', in Apollonio (note 9), pp. 73–4.
16. Carrouges (note 6), p. 24.
17. *Ibid.*
18. Shattuck (note 1), p. 283.
19. Salvador Dalí, 'Concerning the Terrifying and Edible Beauty of Art Nouveau Architecture', in *Collected Writings of Salvador Dali*, ed. and trans. Haim Finkelstein (Cambridge: Cambridge University Press, 1998), p.195.
20. D'Arcy Wentworth Thompson, *On Growth and Form* (Cambridge: Cambridge University Press, 1917).
21. Mark Burry, 'Gaudi, Teratology and Kinship', in Stephen Perrella, ed., *AD Hypersurface Architecture* (London: Academy,), p. 40.
22. *Ibid.*
23. Dalí (note 19), p. 200.
24. Stephen Bann, ed., *The Tradition of Constructivism* (Milan: Da Capo, 1974), pp.13–14.
25. *Ibid.*, pp. 8–9.
26. *Ibid.*, p.157. I am indebted to Peter Watson's *A Terrible Beauty* (London: Phoenix Press, 2000) for providing some of the chronology for the beginning of the twentieth century.
27. Georges Teyssot, 'The Mutant Body of Architecture', in Diller and Scofidio, *Flesh* (New York: Princeton Architectural Press, 1994), p. 8.
28. Diller and Scofidio, 'The Rotary Notary and His Hot Plate', *AA Files No. 14* (London: AA Publications, 1987), p. 54.
29. Diller and Scofidio, 'The Bridge', *AA Files No. 14* (note 28), p. 60.
30. *Ibid.*
31. *Ibid.*
32. Diller and Scofidio, 'The American Mysteries', *AA Files No. 14* (note 28), p. 58.

The Politics and Cybernetics of Freedom

1. Frederick Kiesler, 'Manifesto of Tensionism: Organic Building The City in Space Functional Architecture', De Stijl (1925).
2. Frederick Kiesler, 'Notes on Architecture as Sculpture', *Art in America* (May 1966).
3. Guy Debord, 'Report on the Construction of Situations', quoted in Mark Wigley, *Constant's New Babylon: The Hyper-Architecture of Desire* (Rotterdam: Witte de With, 010 Publishers, 1998), p. 29.
4. Wigley (note 3), p.14.
5. Constant, 'The Great Game to Come', *Potlatch*, 15 July 1959.
6. *Ibid.*
7. Constant, 'Another City for Another Life', in Wigley (note 3), p. 115.
8. Constant, 'Unitary Urbanism', quoted in Wigley (note 3), p. 131.
9. *Ibid.*
10. Constant, 'New Babylon: Outline of a Culture', quoted in Wigley (note 3), p.160.
11. Wigley (note 3), p. 65.

12. Gordon Pask, 'Theatre Workshop and System Research: Proposal for a Cybernetic Theatre, Price Archive, Canadian Centre for Architecture', quoted by Mary Louise Lobsinger, in 'Cybernetic Theory and the Architecture of Performance: Cedric Price's Fun Palace', in *Anxious Modernisms* (Cambridge, MA: MIT Press, 1991), p. 130.
13. Marcos Novak, 'Next Babylon, Soft Babylon: (trans)Architecture is an Algorithm to play in', in Neil Spiller, ed., *Architects in Cyberspace II: Architectural Design*, 68/11–12 (1998), p. 21.
14. *Ibid.*, p. 23.
15. *Ibid.*
16. Guy Debord, *The Society of the Spectacle*, trans. Donald Nicholson-Smith (New York: Zone Books, 1994; first published in French 1967), Point 179, pp.126–7.
17. *Ibid.*, Point 158, p. 114.
18. *Ibid.*, Point 171, p. 121.
19. *Ibid.*, Point 120, p. 88.
20. Lars Spuybroek, 'Motor Geometry', in Stephen Perrella, ed., *AD Hypersurface Architecture* (London: Academy, 1998), p. 51.
21. *Ibid.*

Iconography Goes POP

1. Richard Hamilton, 'Growth and Form proposal document', quoted in Victoria Walsh, *Nigel Henderson: Parallel of Life and Art* (London: Thames & Hudson, 2001), p. 27.
2. Ron Herron, Interview, 10 January 1983, quoted in David Robbins, ed., *The Independent Group: Postwar Britain and the Aesthetics of Plenty* (Cambridge, MA, 1990), p. 25.
3. Alison and Peter Smithson, *The Charged Void: Architecture* (New York: Monacelli Press, 2002), p. 166.
4. *Ibid.*, p. 178.
5. Group Six, 'This is Tomorrow' exhibition catalogue, quoted in Walsh (note 1), p. 116.
6. Warren Chalk, 'Owing to a lack of interest tomorrow has been cancelled', *Architectural Design* (September

1969).
7. Reyner Banham, 'A Throw-away Aesthetic', in Penny Spark, *Reyner Banham: Design by Choice* (New York: Rizzoli, 1981), p. 90.
8. *Ibid.*
9. Lawrence Alloway, 'Notes on Abstract Art and the Mass Media, February 1960', quoted in David Robbins, *The Independent Group and the Aesthetics of Plenty* (Cambridge, MA: MIT Press, 1990), p. 168.
10. Lawrence Alloway, 'Personal Statement', *Ark*, 19 (Spring 1957), quoted in Robbins (note 9), p. 165.
11. Richard Hamilton, 'Letter to Alison and Peter Smithson', from 'Collected Words 1953–1982', quoted in Robbins (note 9), p. 182.
12. John McHale, *The Expendable Ikon: Works by John McHale*, exh. cat. (Albright-Knox Art Gallery, Buffalo, 1984), p. 10.
13. *Ibid.*, p 20.
14. *Ibid.*, p .21.
15. Lawrence Alloway, in *ibid.*, p. 31.
16. *Ibid.*, p. 32.
17. 'Asymptote', in Marie-Ange Brayer and Beatrice Simonot, *Archilab's: Future House* (London: Thames & Hudson, 2002), p. 68.

The Second Poverty of Heroic Structures and Arcadian Networks

1. Paolo Soleri, *The City in the Image of Man* (Cambridge, MA: MIT Press), 1970, p. 14.
2. *Archigram*, 1 (May 1961).
3. David Greene, in *ibid.*
4. *Ibid.*
5. *Living Arts*, no. 2 (June 1963), quoted in *Archigram* (New York: Princeton Architectural Press, 1999), p. 20.
6. *Ibid.*
7. Peter Cook, 'Editorial', *Archigram*, 3 (1963).
8. Peter Cook, 'Plug-in City', in *Archigram* (note 5), p. 36.
9. *Archigram* (note 5), p. 44.
10. David Greene, 'Living Pod', in *Archigram* (note 5), p. 52.
11. Peter Reyner Banham, 'A Home is Not a House', *Art in America* (April 1965).

12. Michael Webb, 'The Cushicle', *Archigram* (1966), p. 64.
13. *Ibid.*, p. 80.
14. Coop Himmelb(l)au, *Arthropods*, ed. Jim Burns (London: Studio Vista, 1973), p. 100.
15. Christiano Toraldo di Francia, 'Memories of Superstudio', in Peter Lang and William Menking, *Superstudio: Life without Objects* (Milan: Skira, 2003), p. 66.
16. Coop Himmelb(l)au (note 14), p.145.
17. Toraldo di Francia (note 15), p. 69.
18. *Archigram* (note 7), p. 78.
19. Peter Reyner Banham, *Megastructure: Urban Futures of the Recent Past* (London: Thames & Hudson, 1976), p. 160.
20. *Archigram* (note 7), p. 88.
21. Greene (note 10), p. 110.
22. *Ibid.*, p. 113.
23. Ron Herron, Warren Chalk, David Greene, in *Archigram* (note 7).
24. *Ibid.*
25. Webb (note 12), p. 129.
26. Christine Hawley, *Beyond Elegance*, unpublished essay (1995), pp. 8–11.
27. Peter Cook, in *Korean Architects*, 148 (1996), pp. 41–5.

A Gizmology of Visionary Housing

1. John McHale, in *Architectural Design* (March 1960), pp. 5–6.
2. *Ibid.*, p. 7.
3. Cedric Price, 'Towards a 24-hour Economic Living Toy', *Interior Design* (September 1967).
4. Peter Eisenman, 'The End of the Classical', *Perspecta*, 21 (1984).
5. Peter Cook, 'Beyond the Normal Limits of Twentieth Century Architecture', *AA Files*, no. 7 (September 1984).
6. Michael Sorkin, *Post Rock Propter Rock: A Short History of the Himmelblau Blaubox* (London: AA Publications, 1988), p. 8.
7. Ben Nicholson, 'A Method for Architecture', in 'Work of Cranbrook Studio 1981–1982', ed. Daniel Libeskind, *Parametro* (August-September 1983), p. 26.
8. *Ibid.*
9. Lebbeus Woods, *Radical Reconstruction*

(New York: Princeton Architectural Press, 1997), p. 18.

10. *Ibid.*, p. 21.

11. Alberto Perez-Gomez, *Polyphilo or the Dark Forest Revisited: An Erotic Epiphany of Architecture* (Cambridge, MA: MIT Press, 1992), p. 85.

12. Ben Nicholson, 'War and Peacefare at the Loaf House', in Neil Spiller, ed., *Integrating Architecture* (London: Academy, 1996), p. 39.

13. *Ibid.*, p. 41.

Transcripts for a New *Détournement*

1. Kurt Schwitters, quoted in John Elsner and Roger Cardinal, eds, *The Cultures of Collecting* (Cambridge, MA: Harvard University Press, 1994), p. 72.

2. Cherry Gilchrist, *Elements of Alchemy* (London: Element Books, 1991), p. 41.

3. Max Ernst, quoted in Patrick Walberg, *Surrealism* (Paris: Skira, 1962), p. 64.

4. Ben Nicholson, 'The Appliance House', in *The Idea of the City* (Cambridge, MA: MIT Press, 1991), p. 127.

5. Ben Nicholson, *The Appliance House* (Cambridge, MA: MIT Press, 1990) p. 17.

6. *Ibid.*, p. 16.

7. *Ibid.*, p. 35.

8. *Ibid.*, p. 37.

9. *Ibid.*, p. 39.

10. Bernard Tschumi, *Questions of Space: Text 5* (London: AA Publications, 1995), p. 17.

11. *Ibid.*, p. 21.

12. *Ibid.*, p. 88.

13. *Ibid.*, p. 26.

14. *Ibid.*, p. 35.

15. *Ibid.*, p. 53.

16. Bernard Tschumi, *Manhattan Transcripts: Theoretical Projects* (London: Academy, 1981), p. 8.

17. *Ibid.*

18. *Ibid.*, p. xxvi.

19. Nigel Coates, 'Street Signs', in John Thackera, ed., *Design after Modernism* (London: Thames & Hudson, 1988), p. 96.

20. *Ibid.*, p. 97.

21. *Ibid.*

22. *Ibid.*

23. *Ibid.*, p. 98.

24. *Ibid.*, p. 100.

25. *Ibid.*

26. Guy Debord, 'Detournement as Negation and Prelude', in Iwona Blazwick, ed., *An Endless Adventure … An Endless Passion … An Endless Banquet: A Situationist Scrapbook*, exh. cat., ICA, London (London and New York: Verso, 1989), p. 29.

27. *Ibid.*

28. Coates (note 19), p. 101.

29. Nigel Coates, *Gamma City Special Issue: Narrative Architecture Today* (London: AA Publications, 1985).

30. *Ibid.*

31. Kevin Rhowbotham, 'A Collection of Writings, 1985–94', in Martin Pearce and Maggie Toy, eds, *Educating Architects* (London: Academy, 1995), p. 96.

32. *Ibid.*

33. *Ibid.*, p. 97.

34. *Ibid.*, p. 98.

35. Kevin Rhowbotham, 'Aspects of a Prospective Pedagogical Economy – New Technologies, New Markets', in Neil Spiller, ed., *Architects in Cyberspace II : Architectural Design* (London: Academy, 1998), p. 74.

36. Kevin Rhowbotham, *Field Event /Field Space*, Serial Books: Architecture and Urbanism (London: Black Dog, 2001), p. 33.

37. Vilem Flusser, *The Shape of Things: A Philosophy of Design* (London: Reaktion Books, 1999), p. 103.

Walking in a Parkland of Ecstasy, Delirium and Disjuncture

1. Michael Sorkin, 'Post Rock Propter Rock: A Short Story of Coop Himmelblau', in *Blaubox* (London: AA Publications, 1988), p. 4.

2. Bernard Tschumi, 'La Case Vide', *AA Files*, no. 12 (1986), p. 66.

3. *Ibid.*

4. Bernard Tschumi, *La Case Vide La Villette 1985 Folio* (London: AA Publications, 1986), p. 25.

5. Anthony Vidler, 'The Body in Pain: The Body and Architecture in Post-Modern Culture', *AA Files*, no. 19 (1990), p. 8.

6. *OMA Rem Koolhaas Architecture 1970–1990* (New York: Princeton Architectural Press, 1991), p. 90.

7. Peter Wilson, 'OMA, The Park the Peak – Two International Competitions', *AA Files*, no. 4 (1983), p. 79.

8. Cedric Price, *Works II* (London: AA Publications, 1984), p. 69.

9. 'Zaha Hadid, Parc de la Villette 1982–3', in *GA Architect* (1990), p. 58.

10. Mark Wigley, in Philip Johnson and Mark Wigley, *Deconstructivist Architecture*, exh. cat. (Museum of Modern Art, New York, 1988), p.11.

11. Kenneth Frampton, 'A Kufic Suprematist: The World Culture of Zaha Hadid', *AA Files*, no. 6 (1984), p. 101.

12. Peter Cook, in *RIBA Journal* (Jan. 1980).

13. Christine Hawley, 'Peter Cook, 21 Years – 21 Ideas', *Folio VI* (London: AA Publications, 1985), p. 11.

14. Daniel Libeskind, *Between Zero and Infinity* (New York: Rizzoli, 1982).

15. *Ibid.*, p. 29.

16. *Ibid.*, p. 27.

17. Daniel Libeskind, *Theatrum Mundi: Through the Green Membranes of Space* (London: AA Publications, 1985), back page.

18. Daniel Libeskind, *The Space of Encounter* (London: Thames & Hudson, 2001), p.180.

19. *Ibid.*, p. 181.

20. Wigley, in Johnson and Wigley (note 10), p. 34.

21. Jiri Kolar, *The End of Words: Selected Works 1947–1970*, exh. cat., ICA, London (1990), p. 68.

22. Peter Eisenman, 'Choral Works: Parc de la Villette 1986–7', *A+U* (August 1988), p. 136.

23. Peter Eisenman, 'Moving Arrows, Eros and Other Errors – An Architecture of Absence', *AA Folio* (1986), p. 5.

24. *Ibid.*, p. 6.

25. Daniel Libeskind, 'Between the Lines', in Libeskind (note 18), p.28.

26. *Ibid.*, p. 26.

27. *Ibid.*, p. 28.

28. 'Morphosis, Comprehensive Cancer Centre', in Andreas Papadakis, *Deconstruction II* (London: Academy, 1989), p. 89.

29. 'Morphosis, Kate Mantilini Restaurant: Santa Monica', in *Papadakis* (note 30), p. 93.

War and Relativity in the Age of Memorial Mechanics

1. Alberto Perez-Gomez, *Polyphilo or the Dark Forest Revisted : An Erotic Epiphany of Architecture* (Cambridge, MA: MIT Press, 1994), p. 284.
2. Raoul Bunschoten, 'oTOTEMan, or he is my relative', *AA Files*, no. 13 (1986), p. 73.
3. John Hejduk, *Victims* (London: AA Publications, 1986), n.p.
4. Elias Canetti, *The Conscience of Words & Earwitness* (London: Picador, 1987), p. 177.
5. *Ibid.*, p. 185.
6. John Hejduk, *Pewter Wings, Golden Horns, Stone Veils* (New York: Monacelli Press, 1997), p. 12.
7. *Ibid.*, p. 23.
8. Lebbeus Woods, *Origins* (London: AA Publications, 1985), p. 55.
9. Peter Cook, 'Lebbeus Woods – The Craggy Optimist', in *ibid.*, p. 4.
10. Woods (note 8), p. 10.
11. *Ibid.*, p. 19.
12. *Ibid.*, p. 48.
13. Lebbeus Woods, *One Five Four* (New York: Princeton Architectural Press, 1992), p. 6.
14. *Ibid.*, p. 7.
15. *Ibid.*, p. 10.
16. Lebbeus Woods, *Radical Reconstruction* (New York: Princeton Architectural Press, 1997), p. 18.
17. *Ibid.*, p. 20.
18. *Ibid.*, p. 21.
19. *Ibid.*
20. *Ibid.*
21. *Ibid.*, p. 22.
22. *Ibid.*, p. 21.
23. *Ibid.*, p. 22.
24. Michael Webb, *Temple Island: A Study by Michael Webb* (London: AA Publications, 1987), p. 1.
25. Lebbeus Woods, 'Henley and the Enigma of Michael Webb', in *ibid.*, p. 54.
26. *Ibid.*
27. Michael Sorkin, 'Canticles for Mike', in Webb (note 24), p. 5.
28. *Ibid.*, p. 6.
29. Felix Robbins, Unpublished text, 2003.
30. *Ibid.*

The Poetry of Small Things

1. 'Superstudio, Extra-Urban Material Culture', in Peter Lang and Bill Menkin, *Superstudio: A Life without Objects* (Milan: Skira, 2003), p. 224.
2. *Ibid.*, p. 222.
3. *Ibid.*, p. 226.
4. Raoul Bunschoten, 'Work of Cranbrook Studio', *Parametro* (1983).
5. Raoul Bunschoten, 'Spinoza's Garden', *AA Files*, no. 11 (1986).
6. Raoul Bunschoten, 'The Skin of the Earth', in *The Idea of the City* (Cambridge, MA: MIT Press, 1991), p. 181.
7. Alvin Boyarsky, Interview with Peter Wilson: 'Buildings and the Shipshape', *AA Folio* (1984), p. 7.
8. Peter Wilson, Letter to the author, 17 May 2000.
9. *Ibid.*
10. Peter Wilson, *The Clandeboye Report* (London: AA Publications, 1985), p. 5.
11. Wilson (note 8).
12. Peter Wilson, in *The Idea of the City* (note 6), p.102.
13. Peter Wilson, *Western Objects: Eastern Fields – Recent Projects by Architekturburo Bolles Wilson* (London: AA Publications, 1989), p. 37.
14. 'Toyo Ito', in *ibid*, p. 41.
15. Wilson (note 13), p. 11.
16. Peter Salter, in *The Idea of the City* (note 6), p. 200.
17. Peter Salter and Chris Macdonald, *Macdonald and Salter: Building Projects 1982–1986* (London: AA Publications, 1987), n.p.
18. Peter Salter, in *The Idea of the City* (note 6), p. 201.
19. Anthony Dunne, *Hertzian Tales: Electronic Products, Aesthetic Experience and Critical Design* (London: RCA CRD Research, 1999).
20. Anthony Dunne and Fiona Raby, *Design Noir: The Secret Life of Electronic Objects* (London: August/Birkhauser, 2002).

Soft Machines and Virtual Objects

1. Erik Davis, *Technosis: Myth, Magic and Mysticism in the Age of Information* (London: Serpents Tail, 1998), p. 195.
2. Stephen Bann, *The Tradition of Constructivism* (Milan: Da Capo, 1974), pp. 248–9.
3. Nicholas Schoffer, 'Spatiodynamism, Luminodynamism and Chronodynamism', quoted in *ibid.*, p. 255.
4. *Bann* (note 2), p. 257.
5. Gordon Pask, 'The Architectural Relevance of Cybernetics', *Architectural Design* (1969).
6. *Ibid.*
7. Nicholas Negreponte, *Architecture Machine* (Cambridge, MA: MIT Press, 1970), p. 3.
8. *Ibid.*, p. 117.
9. Gordon Pask, 'Aspects of Machine Intelligence', in Nicholas Negreponte, *Soft Architectural Machines* (Cambridge, MA: MIT Press, 1975), pp. 7–8.
10. John Frazer, *An Evolutionary Architecture: Themes VII* (London: AA Publications, 1995), p. 9.
11. *Ibid.*, p. 118.
12. *Ibid.*, p. 40.
13. *Ibid.*, p. 56.
14. *Ibid.*, p. 103.
15. Marcos Novak 'Liquid Architectures in Cyberspace', in Michael Benedikt, ed., *Cyberspace: First Steps* (Cambridge, MA: MIT Press, 1991), p. 2.
16. Marcos Novak, 'Liquid~, trans~, invisible~: The Ascent and Speciation of the Digital in Architecture', unpublished manuscript, 2001.
17. Novak (note 15), p. 248.
18. *Ibid.*, p. 251.
19. Cynthia Davidson, ed., *Anyone* (New York: Rizzoli, 1991), p. 11.
20. Neil Spiller, 'Introduction', in Neil Spiller, ed., *Cyber Reader: Critical Writings for the Digital Era* (London: Phaidon, 2002), p. 96.
21. Greg Lynn, 'Architectural Curvilinearity: The Folded, the Pliant and the Supple', in *idem, Folding in Architecture*, Architectural Profile No. 102 (London: Academy, 1993), pp. 9–10.
22. Greg Lynn, 'Stranded Sears Tower', in Lynn (note 21), p. 83.
23. RAA Um (Jesse Reiser, Stan Allen, Polly Apfelbaum, Nanako Umemoto),

in Lynn (note 21), p. 87.

24. Michael Benedikt, 'Unreal Estates', in
    ANY: Electrotecture, no. 3 (1992), p.
    56.

25. William Mitchell, in *ANY: Electrotecture*
    (note 24), p. 33.

26. Novak (note 15), p. 15.

27. Marcos Novak, 'Transmitting
    Architecture: transTerraFirma/
    TidsvagNoll v2.0', in Neil Spiller and
    Martin Pearce, eds, *Architects in
    Cyberspace*, Architectural Design
    Profile No. 118 (London: Academy,
    1995), p. 45.

28. Neil Spiller, *Digital Dreams:
    Architecture and the New Alchemic
    Technologies* (London: Watson-Guptill
    Publications, 1998), p. 9.

29. 'Greg Lynn: Projects', in Stan Allen with
    Kyong Park, *Sites and Stations:
    Provisional Utopias*, Lusitana No. 7
    (New York: Lusitania, 1995), p.127.

30. Greg Lynn, 'Embryologic Houses', in Ali
    Rahim, ed., *Contemporary Processes in
    Architecture*, *Architectural Design*,
    70/3 (2000), pp. 31–2.

31. Novak (note 15), p. 16.

32. Marcos Novak, 'Eversion: Brushing
    against Avatars, Aliens and Angels', in
    Stephen Perrella, ed., *Hypersurface
    Architecture II*, *Architectural Design*,
    69/9–10 (1999), p. 72.

Bibliography

Archigram

Archigram, *Archigram* (Paris: Centre Georges Pompidou Service Commercial, 1998)
Cook, Peter, ed., *Archigram* (New York: Princeton Architectural Press, 1999)
Sadler, Simon, *Archigram: Architecture without Architecture* (Cambridge, MA: MIT Press, 2005)

Raoul Bunschoten

Chora, ed, *Urban Flotsam* (Rotterdam: Uitgeverij 010 Publishers, 2000)
—, *Meta-spaces: Material Modelling of Proto-urban Conditions* (London: Black Dog, 2001)
—, *A Passage Through Silence and Light: Daniel Libeskind's Extension to the Berlin Museum* (London: Black Dog, 2001)
—, and Duncan McCorquodale, ed, *Public Spaces: Prototypes,* Serial Books: Architecture & Urbanism (London: Black Dog, 2002)
—, *Chora/Raoul Bunschoten: From Matter to Metaspace – Cave, Ground, Horizon, Wind,* Consequence Book Series on Fresh Architecture (Vienna: Springer-Verlag, 2006)

Nat Chard

Chard, Nat, *Drawing Indeterminate Architecture, Indeterminate Drawings of Architecture, Consequence* Book Series on Fresh Architecture (Vienna: Springer-Verlag, 2005)

Nigel Coates

Coates, Nigel, *Nigel Coates: The City in Motion* (New York: Rizzoli International Publications, 1989)
—, *Guide to Ecstacity* (London: Lawrence King, 2003)
—, and Martin Benson, eds, *Discourse of Events*, Themes (London: AA Publications, 1983)

Peter Cook

Cook, Peter, *The Primer* (New York: Wiley Academy, 1996)
—, *The City Seen as a Garden of Ideas* (New York: Monacelli, 2004)
—, ed., *Archigram*, intro. Michael Webb (New York: Princeton Architectural Press, 1999)
Fournier, Colin, *et al., Friendly Alien* (Ostfildern: Hatje Cantz, 2003)

Coop Himmelb(l)au

Coop Himmelb(l)au, *The End of Architecture?: Documents and Manifestos,* Vienna Architecture Conference, Architecture & Design (London: Prestel Publishing, 1993)
—, *Architectural Monographs* (London: Wiley Academy, 1995)

Guy Debord

Debord, Guy, *Society of the Spectacle*, trans. Donald Nicholson-Smith (New York: Zone Books, 1994, first published in French 1967')
McDonough, Tom, ed., *Guy Debord and the Situationist International: Texts and Documents*, October Books (Cambridge, MA: MIT Press, 2002)

Neil Denari

Denari, Neil M., *Gyroscopic Horizons* (New York and London: Princeton Architectural Press and Thames & Hudson, 1999)

Diller and Scofidio

Diller, Elizabeth, and, Ricardo Scofidio, *Flesh: Architectural Probes* (London: Triangle Architectural Pubs, 1995)
—, *Back to Front: Tourisms of War* (New York: Princeton Architectural Press, 1996)
—, *Blur: The Making of Nothing* (New York: Abrams, 2002)
Hays, K. Michael, and Aaron Betsky, *Scanning: The Aberrant Architectures of Diller and Scofidio* (New York: Abrams, 2003)

Dunne & Raby

Dunne, Anthony, and Giles Lane, *Hertzian Tales: Electronic Products, Aesthetic Experience, and Critical Design* (London: RCA CRD Research, 1999)
—, and Fiona Raby, *Design Noir: The Secret Life of Electronic Objects* (London: August/Birkhauser, 2002)
Raby, Fiona, *et al., Project 26765-flirt: Flexible Information and Recreation for Mobile Users* (London: RCA Computer Related Design Research, 2000)

Peter Eisenman

Eisenman, Peter, *Diagram Diaries, Architecture* (London: Thames & Hudson, 1999)
—, *Tracing Eisenman: Peter Eisenman Complete Works* (London: Thames & Hudson, 2006)
—, and Leon Krier, *Reconstruction/ Deconstruction,* Architectural Design Profile (London: Academy, 1994)
Grosz, Elizabeth, *Architecture from the Outside: Essays on Virtual and Real Space*, foreword Peter Eisenman, Writing Architecture (Cambridge, MA: MIT Press, 2001)

John Frazer

Frazer, John, *An Evolutionary Architecture: Themes VII*, Themes (London: Architectural Association Publications, 1995)

Zaha Hadid

Dochantschi, Markus, ed., *Zaha Hadid: Space for Art: Contemporary Arts Centre, Cincinnati – Lois & Richard Rosenthal Centre for Contemporary Art* (Baden: Lars Müller Publishers, 2004)
Fawcett, Anthony, ed., *New British Interiors: Zaha Hadid and Nigel Coates* (Kyoto: Kyoto Shoin International, 1991)
Fontana Giusti, Gordana, and Patrick Schumacher, *Zaha Hadid: The Complete Works* (London: Thames & Hudson, 2004)
Hadid, Zaha, and Aaron Betsky, *Zaha*

Hadid: The Complete Buildings and Projects (London: Thames & Hudson, 1998)

John Hejduk

Hejduk, John, *Architectures in Love* (New York: Rizzoli International Publications, 1995)
–, *Pewter Wing, Golden Horns, Stone Veils: Wedding in a Dark Plum Room* (New York: Monacelli, 1997)
–, *Such Places as Memory: Poems 1953-96*, foreword David Shapiro, Writing Architecture (Cambridge, MA: MIT Press, 1998)
–, *Education of an Architect: Point of View – The Cooper Union School of Art and Architecture, 1964–1971* (New York: Monacelli, 2000)
–, and Kim Shkapich, *Vladivostok: A Trilogy* (New York: Rizzoli International Publications, 1989)

Ron Herron

Cook, Peter, *et al., Spirit and Invention*, Themes (London: Architectural Association Publications, 1982)
Peter Reyner Banham and Isozaki, Arata, *The Visions of Ron Herron*, (London: Architectural Press, 1990)

Wes Jones

Jones, Wes, *Instrumental Form (Boss Architecture)* (New York: Princeton Architectural Press, 1998)

Rem Koolhaas/OMA

Koolhaas, Rem, *Delirious New York: A Retroactive Manifesto for Manhattan* (New York: Thames & Hudson, 1979)
–, and Bruce Mau, *S,M,L,XL* (New York: Monacelli Press, 1995)

Daniel Libeskind

Libeskind, Daniel, *Between Zero and Infinity* (New York: Rizzoli International Publications, 1982)
–, *The Space of Encounter* (London: Thames & Hudson, 2001)

C. J. Lim

Lim, C. J., *Devices* (London: Architectural Press, 2005)

Greg Lynn

Lynn, Greg, *Fold, Bodies and Blobs: Collected Essays* (Lisbon: Exhibitions International, 1998)
–, *Animate Form* (New York: Princeton Architectural Press, 1999)

Morphosis/Thom Mayne

Mayne, Thom, and Val Warke, *Morphosis* (London: Phaidon, 2003)
–, and Fred Orton, *Morphosis: Tangents and Outtakes* (London: Artemis, 1993)
–, *et al., Morphosis: Buildings and Projects v. 3* (New York: Rizzoli International Publications, 1999)

Nicholas Negroponte

Negroponte, Nicholas, *Architecture Machine* (Cambridge, MA: MIT Press, 1970)
–, *Being Digital* (New York: Alfred A. Knopf, 1995)

Gordon Pask

Pask, Gordon, *Approach to Cybernetics*, Radius Books (London: Hutchinson, 1968)
–, *Cybernetics of Human Learning and Performance* (London: Crane Russak & Co., 1975)
–, *Conversation Theory: Applications in Education and Epistemology* (London: Elsevier, 1976)
–, and Susan Curran, *Micro Man: Living and Growing with Computers* (London: Century, 1982)

Giovanni Battista Piranesi

Wilton–Ely, John, *Mind and Art of Giovanni Battista Piranesi* (London: Thames & Hudson, 1978)
–, *Piranesi as Architect and Designer* (New Haven: Yale University Press, 1993)
Piranesi Diary: 2002 (Cologne: Taschen, 2001)

Cedric Price

Hardingham, Samantha, *Cedric Price – Opera* (London: Wiley, 2003)
Price, Cedric, *The Square Book* (London: Wiley-Academy, 2003)

Hani Rashid

Lynn, Greg, and Hani Rashid, *Architectural Laboratories* (Rotterdam: Netherlands Architecture Institute, 2003)
Rashid, Hani, *et al., Asymptote: Hani Rashid and Lise Anne Couture – Architecture at the Interval* (New York: Rizzoli International Publications, 1995)

Reiser and Umemoto

Benjamin, Andrew, and Daniel Libeskind, *Reiser and Umemoto, Architectural Monographs* (London: Academy, 1998)

Peter Reyner Banham

Reyner Banham, Peter, *Theory and Design in the First Machine Age* (London: Architectural Press, 1970)
–, *Architecture of the Well-tempered Environment* (London: Architectural Press, 1969)
–, *Los Angeles: The Architecture of Four Ecologies* (London: A Lane, 1971)
–, *Megastructure: Urban Futures of the Recent Past* (London: Thames & Hudson, 1976)

Kevin Rhowbotham

Rhowbotham, Kevin, *Form to Programme* (London: Black Dog, 1995)
–, *Field Event/Field Space*, Serial Books: Architecture & Urbanism (London: Black Dog, 2001)

Peter Salter

Beard, Peter, *4 + 1: Peter Salter Building Projects* (London: Black Dog, 2001)

Boyarsky, Alvin, and Peter Salter, *Intuition and Process*, Themes (London: Architectural Association Publications, 1989)

Peter Salter: Four Japanese Projects 1990–1993 (London: Architectural Association Publications, 1996)

Salter, Peter, *et al.*, *Climate Register* (London: Architectural Association Publications, 1994)

Antonio Sant'Elia

Da Costa Meyer, Esther, *The Work of Antonio Sant'Elia: Retreat into the Future*, Yale Publications in the History of Art (New Haven: Yale University Press, 1995)

Smithsons

Smithson, Alison, and Peter Smithson, *The Charged Void: Architecture* (New York: Monacelli Press, 2002)

Neil Spiller

Cook, Peter, and Neil Spiller, *The Power of Contemporary Architecture* (London: Wiley-Academy, 1998)

Spiller, Neil, *Digital Dreams: Architecture and the New Alchemic Technologies* (New York: Watson-Guptill Publications, 1998)

—, *Further Architects in Cyberspace I I: Architectural Design* (London: Academy, 1998)

—, *Maverick Deviations* (London: Wiley-Academy, 1999)

—, *Lost Architectures* (London: Wiley-Academy, 2001)

—, *Young Blood*, Architectural Design (London: Wiley-Academy, 2001)

—, *Reflexive Architecture*, Architectural Design (London: Wiley-Academy, 2002)

—, ed., *Cyber Reader: Critical Writings for the Digital Era* (London: Phaidon, 2002)

—, and Martin Pearce, *Architects in Cyberspace*, Architectural Design Profile (London: Wiley-Academy, 1995)

Lars Spuybroek

—, *et al.*, *NOX: Machining Architecture* (London and New York: Thames & Hudson, 2004)

Superstudio

Lang, Peter, and William Menking, *Superstudio: A Life Without Objects* (Milan: Skira Editore, 2003)

Bernard Tschumi

Hays, K. Michael, *et al.*, *Bernard Tschumi, Architecture/Design* (London and New York: Thames & Hudson and Rizzoli International Publications, 2003)

Tschumi, Bernard, *Manhattan Transcripts: Theoretical Projects* (London, Academy, 1981)

—, *Questions of Space: Text 5* (London: Architectural Association Publications, 1995)

—, *Architecture and Disjunction* (Cambridge, MA: MIT Press, Cambridge, 1996)

—, *Columbia, Documents of Architecture and Theory: Vol. 6* (London: Art Data, 1998)

—, *Event – Cities 2* (Cambridge, MA: MIT Press, Cambridge, 2001)

—, *Event-Cities: Concept Vs. Context Vs. Content: No 3* (Cambridge, MA: MIT Press, 2005)

Lebbeus Woods

Woods, Lebbeus, *One Five Four* (New York: Princeton Architectural Press, 1992)

—, *The New City* (New York: Pocket Books, 1992)

—, *War and Architecture*, Pamphlet Architecture (New York: Princeton Architectural Press, 1996)

—, *Radical Reconstruction* (New York: Princeton Architectural Press, 1997)

—, *Earthquake!: A Post-biblical View* (Vienna: Springer-Verlag, 2002)

Photographic Credits

407 Courtesy Mark Burry
408 Collection of Gemeentemuseum den
Haag
409 Courtesy Peter Cook
410–11 Courtesy Coop Himme(l)blau
412 Courtesy Marcos Novak
413–14 Courtesy Neil Denari
415 Gunter Domenig/Neumueller
416 Courtesy Diller + Scofidio
417–19 Courtesy Dunne & Raby
420 Courtesy Peter Eisenman
421–2 Courtesy John Frazer
423 Courtesy Future Systems
424–5 Courtesy Mark Burry
426 Fronds John Hejduk, Collection
Centre Canadien d'Architecture/Canadian
Centre for Architecure, Montreal
428 Austrian Frederick and Lillian Kiesler
Foundation, Vienna
430 Courtesy Studio Daniel Libeskind,
Architect
431 Courtesy C. J. Lim
432 Courtesy Greg Lynn/FORM
433 Courtesy Morphosis/Tim Street-
Porter
434 Courtesy Ben Nicholson
436–7 Courtesy Marcos Novak
438 Reiser and Umemoto
439 Courtesy John Puttick
440 Courtesy Kevin Rhowbotham
441 Courtesy Peter Salter
442 Courtesy Felix Robbins
443 Courtesy Neil Spiller
444 Courtesy Peter Wilson
445 Courtesy Lars Spruybroek/NOX
446–7 Christiano Toraldo di Francia/
Superstudio
448–9 Courtesy Peter Wilson
450 Courtesy Lebbeus Woods
451–2 Courtesy Michael Webb
453 Courtesy Studio Daniel Libeskind

frontispiece
**Maldoror's Equation
from 'Micromegas'**
Daniel Libeskind,
1979

Acknowledgments

This book is dedicated to Arthur George Spiller (1920–2000).

This book would not have been possible without the 2002 John and Magda McHale
Fellowship at the University of Buffalo, State University of New York. My work has also
benefited from the Bartlett's Architectural Research Fund.

Many people have helped in different ways during the gestation of this book.
Thank you to:
My wife, Melissa Jones, for love, support and editing
My son Edward for noise, early-morning hugs and the experience of fatherhood
My son Tom for happy two-toothed smiles and licky kisses
Phil Watson for 'Pataphysical genuis, support and friendship
Peter Cook for Italian and Japanese impersonations, and all the other stuff
Magda McHale for her interest in my work and inspirational conversations
Hadas Steiner for being my Buffalo theory buddy
Paula Paradise for wine advice and pool-hall hip flasks
Jean LaMarche for Futurist suppers and the Islands of Dr Moreau
Omar Khan for Paskian anecdotes
Ben Nicholson for showing me his secret weapons
Ranulph Glanville for historical cybernetic guidance
Cedric Price for just being Cedric
Lucas Dietrich for having the idea and editorial direction
Cat Green for keeping everyone's eye on the manuscript ball
Manuel Rivera III for image-scanning Stateside
Stuart Munro for image-scanning Blighty-side
Andrea Belloli for making the manuscript fluent and making me conform to her
high levels of perfection.

Also, thank you to all the architects who provided me with illustrations of their
visionary work.

First published in the United Kingdom in 2006
by Thames & Hudson Ltd, 181A High Holborn,
London WC1V 7QX

www.thamesandhudson.com

British Library Cataloguing-in-Publication Data
A catalogue record for this book is available from the
British Library.

ISBN-13: 978-0-500-28655-5
ISBN-10: 0-500-28655-8

Designed by Roger Fawcett-Tang at Struktur

Printed and bound in Singapore by Star Standard
Industries (Pte) Ltd